The Mountain
Man of Letters

Essays on the Works of
Howard O'Hagan

ESSENTIAL WRITERS SERIES 57

Canadä

ONTARIO ARTS COUNCIL
CONSEIL DES ARTS DE L'ONTARIO

an Ontario government agency
un organisme du gouvernement de l'Ontario

Canada Council   Conseil des arts
for the Arts   du Canada

Guernica Editions Inc. acknowledges the support of
the Canada Council for the Arts and the Ontario Arts Council.
The Ontario Arts Council is an agency of the Government of Ontario.

We acknowledge the financial support of the Government of Canada.

The Mountain Man of Letters

Essays on the Works of
Howard O'Hagan

Edited by
Sergiy Yakovenko

GUERNICA
EDITIONS

TORONTO • CHICAGO
BUFFALO • LANCASTER (U.K.)
2024

Guernica Founder: Antonio D'Alfonso

Sergiy Yakovenko, editor
Michael Mirolla, general editor
Joseph Pivato, series editor
Cover and Interior Design: Rafael Chimicatti
Cover image: sergey pesterev/unsplash

Guernica Editions Inc.
1241 Marble Rock Rd., Gananoque (ON), Canada K7G 2V4
2250 Military Road, Tonawanda, N.Y. 14150-6000 U.S.A.
www.guernicaeditions.com

Distributors:
Independent Publishers Group (IPG)
600 North Pulaski Road, Chicago IL 60624
University of Toronto Press Distribution (UTP)
5201 Dufferin Street, Toronto (ON), Canada M3H 5T8

First edition.
Printed in Canada.

Legal Deposit—First Quarter
Library of Congress Catalog Card Number: 2023944467
Library and Archives Canada Cataloguing in Publication
Title: The mountain man of letters :
essays on the works of Howard O'Hagan / edited by Sergiy Yakovenko.
Names: Yakovenko, Sergiy (College teacher), editor.
Description: Includes bibliographical references.
Identifiers: Canadiana (print) 20230522955 | Canadiana (ebook) 2023052303X
ISBN 9781771838733 (softcover) | ISBN 9781771838740 (EPUB)
Subjects: LCSH: O'Hagan, Howard—Criticism and interpretation.
Classification: LCC PS8529.H35 Z66 2024 | DDC C813/.5409—dc23

Contents

Introduction
Howard O'Hagan and Critics

Sergiy Yakovenko

Apophatic synesthesia may be a pretentious yet correct term to describe *Tay John*'s most appealing portrayal of a snowy landscape, paraphrased in the apposite title of Margery Fee's edited volume on Howard O'Hagan: *Silence Made Visible*. The snowflakes "were like immense moths winging down in the twilight, making the silence about me visible" (*Tay John* 68)—this is how the lack of sound *looks like*, visualized. To name another aspect of that apophatic quality of O'Hagan's prose, we can borrow Arnold Davidson's phrase "silencing the word"—the paradoxical using of *words* to silence *the word*. Almost like in Robert Frost's famous poem "Fire and Ice," the end of Red Rorty's quasi-ministerial "word" comes by way of fire, and a stone in the open jaw of his bare skull, while Father Thomas Rorty is silenced with a frozen froth on his lips. Not only Tay John's putative father and uncle, but also his partner Ardith Aeriola, who knew him most intimately of all and bore his child, ends up with her mouth "chock-full of snow" (*Tay John* 199). There is something in it from Joseph Conrad, one of O'Hagan's literary mentors: the horror of Kurtz's wide-open mouth and his soundless scream, and the grotesque irony of Kayerts, "hanging by a leather strap from the cross" and, "irreverently ... putting out a swollen tongue at his Managing Director" (Conrad 25).

O'Hagan seems to cultivate the irreverence of these apophatic, negative gestures. Conrad's "Managing Director" (from "An Outpost of Progress") is not only *Tay John*'s chief narrator, Jack Denham, but also all of us, the readers, who forever are doomed to be satisfied with, or unnerved by, "Evidence—Without a Finding" (*Tay John* 119). Having learned, or inherited, something from the great masters of ambiguity and style, like Henry James and Joseph Conrad, O'Hagan invites his reader to share in Keats's "*Negative Capability*, that is when man is capable of being in uncertainties, Mysteries, doubts, without any irritable reaching after fact & reason" (Keats 109). With *Tay John*'s author, as "with a great poet the sense of Beauty overcomes every other consideration" (Keats 109). From the first Canadian edition of the novel (1974), critics have noticed the oxymoronic negativity of O'Hagan's sense of beauty. Patricia Morley starts her "Introduction to the New Canadian Library Edition" by addressing Father Rorty's philosophy of truth and beauty as "unavoidably linked to violence and suffering" (vii). Michael Ondaatje, also in a 1974 study, "O'Hagan's Rough-Edged Chronicle" (later repeated in his afterword to the 1989 and 2008 editions), insightfully compares O'Hagan's narrative technique and the conception of the hero with those of Greek tragedy, whose power was "caused by the very fact that the narrators, Chorus, had no true understanding ... of the central character" (24). In a most recent comparative study, "Forests of Symbols: *Tay John* and *The Double Hook*" (2015), Joseph Pivato writes about both O'Hagan's and Sheila Watson's "deceptively simple styles" that "hide many levels of meaning," and cites Barbara Godard's description of Watson's "divesting language of associations—thus creating a new way of seeing—with its awareness of silence ..." (qtd. in Pivato 192).

The first collective monograph on O'Hagan, Fee's *Silence Made Visible: Howard O'Hagan and* Tay John (1992), to which our volume is indebted in many ways, also does justice to the paradox of this language of vision "with its awareness of silence." At the conclusion of *Silence Made Visible*, Ronald Granofsky's chapter "The Country of Illusion: Vision, Change, and Misogyny in Howard O'Hagan's *Tay John*" articulates the novel's landscape symbolism of a mountain country, "in which vision is unreliable and illusion endemic" (109). Granofsky traces back the connections between the complex imagery of *Tay John*, entwined with the incidents of the plot, and the narrative's doubtful vision, which contributes to the novel's dialectic of stasis and change—a male, imperialistic urge "to name, to reify" "the unknown and the unreal" and, therefore, the menacing, which is represented by female figures with "their illusory promise of the most desirable of all states of stasis, immortality" (109).

In fact, a few of Granofsky's insights had already been vocalized in some earlier publications, among which the most prominent are two articles that appeared in 110th issue of *Canadian Literature* (Fall 1986)—Fee's "Howard O'Hagan's *Tay John*: Making New World Myth" and Davidson's "Silencing the Word in Howard O'Hagan's *Tay John*"—as well as Jack Robinson's studies "Myths of Dominance Versus Myths of Re-Creation in O'Hagan's *Tay John* (1988) and "Dismantling Sexual Dualities in O'Hagan's *Tay John*" (1990). Already in his earlier pioneering essay "Being and Definition in Howard O'Hagan's *Tay John*" (1983), Davidson tackles the problem of naming as a colonial metaphysics, whose outcome is a creation of "inauthentic map of words" (138). Indeed, the disbalanced complexity of the novel's narrative structure and the narrator Denham's own speculations on the nature of all stories as inconclusive have provoked an array of critical responses defining the novel as a postmodernist precursor. In "Making New World Myth," Fee suggests that "O'Hagan's text, in its self-consciousness about the fictive quality of *all* versions of reality, elicits the label 'post-modernist' despite its 1939 publication date" (9).

In the second half of the 1980s and the first half of the 1990s, the most prolific period in *Tay John* studies to date, scholars such as Fee, Davidson, Robinson, W. J. Keith, Stephen Scobie, and D. M. R. Bentley used poststructuralist and deconstructionist approaches to address O'Hagan's explicit and implicit intertextuality, which, in Fee's words, replaced "divine authority in the making of myth" ("Making New World Myth" 9). Davidson investigates how O'Hagan deconstructs his own story "by telling it in terms of … the most unquestionably accepted legend or story in the western world"—the Gospels ("Silencing the Word" 31). Both Fee and Robinson use the verb "dismantle" to signify O'Hagan's strategy concerning "the old myths" (Fee, "Making" 11), and "especially the world-explaining myth of ideology itself" (Robinson, "Myths of Dominance"). In Robinson's view, "ironies, paradoxes, parodies, and other strategies for the dispersion of meaning" are employed in *Tay John* for deconstructing the work of "sexual dualities," such as "spirit/body, possessor/possessed, civilized/natural, and maternal/adult love," at the very core of the western colonial culture ("Dismantling Sexual Dualities" 95, 106). More specifically, the main ideologies of this culture are "the Christian division of spirit and flesh, the egocentric self, the use of language and story as means of subduing nature, the process of knowing through intellectual dominance, the myth of the world-dominating male, the centralist and imperialist concepts of culture, and ideology as *teleos*" (Robinson, "Myths of Dominance"). A little outside of the postmodernist interpretive vein, but in accord with the accepted notion of the novel's intertextuality, is Bentley's 1993 article "The Wide Circle and Return: *Tay John* and Vico" (an underrated and undeservedly forgotten text, which is reprinted in this volume).

At the beginning of the twenty-first century, Francis Zichy puts into doubt not only the premature postmodernist awareness of *Tay John* but also its qualities as a modernist novel. In "Crypto-, Pseudo-, and Pre-Postmodernism: *Tay John*, *Lord Jim*, and the Critics," Zichy takes issue with such a high valuation of O'Hagan's novel and dismisses *Tay John* as merely a "wilderness story" in the spirit of Jack London's northern tales (194; 204). Comparing "the handling of the narrative" in *Tay John* and Joseph Conrad's *Lord Jim* to the former's disadvantage in terms of "the comparative simplicity of O'Hagan's narrative art" (193), Zichy shifts his focus toward the moral character of Jack Denham, whose "authority is much less clearly established" than Marlow's (197). In his diagnosis of "a large admixture of self-serving idealization in Denham's portrait of his 'hero'" (216), Zichy does not seem to dissent much from the opinion of other scholars, but his assertion of Denham's failure to live up to Marlow's moral romantic ideal ascribes to O'Hagan an agenda that would contradict the novel's unmasking and satirical intentions: "O'Hagan's novel drastically discounts not only the romantic character but also all human aspiration" (208). While a few of Zichy's comparative observations are shrewd and thought-provoking, including his scathing criticism of Denham's character, the scholar appears less convincing when, especially in "The 'Complex Fate' of the Canadian in Howard O'Hagan's *Tay John*," he accuses O'Hagan of positing such an unheroic, mediocre, and self-deprecating narrator as Denham "as exemplary of the Canadian character" ("The 'Complex Fate'" 201). Zichy has a point in asserting that "the novel is in fact grounded in the psychology of Denham's character" (201), but in his findings, he allows for little difference between the narrator and the author, thus making O'Hagan complicit in Denham's "state of self-serving illusion" (212).

One tendency of O'Hagan scholarship in recent years, also reflected—and even emphasized—in this volume, is a noticeable turn to the problem of the Indigenous. In the "golden age" of *Tay John* criticism, scholars approached this topic mostly from the poststructuralist perspective—to explicate the complex knot of the protagonist's identity, his name, and the intricacies of the narrative. Ralph Maud's "Ethnographic Notes on Howard O'Hagan's *Tay John*" (in *Silence Made Visible*) is an important guide to the Indigenous roots of O'Hagan's story. In "Forests of Symbols," Pivato points to a subtle network of "allusions to the folklore of First Nations and the common places of epics and western tall tales" (191). Robinson in his studies of the novel has given attention to O'Hagan's use of First Nations' folktales and symbolic imagery (like the owl, symbol of woman). More broadly, Indigenous motifs are referred to in the postcolonial critique of *Tay John* and in those interpretations that regard the novel as a pioneering postcolonial work of fiction. Robinson, for example, qualifies Red Rorty's preaching among the Shuswap as "a verbal rape, a paradigm for the taking of the land and the suppression of the Indigenous cultures by the invading white culture" ("Myths of Dominance"). At the same time, in his 2013 essay "Fictions of Mixed Origins: *Iracema*, *Tay John*, and Racial Hybridity in Brazil and Canada," Albert Braz points out that, "while O'Hagan dramatizes the manner in which the dominant society silences Indigenous voices," Indigenous people do "not have much of a voice" in the novel (7).

The current volume is the second collective monograph which aims at presenting the most recent scholarship on O'Hagan. The first one, Fee's *Silence Made Visible*, was published thirty years ago—a pioneering, and unique in its kind, book that includes a detailed chronology of O'Hagan's life (by Fee and Peter James Clark), an annotated bibliography (by Richard Arnold), a few documents and O'Hagan's early and less known short stories, Keith Maillard's extensive interview with O'Hagan, and critical articles by Fee, Keith, Maud, and

Granofsky. As the full title of the book suggests, *Silence Made Visible: Howard O'Hagan and* Tay John, its critical focus is narrowed down to O'Hagan's most celebrated work—the novel *Tay John*. Fee offers a detailed "Note on the Publishing History of O'Hagan's *Tay John*" and explains the novel's road to canonization ("The Canonization of Two Underground Classics: Howard O'Hagan's *Tay John* and Malcolm Lowry's *Under the Volcano*"). The purpose of our collection is not only to refresh *Tay John* scholarship (the novel is still—deservedly—in the centre of the volume) but also to break the vicious circle of ignoring O'Hagan's other works—his later novel *The School-Marm Tree* (1977) and his short stories and sketches, collected in *Wilderness Men* (1958) and *The Woman Who Got on at Jasper Station, and Other Stories* (1963). Up until now, *The School-Marm Tree* and O'Hagan's short prose have been briefly discussed only in book reviews and—tangentially—in *Tay John* studies. This volume offers two original articles on *The School-Marm Tree*, by Renée Hulan and Carl Watts, and Albert Braz's profound study of O'Hagan's *Wilderness Men*. As a matter of fact, Keith, in "Howard O'Hagan, *Tay John*, and the Growth of Story" (in *Silence Made Visible*), shows how the story of *Tay John* grows from "an oral tradition of tale-telling among the 'wilderness men'" (74), and how O'Hagan's versions of these tales appear both in *Tay John* and in his short fiction. It is a little ironic that one of the two articles that were published earlier and are now reprinted in this book, Kylee-Anne Hingston's "The Declension of a Story: Narrative Structure in Howard O'Hagan's *Tay John*" (2005), demonstrates that the novel's narrative betrays a dynamic contradictory to "the growth of story": O'Hagan intentionally orchestrates "a declension from an elusive but indisputable legend to corporeal but uncertain facts" (181).

This volume is structured thematically rather than chronologically. It begins with Joseph Pivato's "Teaching *Tay John* on the Yellowhead Highway." In his article, Pivato places *Tay John* in an important cultural, literary-historical, and educational context of the 1970s, when, in the wake of its publication by McClelland and Stewart (1974), the novel started to be included in the newly developed university English courses. In particular, he shares his memories of opening the first course in Canadian Literature at Athabasca University in 1978—with O'Hagan's *Tay John*.

Pivato describes teaching the novel in 1978-79 as a truly "pioneering adventure." The rediscovery of *Tay John* after its publication as part of the New Canadian Library series coincided with, and contributed to, the revival of Canadian Literature on university English curricula in Canada, which for decades had been dominated by English and American studies. In the context of this reanimation, it was also important to break the stereotype of the Canadian literary imagination as governed by "a garrison mentality"—Northrop Frye's highly influential notion that was first described in his contribution to the *Literary History of Canada* (1965) and later popularized by Margaret Atwood's *Survival: A Thematic Guide to Canadian Literature* (1972). Teaching *Tay John* in the 1970s and onward, alongside such works as John Richardson's *Wacousta* and Louis Hémon's *Maria Chapdelaine*, Pivato, together with E. D. Blodgett, took a challenge to demonstrate that the notions of the garrison mentality and survival represented "reductionist views of the Canadian literary imagination." One major factor responsible for this reduction was a neglect of the Indigenous component in Canadian literature, especially the relationship with the natural environment that the First Nations have built throughout the centuries—drastically different from the one suggested by the second chapter of Atwood's *Survival*: "Nature the Monster." Pivato demonstrates that, although on the surface the garrison theme may apply to the image of the fort in

Wacousta, "the Indigenous people outside are often depicted as morally superior to the British." Like Wacousta, Tay John considers himself an outsider of his own society, but both are in perfect accord with nature.

Pivato argues that the many scenes of Tay John's spiritual communion with the land allude to "the history of the French-Canadian *coureurs des bois* and *voyageurs*, who travelled into the interior of Canada to trade with the Indigenous people"—characters that are not uncommon in Quebec novels of the soil, like Hémon's *Maria Chapdelaine*. Pivato concludes that the environmental imagination evoked by *Tay John* has inspired a number Canadian novelists, such as Robert Kroetsch, Michael Ondaatje, Rudy Wiebe, and Jack Hodgins.

No serious discussion of *Tay John* can leave out the novel's tripartite structure. In "The Wide Circle and Return: *Tay John* and Vico," D. M. R. Bentley offers an original key to "some intriguing shifts in narrative mode," style and themes of *Tay John*'s three parts: "Legend," "Hearsay," and "Evidence—Without a Finding." This key is the three ages—the "age of the gods," the "age of the heroes," and the "age of men"—which, according to Giambattista Vico, comprise the recurring cycles of history. Bentley contends that this is not just a typological comparison: O'Hagan could have read Vico's *Scienza Nuova* either in the original Italian or French translation.

The first part of *Tay John* corresponds with the "age of gods" based on multiple factors that describe the Shuswap community in accordance with Vico's characteristics of this period's culture, such as the "strong sense of the divine" and the practice of divination, mankind's "civic nature" (the Shuswap "We" as "the greatest magic"), the "admixture of religion and cruelty" (the execution of Red Rorty), the metonymical language, testifying to incapability for abstract thinking (the naming of Tay John by the color of his hair). By contrast, the title of the second part, "Hearsay," reflects the separation of names and things in the abstract forms pertaining to the language of the "age of heroes." Enriched, according to Vico, by "metaphors and comparisons in ... articulated speech," this language finds an appropriate expression in "Jackie's Tale" and its narrator of aristocratic lineage, Jack Denham. The heroic and aristocratic motifs are expanded by a few allusions to Arthurian legend, with Arthur Alderson—naturally—as the legendary Arthur, Tay John as Lancelot, and Julia Alderson as Guinevere. Arthur's apology to Tay John after an improvised trial is an example of Vico's "heroic jurisprudence," which stands in opposition to both Red Rorty's brutal execution by the rules of "divine law," in the first part of the novel, and the emasculation of jurisprudence in the third part, corresponding to the Viconian "age of men." The "dissolution of culture," associated with that age, finds its expression in the diffused morality and unstable faith of Father Rorty, whose name "Thomas" is an allegory of doubt, and in the image of the protagonist, Tay John, who seemed to Denham as neither divine nor heroic anymore but "as merely human."

The "maturity" of the third age, but also the "decadence" that accompanies it, prompts Bentley to conclude that the disintegration of Dobble's entrepreneurial dream "was especially irresistible when O'Hagan wrote and published *Tay John* in the late 1930s, in the midst of the Great Depression and on the brink of the Second World War."

Bentley's insight that *Tay John*'s tripartite structure mirrors Vico's stages of the declining human society may find its ally in Kylee-Anne Hingston's "'The Declension of a Story: Narrative Structure in Howard O'Hagan's *Tay John*." Contrary to an established view that in his narrative O'Hagan transforms tangible facts into an intangible new myth, Hingston argues that the author's intention is to represent storytelling as a "declension," or degeneration, from an absolute story of the legend to a material but dubious evidence.

Hingston reads the narrator's Platonist explication of Shuswap basket making as O'Hagan's metaphor for storytelling: a physical basket is a shadow of an absolute basket that exists in the ideal realm as a Platonic Eidos, and likewise, storytelling brings down the ideal, original story to a material level. Naming, as Hingston argues, is comparable with storytelling, with the debasing of the original, rather than with myth-making. The figure of the enigmatic and elusive protagonist, Tay John, along with the associated with him images of wilderness, darkness, and shadow, is an allegory of the authoritative legend. That is why the naming of Tay John and the naming of the wilderness as a form of appropriation are "a weak articulation" of their essence. Shadow and darkness as Tay John's true origins stand for humankind's "universal subconscious," an eternal story that exists outside its various material representations—both the tales and the taletellers. Hingston argues that O'Hagan invites his reader to appreciate the very inconsistency among the versions of Tay John's story as a testimony to the existence of an immutable myth outside the changeable material realm. Neither names nor narratives are able to capture Tay John: born from the darkness of the grave, being of an uncertain racial and social status, he manages to dodge all the imposed roles extended to him by the Shuswap messiah myth, or the Arthurian narrative, or Dobble's entrepreneurial imagination.

This "refusal to be narrated" makes Tay John a central allegory of O'Hagan's concept of story. Although unable to capture the "elusive heart of the story," storytelling betrays its "negative capability" through O'Hagan's respect for the beauty and power of language. Manifested, among others, in Denham's praise for the metaphor of "snow flies," this power of words, in Hingston's view, proves that O'Hagan in his novel acknowledges and asserts the ability of tales to "relate" the ideal, elusive, and impalpable to "the known world," and thus advocates for a balance between the story and storytelling.

In his profound chapter "Satirical Echoes: Re-Considering Howard O'Hagan's *Tay John* as Influenced by Joseph Conrad's *Heart of Darkness*," Jack Robinson interprets a few "echoes" of Conrad's novella in O'Hagan's *Tay John* as a continuation of Conrad's discourse "on empire, gender, and otherness." While both authors, Conrad and O'Hagan, expose "the self-enclosed" and self-serving world of European colonialism, the forty-year chronological divide between the two works accounts for O'Hagan's more forward-thinking insights about Indigenous values and "the problematic nature of cultural hybridity that is still relevant today but was unheard of in his time."

Considering both *Heart of Darkness* and *Tay John* as satirical novels, Robinson in his comparative analysis focuses on such elements of satire as sardonic wit and irony. Like Conrad's Marlow, who derides imperialist misconceptions about the wilderness resulting from the fear of the unknown, O'Hagan's narrator Denham wittily ridicules Dobble's folly of possession and the complacent delusion of his mastership of nature, Western Christianity as an instrument of colonization and a set of self-serving yet destructive abstractions (Father Rorty), and false rationality that is based on racial and social prejudice (inspector Jay Wiggins). At the same time, we can detect the authors' ironic attitude toward their first-person narrators: both Marlow and Denham perpetuate the stereotypes of women as defined by nature and sexuality (and nature also as feminized and sexualized), and thus as objects of possession. Moreover, while recognizing some postcolonial glimpses of Conrad and O'Hagan, Robinson admits that both "purvey stereotypes" themselves: "just as Africa had to remain

wild and primitive for Conrad, the Indigenous for O'Hagan had
to be hypermasculine and identified with nature." A shared
symbolic image of the streams separating Denham from the
Tay John-grizzly battle, and Marlow from Kurtz's Indigenous
mistress, is representative of Western "ideology of a separation
from nature and otherness." Among the shared motifs that are
informed by irony are naming and sight as delusory tools of
appropriation, the meta-narrative commentary, unmasking a
fallacious simplicity of the relationship between the tale and
reality, and the derisive technique of twinning, represented by
the two women whom Marlow encounters in the company's
office, by the Rorty brothers, and by the two gold prospectors
who initiate Tay John into the world of Western materialism.

   In Robinson's view, satire in both *Heart of Darkness* and
Tay John generates the uneasiness of unresolved problems,
revealing the "darkness" of the imperial lies and delusions
by the allegories of open mouths or misleading names. One
of these points of uneasiness in *Tay John* is "the colonial trap
of cultural hybridity," which the protagonist falls victim to.
Nevertheless, as Robinson asserts, O'Hagan's narrative strategy in the novel embraces at least some Indigenous values:
the story of Tay John, told from a variety of perspectives as a
communal enterprise, is consistent with the Shuswap "We"
spirit rather than with the "self-doubt, fear, self-consciousness,
and self-dramatization" comprising "the western self."

   In his essay "Fantasy and Sovereignty in Howard O'Hagan's
Tay John: A Postcolonial Reading," Sergiy Yakovenko focuses
on the narrator Jack Denham's attempt to appropriate Tay
John, the protagonist of his tale, for his own fantasies that
are steeped in the colonialist ideology of enlightenment. Even
though Denham may be right about his hero's interstitial position between the two worlds, the Indigenous and the colonial,
O'Hagan's narrative irony consists in Tay John's resistance to

such forms of appropriation and his ultimate privacy as a modern individual *self*.

Yakovenko emphasizes the importance of Denham's initial narrative scene—Tay John's battle with a bear—as a moment revealing an ideological lining of the narrator's fantasies that involve the "other." Comparing and contrasting Denham with Joseph Conrad's Marlow, as well as with Jack London's and Georges Bugnet's characters' attitudes toward the wilderness, Yakovenko analyzes such colonialist stances as "the sexualization of the wilderness, the Enlightenment supremacy of vision, language as a tool of colonization, and the juxtaposition of idea and instinct." Denham resembles the figure of Odysseus in Theodor Adorno's illustration of the Hegelian Master-Slave dialectic: enjoying from a safe distance what appears to him as an epic battle between man and the dark forces of nature, O'Hagan's narrator appropriates Tay John's victory as the Master who uses the Slave's labour to define his own relationship with the world. Denham's fantasy is thwarted, however, by Tay John's refusal to return the gesture, or the gaze, of recognition; the latter's noncompliance as a projected "Slave" figure establishes his sovereignty and sets the tone for the remainder of Jackie's tale as constituted by enigmatic and evasive character of Tay John rather than by Denham's colonialist fantasies.

Tay John's departure from the cyclic time and collective tribal identity of his native culture opens the world of new opportunities and delights, but his fascination with some elements of Western civilization does not annihilate his powers of resistance to the patterns of identity that civilization tries to impose on him. In his pursuit of individual happiness and freedom, as a modern self emerging from the bondage of myth, Tay John can still resort to a potlach bargain in a foolhardy act of severing his own hand—to take possession of the desired object, but also he is able to abandon his beloved Stetson hat in a gesture of insulted dignity. Always equal to himself, Tay John escapes into his privacy whenever Denham or we as readers want to align him with something familiar.

Renée Hulan's chapter "The Constant Craving of Howard O'Hagan's Wilderness Women" makes for a smooth transition from the *Tay John* section of this volume to the discussion of *The School-Marm Tree*. One of Hulan's goals is to revisit the position of women in O'Hagan in relation to the modernist and postmodernist poetics. For this reason, she dedicates nearly half of her essay to a thorough account of the existing *Tay John* criticism, with particular attention to the discussion of O'Hagan's conception of the female. The novelist's misogynistic tendencies, noted by a few critics, proceed from the fact that *Tay John* creates an environment characterized by a fear of women. As Hulan points out, there is a strong association of the notions of the "uncanny" and "mystic" with the feminine, which must always be subdued by the masculine. The novel's "narrative femicide," represented by the death of the female grizzly and of the pregnant Ardith, testifies to the fact that "*Tay John* conforms to the sacrificial mode of Modernism."

Hulan finds it compelling that in *The School-Marm Tree*, O'Hagan departs from the mainstream Modernism by attempting to explore female subjectivity in all its "psychological complexity of *being* the Other in the Western novel, a genre in which women are always stereotypically cast as the civilizing presence against the male protagonist's flight towards individuality." Hulan makes a point that femicide is absent from the novel; moreover, the heroine is not even punished either for "enjoying her sexuality" or "transgressing boundaries of social class." A typical victim of gender and class stereotypes between the two wars, Selva is denied the freedom of the frontier life that men can enjoy. Her body is represented as a passive object of external forces, and her desire is symbolized by the school-marm tree, but passivity is not her true character. She proves herself able to fight, and she dreams of escape to the fantasized fine life in the East. With the death of Peter, however, she has to relinquish her fantasies and "finds freedom in the dark enclosure of the forest." Hulan emphasizes that O'Hagan does not make the heroine's growing love for the outdoors a fact exceptional for a woman. Neither is Selva defined by her refuge to the safe partnership with a "mountain man," Clay. Her name suggests an association with "forest" but also with "self," which represents that "constant craving" of "O'Hagan's wilderness women," their Unheimlich, unhomeliness in the world defined by masculinity.

Carl Watts begins his article "Myth Demystified: Realism and Settler Society in Howard O'Hagan's *The School-Marm Tree*" with an inquiry into the reason behind a somewhat wary critical response that this late O'Hagan's novel has received so far. Compared with *Tay John*, whose myth-dismantling and myth-making aspirations have secured a stable interest in the novel from poststructuralist and thematic-critical scholarship, *The School-Marm Tree* has been described as rather a simplistic and predictable tale, on the border of romance and realism. In his revision of these terms—romance and realism—Watts draws on Fredric Jameson's conception of realism as a movement dominated by "the function of demystification" and on Glenn Willmott's interpretation of the realism-romance dichotomy as an interpenetrating, self-ironizing formation that registers the uncertainties of modernity in Canadian literature.

Watts reads *The School-Marm Tree* as a culmination of the work of demystification that O'Hagan started in his previous novel: the establishment of the mainstream "settler-colonial hegemony" reconfigures and problematizes "the identities, relationships, and binaries" of the myth that were depicted in *Tay John*. Instead of the latter's modernist individualism associated with the frontier-settler self-seeking subject, *The School-Marm Tree* suggests a uniformity and totality of the settler-colonial society, which blot out regional and social-class differences and produce an array of "interchangeable characters instead of archetypes." This narrative and behavioural interchangeability regardless of class differences becomes evident in the doubling of characters such as "Slim and Clay, Wrogg and Branchflower, Edna and Rosie," in the gradual dissolution of the individual into the type, and in "the half-heartedly instrumental relationships that obtain among many of the novel's main characters." The characters' unusual fixation on the mundane idiosyncrasies of personal appearance (a conversation between Rosie and Peter) or Clay's awkward joke comparing a human with an—exotic and "cartoonish" in that context—animal, kangaroo, downplay the socio-economic, regional, and cultural differences.

Finally, the prevailing materialism and narcissism of the homogenized colonial-settler community add to the self-reflexive and self-ironizing unmasking of "realist mechanisms such as supposedly transparent and objective description"—for example, the novel's extended descriptions of consumer products. Watts argues that the inversion of realism and romance, incipient in the quasi-mythical narrative of *Tay John* and deliberately problematized in *The School-Marm Tree*, accounts for a dissolution of the modernist frontier individualism into "the newly epic predictability of an increasingly totalized settler-colonial world."

In his chapter "Legendary Loners and Lonely Acts: Civilization, Freedom, and Sovereignty in *Wilderness Men*," Albert Braz analyzes short fiction and sketches that appear in O'Hagan's collection *Wilderness Men* (1958). Based on their author's personal experience or research, most of these stories capture the conflicts that arise from Canada's colonial roots: between civilization and nature, between organized society and solitary men trying to escape its constraints, and between the settlers and First Nations. Braz states that, addressing some systemic social contradictions that pervade Canadian society, O'Hagan demonstrates forward-looking insights but is not always "able to rise above the dominant stereotypes of the day."

The first and the last sketches in the *Wilderness Men*—"The Black Ghost" and "I Look Upward and See the Mountain"—depict two "truly" wilderness men, the old trapper MacNamara and the painter Jan Van Empel, respectively, whose many outdoor experiences include bonding with a wild animal. The theme of this "community of interest" between humans and nonhumans stays central in "Grey Owl," which follows a life story of the famous writer and impersonator Archibald Belaney. Braz emphasizes O'Hagan's point that Belaney's metamorphosis into Indigenous person "is not so much an act of cultural appropriation" as an act of self-reinvention and rediscovery of a new identity, which also makes this figure "a literary precursor" of Tay John. *Tay John*'s motif of naming and its illusory connection with identity is also relevant for "The Man Who Chose to Die," O'Hagan's variation on the story of Mad Trapper, Albert Johnson.

Braz points out that, according to O'Hagan, the term "wilderness men" can only be properly applied to colonial settlers who rejected their own "civilized" society, but not to the Indigenous subjects whom the Canadian Confederation made outcasts in their own country. For this reason, O'Hagan's sketches dedicated to Indigenous historical figures depict lonely acts rather than "loners." Almighty Voice and Simon Gunanoot, the protagonists of "The Singer in the Willows" and "The Little Bear That Climbs Trees," respectively, "are obviously not loners who try to flee civilization but rather casualties of a political and legal system that appears to be structurally designed not to deal with Indigenous people in an equitable manner." On the other hand, Indigenous female characters as the focus of the sketch "Shwat—The End of Tzouhalem" throw into relief the limitations of the male-dominated world of the author's other stories. Besides cultural oppression and gender domination, Braz draws attention to the evanescence of life in O'Hagan's writings, especially to the "nonchalance about killing" the nonhuman animals, which historically underlies the colonialist economy.

The collection concludes with a chapter titled "Howard O'Hagan in His Own Words," which offers a thematic highlight reel of O'Hagan's statements on his own work, and is largely based on his 1979 interview to Keith Maillard, published in *Silence Made Visible*. In this interview, O'Hagan observes that "a writer has a wonderful privilege. He can live his life twice" (33). It seems significant that the author, who lived for many years in places as diverse as Montreal, Jasper, New York, Australia, Argentina, Sicily, and British Columbia, in his best works chose to relive his life as a writer in the Canadian Rockies. David Stouck considers O'Hagan one of the most original representatives of the genre of the "mountain man novel," "which is central to the literary traditions of the West" (221). Geoff Hancock testifies that as O'Hagan "continued to write ... he became known as the mountain man of Canadian letters, and one of the best prose stylists of western Canada" (880). Although *The Mountain Man of Letters* is on the front cover of this book, the essays that comprise our volume go far beyond this regional definition to situate O'Hagan's works in broad theoretical contexts.

Works Cited

Braz, Albert. "Fictions of Mixed Origins: *Iracema*, *Tay John*, and Racial Hybridity in Brazil and Canada." *AmeriQuests*, vol. 10, no. 1, 2013, pp. 1-9.

Conrad, Joseph. *Heart of Darkness and Other Tales*. Edited with an Introduction and Notes by Cedric Watts, Oxford UP, 2008.

Davidson E. Arnold. "Being and Definition in Howard O'Hagan's *Tay John*." *Études Canadiennes*, vol. 15, 1983, pp. 137-47.

----. "Silencing the Word in Howard O'Hagan's *Tay John*." *Canadian Literature*, vol. 110, Fall 1986, pp. 30-44.

Fee, Margery. "Howard O'Hagan's *Tay John*: Making New World Myth." *Canadian Literature*, vol. 110, Fall 1986, pp. 8-27.

----. "A Note on the Publishing History of O'Hagan's *Tay John*." Fee, *Silence*, pp. 85-91.

----, ed. *Silence Made Visible: Howard O'Hagan and* Tay John. ECW, 1992.

----. "The Canonization of Two Underground Classics: Howard O'Hagan's *Tay John* and Malcolm Lowry's *Under the Volcano*." Fee, *Silence*, pp. 97-108.

Granofsky, Ronald. "The Country of Illusion: Vision, Change, and Misogyny in Howard O'Hagan's *Tay John*." Fee, *Silence*, pp. 109-126.

Hancock, Geoff. "O'Hagan, Howard." *The Oxford Companion to Canadian Literature*, 2nd ed., edited by William Toye, Oxford UP, 1997, pp, 880-81.

Hingston, Kylee-Anne. "The Declension of a Story: Narrative Structure in Howard O'Hagan's *Tay John*." *Studies in Canadian Literature/Etudes en Litterature Canadienne*, vol. 30, no. 2, 2005, pp. 181-92.

Keith, W. J. "Howard O'Hagan, *Tay John*, and the Growth of Story." Fee, *Silence*, pp. 73-84.

Keats, John. *Keats's Poetry and Prose*. Selected and edited by Jeffrey N. Cox, Norton, 2009.

Maud, Ralph. "Ethnographic Notes on Howard O'Hagan's *Tay John*." Fee, *Silence*, pp. 92-96.

Morley, Patricia. "Introduction to the New Canadian Library Edition." *Tay John*, by Howard O'Hagan, McClelland and Stewart, 1974, pp. vii-xiv.

Ondaatje, Michael. "Howard O'Hagan and the 'Rough-Edged Chronicle.'" *Canadian Literature*, vol. 61, Summer, 1974, pp. 24-31.

O'Hagan, Howard, and Keith Maillard. "An Interview with Howard O'Hagan." Fee, *Silence*, pp. 21-38.

----. *Tay John.* 1939. Afterword by Michael Ondaatje, McClelland and Stewart, 1989.

Pivato, Joseph. "Forest of Symbols: *Tay John* and *The Double Hook*." *Sheila Watson: Essays on Her Works*, edited by Joseph Pivato, Guernica, 2015, pp. 181-196.

Robinson, Jack. "Myths of Dominance Versus Myths of Re-Creation in O'Hagan's *Tay John. Studies in Canadian Literature/Etudes en Litterature Canadienne*, vol. 13, no. 2, 1988, https://journals.lib.unb.ca/index.php/scl/article/view/8084/9141

----. "Dismantling Sexual Dualities in O'Hagan's *Tay John*." *Alberta*, vol. 2, no.2, 1990, pp. 93-108.

Scobie, Stephen. *Signature, Event, Context.* NeWest, 1989.

Stouck, David. "The Art of the Mountain Man Novel." *Western American Literature*, vol. 20, 1985, pp. 211-22.

Zichy, Francis. "Crypto-, Pseudo-, and Pre-Postmodernism: *Tay John, Lord Jim,* and the Critics." *Essays on Canadian Writing*, vol. 81, Winter 2004, pp. 192-221.

---. "The 'Complex Fate' of the Canadian in Howard O'Hagan's *Tay John*." *Essays on Canadian Writing*, vol. 79, Spring 2003, pp. 199-225.

Teaching *Tay John*
on the Yellowhead Highway

JOSEPH PIVATO

In 1978 at, then new, Athabasca University we created our first course in Canadian Literature by beginning it with Howard O'Hagan's *Tay John*. Though set in western Canada, O'Hagan's 1939 novel was not well-known in Alberta. This almost forgotten work was rediscovered by readers in 1974 when McClelland and Stewart reprinted it in their New Canadian Library series as number 105. At the 1978 Calgary Conference on the Canadian Novel the organizers published the results of a survey of the most significant Canadian novels. On the list of the one hundred most important novels *Tay John* was number 76, that is, with the bottom twenty-five titles.[1]

Teaching *Tay John* in 1978-79 was a pioneering adventure. As the first novel in the course along with Richardson's *Wacousta* and Hemon's *Maria Chapdelaine*, this novel set the tone for the entire twenty-four weeks of readings and discussions. In those early years of teaching the first courses in

---

1   In the 1965 version of the *Literary History of Canada* edited by Carl F. Klink, there are no references to Howard O'Hagan or *Tay John* in any of its 945 pages. In 1977 poet Gary Geddes' short article "The Writer that CanLit Forgot," *Saturday Night* (Nov. 1977) 86, was devoted to Howard O'Hagan.

Canadian Literature we were not aware of the influence that O'Hagan's mythic novel was having on other Canadian authors who were beginning to publish novels. Only later did Robert Kroetsch, Michael Ondaatje and Rudy Wiebe reveal their debt to *Tay John*. Our growing awareness of this broad influence would change our reading of O'Hagan's novel and of other novels such as Sheila Watson's *The Double Hook* (1959) and Jack Hodgins' *The Invention of the World* (1977). These are revealing examples of T.S. Eliot's observation about "Tradition and the Individual Talent": "The existing order is complete before the new work arrives; for order to persist after the supervention of novelty the whole existing order must be, if ever so slightly, altered ... readjusted" (Eliot 50).

For the first fourteen years of its existence Athabasca University was housed in several commercial buildings in Northwest Edmonton within sight of the Yellowhead Highway that crosses the northern half of the city from east to west. So we were literally teaching *Tay John* from the highway which bears his name in an English translation of Tête Jaune, which means yellowhead. This highway runs west from Edmonton to Jasper National Park and through the Yellowhead Pass to Mt. Robson and to Tête Jaune Cache. This part of the valley of the Athabasca River is the setting for the story and legend of Tay John. I use the term "we" because I developed this course with my Athabasca colleague Mary Hamilton. Our course consultant was E.D. Blodgett from the Department of Comparative Literature at the University of Alberta.

The Cultural Context 1960 to 1979

The establishment of university courses in Canadian literature in the 1970s was, in part, a patriotic project of creating a national literature for Canada. Up to the 1970s English literature programs were focussed on British authors with one or two courses in American literature. English departments were structured in terms of the historical periods of English literature: Chaucer, Shakespeare and the Elizabethan poets, Milton and Restoration drama, the Romantic poets, the Victorian novelists, the twentieth century divided by two world wars. Faculty members were hired as specialists in each of these periods. There was little room for Canadian writers since many academics believed there were so few literary works of quality that there was little point in studying this writing. In effect, there was no Canadian literature.

This situation began to change after 1967, the centennial year for the confederation of Canada. At Expo 67, the world fair in Montreal, Quebec artists, musicians and writers promoted their distinct culture. The huge pavilion from France featured an entire floor of French literature. These impressive displays made Canadians aware that a country must have a national literature and many people began to rediscover their own writers. By the late 1960s the first university courses in Canadian literature were offered in a few of our universities, often against strong opposition. At York University in Toronto, in 1969 Prof. Clara Thomas and Prof. Eli Mandel taught the first course in Canadian literature. There were so many students registered that the two professors could not accommodate them all. Thomas produced a course manual, *Our Nature, Our Voices: A Guide to English-Canadian Literature,* which she later published in 1972. In addition to promoting several forgotten Canadian women writers, Thomas also included some Quebec writers in English translation, such as Ringuet's *Thirty Acres* and Roch Carrier's *La Guerre, Yes Sir!* She was moving in the direction of Comparative Canadian Literature which was being developed at the Université de Sherbrooke in Quebec (Pivato 2011).

It was in this cultural context of reawakening that O'Hagan's *Tay John* was rediscovered. It was first published in England in 1939 with a publisher who soon went bankrupt, and so O'Hagan never received any royalties. Then the Second World War began. In 1960 *Tay John* was published in New York but it did not sell well, though some copies did circulate in Canada. There are now copies of these early editions in some of the larger university collections such as the University of Alberta Library, University of Toronto Library and the UBC library in Vancouver. Only when McClelland and Stewart brought out the paperback edition of *Tay John* in 1974 was the novel able to circulate and be included in some Canadian literature courses. But by that time it had lots of competition from newer novels such as Mordecai Richler's *St Urbain's Horseman* (1971), Robertson Davies' *The Manticore* (1972), Rudy Wiebe's *The Temptations of Big Bear* (1973), and Margaret Laurence's *The Stone Angel* (1964) and *The Diviners* (1974). So for O'Hagan the blossoming in Canadian literature was both a blessing and a curse.

The Early Theories in Canadian Literature

The dominant approach to literary analysis from the 1940s to the 1970s was the New Criticism, which focused on close reading the language of the text and put aside the author's intentions, his or her psychological state, cultural influences and the social background. This is the way that university professors, teachers and students read Canadian works, that is, as if they did not emerge from the Canadian cultural and social environment. Some of this began to change at the University of Toronto when Professor Northrop Frye published *Anatomy of Criticism* in 1957, a book which influenced criticism in the 1960s primarily with the mythopoeic approach to literary analysis. In 1965 a team of academics at the University of Toronto published the *Literary History of Canada*, to which Frye contributed the final critical essay, "Conclusion."

In a passage that has become famous, Northrop Frye described the dominant quality of the Canadian imagination with the term "a garrison mentality." In a description that could be applied to the people inside the fort in *Wacousta* Frye explains, "Small and isolated communities ... their members have in the way of distinctively human values, and that are compelled to feel a great respect for the law and order that holds them together, yet confronted with a huge, unthinking, menacing, and formidable physical setting—such communities are bound to develop what we may provisionally call a garrison mentality" (830). We can see how such a critical observation can be applied to several early works from Canadian literature, and influence our reading in these narrow environmental terms. In his 28-page essay Frye uses the term, "garrison mentality," four times and implies that it applies to French-Canadian literature as well, though he makes only passing references to three works from Quebec: Hemon's *Maria Chapdelaine*, Gabrielle Roy's *Bonheur d'occasion* and *La poule d'eau*.[2] There are few references to Indigenous people and none to Indigenous writing.

The influence of Frye's thesis about the garrison mentality in the Canadian imagination can be seen in the book *Butterfly on Rock: A Study of Themes and Images in Canadian Literature* (1970) by D.G. Jones, who takes Frye's metaphor and applies it broadly across Canadian writing, even including some Quebec

---

2   The correct title of Roy's novel is *La petite poule d'eau*. The fact that it is incorrectly printed in this edition and in subsequent printings of Frye's "Conclusion" indicates that he and his editors paid little attention to the literature of Quebec.

works. Jones discusses two scenes in *Tay John*, but it is not clear how they are related to the notion of the garrison mentality. The first is Blackie's story about meeting Tay John in the middle of a lake in a blizzard as he is pulling a toboggan with the dead Ardith Aeriola. Jones reads this scene as a mythopoeic allusion to Adam and Eve figures who disappear under the snow and into the earth. The second scene is Father Rorty's loss of faith, his conflict with people and his death on a tree as his cross. Jones reads this as an example of the conflict between the forces of nature and the garrison mentality. Jones did draw attention to *Tay John*.

In 1972 Margaret Atwood published *Survival: A Thematic Guide to Canadian Literature*, a book that took Frye's thesis about the garrison mentality and popularized it by reducing it to four victim postures. Atwood makes several references to Frye and Jones along with many other English language writers. Because of her popularity as a feminist writer, her *Survival* had an impact of the reading of Canadian literature for decades. University students who may never have heard of Northrop Frye or D.G. Jones often would have heard of Atwood and often would have read one of her books. How are they going to read *Wacousta, Tay John* and *Maria Chapdelaine* with an open mind and not under the influence of the narrow thesis of the garrison mentality and survival? This is the challenge for any class in Canadian literature, even to this day.

Critical books that promoted the study of environmental themes dominated the 1970s and included: D.G. Jones' *Butterfly on Rock* (1970), Northrop Frye's *The Bush Garden* (1971), Laurence Ricou's *Vertical Man/ Horizontal World* (1973), John Moss's *Patterns of Isolation in English Canadian Fiction* (1974), Dick Harrison's *Unnamed Country* (1977), Philip Stratford's comparative essay "Canada's Two Literatures: A Search for Emblems," (1979) and countless other articles and book chapters.

In 1985 I wrote a detailed critique of these narrow approaches to Canadian writing in my first book, *Contrasts: Comparative Essays on Italian-Canadian Writing* (22-29), and then in 2015 returned to criticize the shortcomings of Atwood's *Survival* which was still being published, basically unchanged, in 2012 (Pivato 2016).

Given that Atwood's survival thesis is based on an environmental reading of Canadian writing, one might expect that she would give some attention to the writing of Indigenous authors. In chapter 4, "Early People: Indians and Eskimos as Symbols," Atwood's focus is on the depiction of Indigenous people by white writers. In accord with her thesis, she portrays a negative view of the Indigenous person as victim, but a victim who does not speak for himself or herself. In an appendix at the end of this chapter there are five titles of "writing by Indians," a mere token gesture. There is no discussion or even mention of literary works by Indigenous writers such as the Mohawk poet Emily Pauline Johnson (1861-1913), Cree writer Edward Ahenakew (1885-1961), Ojibway writer Basil Johnston, or Metis writer Maria Campbell.

An even more damning criticism of Atwood's survival thesis is that she cannot include any work by Indigenous authors because their work would totally undermine her arguments about the negative views of nature. In her book, chapter two is entitled "Nature the Monster." Indigenous authors and artists would never depict nature in these negative terms that suggest that human beings are constantly in conflict with nature and that it must be destroyed and conquered. In Indigenous culture and belief, the natural environment must be protected and preserved for future generations. Humans are part of the fabric of nature and are responsible for taking care of it. This is also the subtext of the narratives in *Tay John* and *Maria Chapdelaine*.

How do teachers of Canadian literature deal with the environmental readings? We begin by explaining to students that both the thesis of the garrison mentality and that of survival are reductionist views of the Canadian literary imagination, which are often based on selected works that support the argument and by ignoring works that do not support these narrow views. Atwood does not even mention *Tay John* in her book, but she does refer only in passing to Richardson's *Wacousta*, as an example of a garrison in Canadian writing (94). Her reading of *Maria Chapdelaine* is only as an example in Quebec literature of a victim who chooses to stay behind a garrison (218). There is no critical analysis of these texts in greater detail and no information on the historical context. In a 2003 critique of the garrison thesis E.D. Blodgett observes: "The best that could happen, then, to Canada and Québec would be to overcome their mutual origins in the death metaphor of the garrison ...." (173).

Old Stories but Different Styles

In 1979-80 most university students were accustomed to reading conventional narratives in the realistic tradition. Many had read the novels of Charles Dickens in high school. If they began the course by reading *Tay John*, they would encounter a work that was not a conventional novel but a series of tall tales, adventures and unexplained events all told by different narrators. If they began the course with *Wacousta*, they would enter an historical novel set in what was called the "Indian uprising of 1763, specifically the Pontiac Conspiracy." It was a proxy war for the larger conflict between the British and the French for control of central North America. It was part of the Seven Years War, which ended in 1759-60 when the British forces defeated the French forces at Quebec City and at Montreal.

John Richardson's *Wacousta* (1832) is written in the style of a Gothic novel full of melodrama, suspense, danger, violence, treachery and helpless women. The British soldiers and civilians are in Fort Detroit which is partially surrounded by Pontiac's warriors as they fight the British forces over control of the territory. The commander of the Fort, Charles De Haldimar, is not an heroic figure but a man who had betrayed fellow soldiers. Chief Pontiac's main advisor, Wacousta, is actually Reginald Morton, an ex-British soldier whom De Haldimar betrayed and so is out to take revenge on him at no matter what costs.

The dark plot of revenge and the exuberant style of the writing are evident from the opening paragraph of the novel. It begins with a night watch in a period "fearful and pregnant with events of danger," the threat of a "powerful and vindictive foe." The brooding and mysterious atmosphere, inexplicable appearances suggesting the supernatural, terror, suspected treachery, sudden violent action, gloomy midnight settings, are all qualities of the Gothic novel. Even the fort with the drawbridge and the moat-like ditch is a North American stand-in for a mediaeval castle.

Frye's image of the garrison as "Small and isolated communities ... compelled to feel a great respect for the law and order that holds them together, yet confronted with a huge, unthinking, menacing, and formidable physical setting" (830), would seem to apply to the garrison fort in *Wacousta*. However, if we look more closely at the events in the novel, we find that the contrast between the white civility and order inside the garrison and the irrational disorder outside in the forest breaks down. The moral and social order of the fort is questioned by the intrusion of the irrational. There are the mysterious appearances and disappearances within the fort, Ellen Halloway's madness, the discovered treachery of De

Haldimar. Against this background the Indigenous people outside are often depicted as morally superior to the British. Pontiac is described as a great chief of his people. The tall and strong Oucanasta carries the swooning Madeline, and Oucanasta and her brave brother rescue others from danger.

The figure of Wacousta is that of a white man who has rejected corrupt European society and joined the Indigenous people of the new world. He has deliberately chosen to escape into the woods. There is no fear here of the menacing wilderness; in reality, the Indigenous people are another society and culture little known or understood by white Europeans. We find many of these figures who have "gone Indian" in both Canadian and American literature. It is this creative ambiguity that we must use in reading *Tay John* and to do that we must suspend the symbolic structure, the garrison mentality suggested by Northrop Frye.

The melodramatic style of *Wacousta* is full of suspense, nightmarish in places, fantastic in others and so over-the-top that it seems surrealistic, a distortion of nature and the irrational elements suggested by the subconscious. The gothic style is pushed so far that it can be read as a parody, a post-modern parody.

Both *Wacousta* and *Tay John* begin with historical periods in early North American history. In the first sentence O'Hagan gives us the year, 1880, and the location, the Athabasca Valley. The historical event is the building of the Canadian Pacific Railway to the west coast. While Richardson's melodramatic style focuses on a story of revenge, violence and madness, O'Hagan uses a conversational style to relate the story of the legend on Tay John. Because students in Alberta are familiar with the river valleys of the Rocky Mountains, they tend to read the novel as if it were a realistic account of the life of the main character, Tay John. O'Hagan's narrative style tends to support this reading: even though he warns the reader that this is hearsay, and that the story tellers are not reliable, our familiarity with the locations make us want to believe the stories. We should note that every couple of kilometers of the Yellowhead Highway from Edmonton to Jasper has a highway sign with the image of the yellow-headed warrior in profile. It is a subliminal reinforcement of the reality of the historical person who was Tête Jaune. We read the novel with this in the back of our minds.

A Reading of *Tay John*

The first part of O'Hagan's novel is entitled "Legend" and begins by contrasting "men's time" with the timeless nature of legends. This latter temporal dimension is cyclical like the seasons. Tay John's story begins in summer and ends in winter. A legend, in a sense, has no known beginning since it follows a cyclical pattern. The mysterious birth of Tay John has the qualities of a heroic figure, a man with some supernatural qualities, the lack of a shadow, great strength, unusual yellow hair, and visions. He has been given these great talents in order to help his people to survive and thrive. His rite of passage from childhood into manhood indicates his destiny as the long-awaited leader of the Shuswap. They call him Kumkleseem and claim him as the saviour who will take them back to their original lands on the Pacific coast.

After Tay John's encounter with white men, his special relationship with the Shuswap begins to deteriorate. He refuses to share the gifts the white traders gave him as is the custom among Indigenous people. He rejects their rules of conduct and abandons his people. Like Wacousta, Tay John leaves his society in order to go off into the forest by himself. Both men see themselves as outsiders, but also in tune with nature. It is difficult to apply Frye's garrison mentality here.

This narrative is told in a rather simple style with many references to Indigenous beliefs and customs. The legend part of the story is not part of a systemic mythology for us, so it can be classified as a folktale. For the Shuswap in the novel, the story of the warrior with yellow hair is part of a system of beliefs and thus is a myth. It is a very sympathetic depiction of Indigenous people and of the natural settings. O'Hagan is using old myths from Indigenous cultures to create a new mythology for Canada. Margery Fee has published extensively on *Tay John* and explains the author's use of myth in these terms:

> Myth is used here loosely, as O'Hagan appears to use it, to include a wide variety of conventional patterns: native myth and local legend; literary genres, modes, and archetypes; popular stereotypes; and even intellectual categories. All are or have been accepted widely and uncritically as true, and used as valid ways of viewing the world. (9)

The second part of the novel begins with another historical event, the 1904 building of the Grand Trunk Pacific railway through the Yellowhead Pass across the eastern range of the Rocky Mountains. Here we meet men who are sometimes working for railway construction like Jack Denham.

The second part is called "Hearsay" and is narrated by Denham who tells everyone who will listen his story about first meeting Tay John and witnessing him wrestling with, and killing, a grizzly bear with his knife. In "Jackie's Tale" we have the striking image of Tay John getting up after a dramatic fight with the bear:

> A man's head appeared beside it, bloody, muddied, as though he were just being born, as though he were climbing out of the ground. Certainly man had been created anew before my eyes.

Like birth itself it was a struggle against the power of darkness,
and Man had won .... (87)

This image of Tay John rising up out of the ground recalls
his birth near the beginning of "Legend" and suggests the
cyclical structure of a story which begins again. Denham tells
us that after he killed the bear, Tay John just goes back into
the forest: "He vanished, as though he were leaving one form
of existence for another" (89). He soon joins the world of the
white man and becomes the subject of countless stories by
different people: Denham, Colin McLeod, Charlie the cook,
Alderson's story about rescuing Tay John from the river, Julia
Alderson's account of the hunting trip, and Tay John's version
of the trip at the hearing with the Mounted Police.

McLeod tells the story of Tay John running through the
mountain woods on foot for days in search of his run-away
horse. This image, and other scenes of Tay John in the deep
forests and fording rivers, is an allusion to the history of the
French-Canadian *coureurs des bois* and *voyageurs*, who travelled into the interior of Canada to trade with the Indigenous
people. The history and traditions of the *coureurs des bois*
literally "runners of the woods," are totally neglected by Frye's
dead metaphor of the garrison mentality and by Atwood's lists
of victim postures.

In chapter six Tay John goes to visit McLeod in his cabin
to trade for his furs. There he meets another mountain man,
Timberlake with his horses. Tay John wants to trade his furs
for Timberlake's tall sorrel mare. The next day Tay John goes
off with his new sorrel horse. Tay John sees himself as one
with his horse:

Tay John looked upon her, and I suppose saw her as more than a
horse. She would raise him above the ground and his feet would

no longer be the servants of the rocky trails. It seemed he wanted her with his hands, with his feet, with all of him. He saw himself, felt himself, the movement and the smell of horse, sweat and all, riding through the mountain on that sorrel mare. (103)

Later McLeod meets Tay John riding a pinto horse which he has earned by working as a guide for the Aldersons. And later Porter, the young Mounted Police officer, is impressed by Tay John's skills as a tracker, hunter and horseman. Tay John, though a man of the mountains, has a great affinity for horses, a quality which evokes the image of the great Canadian horsemen of the prairies, the Metis hunters of the buffalo herds. Like the Metis, Tay John is half Indigenous and half white, and this link is also suggested by the original French form of the name Tête Jaune. Once more we have the clear indication that this narrative is about a man with strong connections to the wilderness and to animals and with no fear of nature.

The third part of *Tay John* is called "Evidence—Without a Finding." It begins with Denham's philosophical discussion about illusion in contrast with the reality of physical objects. The insubstantial nature of man's ambition and perception sets the tone for the final episode in the story of Tay John. We meet Alf Dobble, who is building a resort in the mountains, a Canadian Lucerne. Dobble wants Tay John to become the resident "Indian guide" for the tourists whom he envisions flocking to his resort. After his experience with the Aldersons, Tay John is wary of Dobble's proposition and of being tied to a town under construction. He would be reduced to an object of curiosity.

We also meet Ardith Aeriola, a woman who has lived on the fringes of society as the kept woman of men with money. When the drunken Dobble makes advances on Ardith, she fights him off and Tay John comes to her rescue. All of Dobble's work camp turns against them and the two outcasts escape into the mountains. Denham, as narrator, learns later that they are living together and that Ardith may be pregnant. Denham is only able to piece together the story bit-by-bit. He finds Father Rorty's letter in Ardith's discarded Spanish bible (210). He hears gossip. And enquires about them at the RCMP office in Edmonton. He learns of Blackie's story. The evidence is questionable. Can we believe gossip and tall tales? Denham defends the uncertain ending:

> Every story—the rough-edged chronicle of a personal destiny— having its source in the past we cannot see, and its reverberations in a future still unlived …. Indeed to tell a story is to leave most of it untold. (166)

Blackie's story is the last that Denham hears about Tay John. Blackie meets Tay John and Ardith in the middle of a frozen lake in a blizzard. Tay John says he is looking for a doctor and then tells Blackie that he is looking for a church and goes off across the lake. As he leaves, Blackie notices that Ardith is tied onto the toboggan and that she is dead (262). Later, Blackie turns to follow them, to try to help them. He traces the tracks of the toboggan into the valley. The tracks become faint in the blowing snow until they disappear, forcing Blackie to give up and turn back:

There was nothing more he could do. He had the feeling, he said, looking down at the tracks, that Tay John hadn't gone over the pass at all. He had just walked down, the toboggan behind him, under the snow and into the ground. (264)

This image of descending into the ground is the opposite of the image of Tay John's mysterious birth. It is part of the cycle of life, of birth and death in nature. In Father Rorty's letter to Ardith Aeriola, Denham finds an apocalyptic vision: "Your face is too close for me to sleep. I have strange visions when I should sleep—of flames, of water flowing, of a long white road" (215).

With the images of the dark grave and the burning forest, there is an implied contrast between man's perception of life and nature. Tay John is born from a grave; Father Rorty dies in the life-giving rain. Howard O'Hagan has taken the consideration of nature far beyond the conflict between those who live with it and those who exploit it. The many dreams and visions in this book lead us to examine our view of life in Canada, our natural environment, our spiritual and social values and our attitudes to our fellow men and women.

A Novel of the Soil: *Maria Chapdelaine*

Based on his experiences of living and travelling in rural Quebec, Louis Hémon wrote *Maria Chapdelaine*, which was published in Montreal in 1914, a year after he was killed when he was hit by a train in Chapleau, Ontario. The novel only achieved success when it was published again in 1921 and translated into other languages. The English translation by W.H. Blake from 1921 is the version we are using here.

Maria Chapdelaine is set in the Lac Saint-Jean area of Quebec. Hémon depicts the people of the settlements of Peribonka and Saint-Gédéon by the detailed recording of customs, values, attitudes towards the land, religion and motivations. It is part of the literary tradition of novels of the soil and so there is no conflict here between man and nature.

The subject of Hémon's narrative is the psychological development of Maria and the important life decision she must make in choosing a husband. Her first love is François Paradis, a woodsman and pioneer, much like her father. Every autumn he leaves the town and travels north by foot and canoe to work in the lumber camps. François evokes the image of the *coureur des bois* that we find in Quebec history and in Quebec novels and in *Tay John*.

After visiting Maria and her family several times, François and Maria go out into the woods to pick wild blue berries. In the forest he proposes marriage to her privately, but no formal engagement is made at that time. He soon goes north to work in the lumber camps for that winter. In the middle of December, he decides to go south for the Christmas holidays, but he finds that the train south is not running because of a problem with the line, so he sets out on foot. Eutrope Gagnon brings the news to the Chapdelaine family:

> François set off alone on snow shoes, pulling his blankets and provisions on a toboggan .... You will remember the weather a week before Christmas—the heavy snow that fell, and after it the nor'west gale .... He went astray ... (90)

Maria has been raised with two different views of the land: one of the settler and farmer who cultivates the soil and develops a farm, and the other of the carefree frontiersman "in whom the vast wilderness awakened distant atavistic instincts for wandering and adventure (25). These words can equally be applied to Tay John, who also wanted to be free to explore and wander.

With the death of François, Maria must make a reasonable choice between two different suitors and consequently between two entirely different lifestyles. With Eutrope Gagnon Maria can look forward to repeating her mother's existence, the hardships of a pioneer style homestead. If Maria chooses the proposal of Lorenzo Suprenant, she will leave rural Quebec for a city in Massachusetts where Suprenant works in a factory.

The life and country values of Gagnon are those voiced by Maria's mother who constantly refers to the old parishes

of settled farms, fine cultivated fields, and life with some social pleasures. While these values are different from those of
François and her father, they nevertheless show an attachment
to rural life, unlike the life with Suprenant in a strange city.

The values of François Paradis and Eutrope Gagnon have a
sense of history of the region, a sense of ancestry in adopting
traditional roles and a spiritual connection to the land. We
can see that there is no garrison mentality here and no sense
of victimhood among the men or the women.

Another important novel of the soil from Quebec is
Ringuet's *Trente Arpents* (1939), which became *Thirty Acres*
(1940) in the English translation. In this tragic story the old
farmer Moisan is devoted to his land but loses it because of
financial problems and is sent by one of his sons to another
son who lives in an American industrial town. There Moisan,
who speaks no English, is unable to communicate with anyone
except his son and spends the rest of his life as a nightwatch-
man in a factory far from his beloved country village.

These Quebec novels of the soil have been compared to
many prairie novels such as those by Frederick Philip Grove:
Settlers of the Marsh and *Fruits of the Earth*.

The Influence of *Tay John*

In the 1989 edition of *Tay John*, there is an "Afterword" by
Michael Ondaatje, in which he identifies four novels which
are the literary touchstones for him:

> The first Canadian novel to reach me this way was Sheila Wat-
> son's *The Double Hook*. The second was *Tay John*. To come later
> were *By Grand Central Station I Sat Down and Wept* by Elizabeth
> Smart and *Swamp Angel* by Ethel Wilson. Seen together they are
> in a way a tradition. (209)

In an article published in 1974, Ondaatje explains that he had first read the novel in 1968, that is when he was 25 years old and just starting out as a writer. "I can think of no other novel that has got as close to that raw power of myth as O'Hagan's book does" (24). We can see the profound effect it had on the young writer. Ondaatje spent the first part of his writing career as a poet. In 1976 he published his first novel, *Coming Through Slaughter*, which demonstrates the influence of Watson's poetic style in *The Double Hook* and the myth-making of O'Hagan's *Tay John*. These influences continue with Ondaatje's *The English Patient* (1992). His 1974 article is the first academic study devoted to *Tay John* in Canada.

The Alberta writer Robert Kroetsch was also an active poet, but his novels *The Studhorse Man* (1970) and *Gone Indian* (1973) demonstrate affinities with *Tay John*. These novels deal with the borderland frontiers and the transformative power of moving across borders. They also have the reader confront the question of blurring ethnic identities.

Another Alberta writer, Rudy Wiebe, has devoted a number of his novels to exploring the lives of Mennonite setters in western Canada, but he has also written about the Indigenous people of the prairies in *The Temptations of Big Bear* (1973) and *The Scorched-Wood People* (1977), stories that evoke the world of *Tay John*.

The stories of British Columbia novelist Jack Hodgins are often set on Vancouver Island and evoke a strong sense of place. In his novel *The Invention of the World* (1977), Hodgins uses new world myths that remind us of *Tay John*.

In my comparative essay "Forest of Symbols: *Tay John* and *The Double Hook*," I explored the many parallels between the two novels. I have no doubt that Sheila Watson had read O'Hagan's novel since there are original 1939 editions in both the libraries at the University of British Columbia and at the

University of Alberta. Not only do the two works have similar
locations in the interior of Rocky Mountain valleys, and similar
characters, they both use myths, and a poetic and ritualistic
language. In writing *The Double Hook*, Watson was inspired
by the example of O'Hagan's narrative, a regional story with
universal implication.[33]

The World of *Tay John* on Campus

In 1985 the Government of Alberta moved Athabasca University
to the Town of Athabasca, which is about 120 km north of the
city of Edmonton. The new campus is about one kilometer
west of the town on the edge of a Boreal Forest and on a rise
above the Athabasca River, which is the site of many events
in *Tay John* as the river flows through the Athabasca valley in
what is now Jasper National Park.

There are trails through the Boreal Forest that border the
campus, which are used by joggers regularly. Several years in
early summer joggers have encountered a brown bear or a
black bear on these trails. Each time the bear had wandered
on to the trail in order to eat the many wild berries which
grow there. And each time the university staff have called the
local Fish and Wildlife Office to have officers come onto the
campus to capture the bear and take it away to be released in
a more remote area away from human habitation. Only to have
the bear or another bear wander back onto the trails and the
university campus the following summer. There is no terror
here; just surprise when the bear comes back.

---

3   For more work in Comparative Canadian Literature from international
    perspectives, see various essays in De Gasperi and Pivato, *Comparative
    Literature for the New Century*, 2018.

Works Cited

Atwood, Margaret. *Survival: A Thematic Guide to Canadian Literature*. House of Anansi Press, 1972, the 2004 and the 2012 editions.

Blodgett, E.D. *Five-Part Invention: A History of Literary History in Canada*. U of Toronto, 2003.

Campbell, Maria. *Halfbreed*. McClelland and Stewart, 1973.

De Gasperi, Gulia & Joseph Pivato. eds. *Comparative Literature for the New Century*. McGill-Queen's U.P., 2018.

Eliot, T.S. "Tradition and the Individual Talent." *The Sacred Wood*, Methuen, 1966.

Fee, Margery. "Howard O'Hagan's *Tay John*: Making New World Myth." *Canadian Literature*, vol. 110, Fall 1986, pp. 8-27.

Frye, Northrop. "Conclusion." *Literary History of Canada: Canadian Literature in English*, edited by Carl F. Klink, U of Toronto P, 1965.

----. *The Bush Garden*. Anansi Press, 1971

Hémon, Louis. *Maria Chapdelaine*. Translated by W.H. Blake, Macmillan, 1969.

Hodgins, Jack. *The Invention of the World*. Macmillan, 1977.

Kroetsch, Robert. *The Studhorse Man*. Macdonald, 1969.

Jones, D.G. *Butterfly on Rock*. U of Toronto P, 1970.

O'Hagan, Howard. *Tay John*. 1939. McClelland & Stewart, 1974.

Ondaatje, Michael. *Coming Through Slaughter*. House of Anansi, 1976.

----. "Howard O'Hagan and 'The Rough-Edged Chronicle'." *Canadian Literature*, vol. 61, 1974, pp. 24-31.

----. Afterword. *Tay John*, by Howard O'Hagan, McClelland & Stewart, 1989, pp. 201-209.

Pivato, Joseph. ed. *Contrasts: Comparative Essays on Italian-Canadian Writing*, Guernica, 1985.

---. "CL History: The Sherbrooke School of Comparative Canadian Literature." *Inquire: Journal of Comparative Literature*, vol. 1, no. 1, 2011, inquire.streetmag.org/articles/25

----. "Forest of Symbols: *Tay John* and *The Double Hook*." *Sheila Watson: Essays on Her Works, edited by* Joseph Pivato, Guernica, 2015, pp. 181-196.

----. "Atwood's *Survival*: A Critique." *Canadian Writers*, Athabasca University, 2016,

Canadian-writers.athabascau.ca/english/writers/matwood/survival.php

Richardson, John. *Wacousta*. McClelland & Stewart, 1972.

Ringuet. *Thirty Acres*. McClelland & Stewart, 1970.

Thomas, Clara. *Our Nature, Our Voices: A Guidebook to English-Canadian Literature*, New Press, 1972.

Watson, Sheila. *The Double Hook*. McClelland & Stewart, 1959.

Wiebe, Rudy. *The Temptations of Big Bear*. McClelland & Stewart, 1973.

The Wide Circle and Return
Tay John and Vico

D. M. R. BENTLEY

The most obvious structural feature of Howard O'Hagan's *Tay John* (1939) is its division into three parts: "Legend," "Hearsay," and "Evidence—Without a Finding." These divisions are accompanied by some intriguing shifts in narrative mode. The first part of the novel, "Legend," is told from an omniscient perspective in a manner that frequently recalls the King James version of the Bible ("He stayed with them, and the people were glad, for they believed that he was a great man" [23]). This narrative mode is briefly continued at the beginning of Part 2, but the remainder of "Hearsay" is recounted in the first person by Jack Denham in a self-reflexive manner that frequently calls attention to narrative matters ("Do you see what I mean?" The "social function" of a "backwoodsman" is "to hand on what he has heard, with the twist his fancy has been able to add" [78, 114]). Denham continues to narrate the third part of the novel, "Evidence—Without a Finding," but now with less emphasis on what he himself has seen and heard than on the stories of various others ("Some of the words, as I have repeated them, may be mine—the gist is his" [216]). It thus seems quite clear that *Tay John* is a novel in which structure and "style" as well as "themes" are "sensitively linked" (Ondaatje, "Afterword" 271). But on what basis and to what end?

The answer proposed here is that the tripartite structure and stylistic shifts of *Tay John* as it moves from the Shuswaps, to the backwoods, to urban culture reflect the three ages that Giambattista Vico discerned in each of the recurring cycles of human history—the "age of the gods," the "age of the heroes," and the "age of men" (20). According to Vico's analysis or "emplotment"[1] of human history in the *Scienza Nuova* (3rd. ed., 1744), each of these three stages has its own type of government and jurisprudence ("theocratic," "aristocratic," and "civil" [339]), as well as its own mode of expression: "[t]he first ... hieroglyphic, sacred or divine; the second, symbolic, by signs or by heroic devices; [and] the third, epistolary, for men at a distance to communicate to each other the current needs of their lives" (140). By explicit analogy with individual human organisms,[2] each of Vico's tripartite cycles *(corsi)* enacts a process of growth, maturity, decline, and return to divine origins *(recorso)*. Thus the "rise [and] progress" of a culture is followed by its "decadence ... dissolution," and, beginning the whole process again, its providentially decreed entry into

---

1   This term comes, of course, from Hayden White (216), who includes two informative essays on Vico and "Croce's Criticism of Vico" in *Tropics of Discourse*. A. M. Klein's "A Shout in the Street," first published in 1951 and recently reprinted in his *Literary Essays and Reviews*, contains a brief summary of Vico's theories followed by "An Analysis of the Second Chapter of Joyce's *Ulysses*" (342). In addition to these and other works mentioned in the body of this essay, Isaiah Berlin's *Vico and Herder: Two Studies in the History of Ideas* and Norman O. Brown's *Closing Time* warrant mention as very different and highly individual discussions of Vico.

2   "It deserves to be noted that in describing the age of the gods our author insists on the analogy between the infancy of the individual and the infancy of the race, and he also draws many of his illustrations from the character and condition of savage peoples. In these respects he was the predecessor of a multitude of later writers" (Flint 221). Towards the end of the first part of *Tay John,* the ageing Shuswap patriarch Smutuksen likens his people to "children" in need of a father (69).

"new divine times" of "primitive simplicity" (415, 399, 424). To students of twentieth-century literature, Vico's ages and cycles are probably best known as the "paradigm" behind the Nestor episode in Joyce's *Ulysses* (Klein 346). They also lie centrally in the background of Northrop Frye's thinking, both in *The Great Code,* which "begins with an avowal of the importance of Vico for his current work" (Bahti 119), and in the *Anatomy of Criticism,* where the "high mimetic" mode of fiction belongs to the "age of the gods" and the "low mimetic" mode to the "age of men" (33-60).[3]

No English translation of Vico was available to O'Hagan when he wrote *Tay John* in the 1930s, and nor was one necessary. Competent enough in Romance languages to work in Buenos Aires (a substantially Italian city) in the early 1930s

---

3   In *The Great Code* 5, Frye acknowledges that "[t]he sequence of literary modes in [the] *Anatomy of Criticism* is ... close ... to Vico," but in the earlier book the Neapolitan philosopher is only mentioned adjectivally in relation to "Joyce and his Viconian theory of history which sees our age as a frustrated apocalypse followed instantly by a return to a period before Tristram" (62). One consequence of Frye's adaptation of Vico in his work on literary modes is that the Frygian analysis of Margery Fee's "Howard O'Hagan's 'Tay John': Making New World Myth" is also profoundly Viconian. "Tay John ... will not stay put," writes Fee: "[h]e moves from myth, to epic romance, to realism; escapes irony by moving into comedy, and finally moves into myth again" (14). Accordingly, the first part of the book is dominated by "religious mythologies," the second is aligned with "aristocratic romance," and the third is centred on "American and materialistic realism" but concludes with a "hint of ... resurrection or cycle" and the "promise of a return of myth in each generation" (12, 20, 16). Echoing Fee, W. J. Keith observes that "(w]ithout a unifying stylistic norm ... *[Tay John]* could easily fall apart. As it is we are confronted with a series of literary forms remarkably compatible with Northrop Frye's theory of modes as they evolve through literary history—from myth through a version of epic ... through varieties of romance ... through the mimetic mode ... to the level of irony ... all this culminating in what Frye calls the 'return of irony to myth'" (36-37).

and to live in Sicily from 1964 to 1974,[4] he could have read the
Scienza Nuova and other writings by Vico either in the original
Italian or in the French translations of Jules Michelet (1835,
1839). Not only did the 1744 edition of the *Scienza Nuova* become available in 1928 in Fausto Nicolini's magisterial edition
of Vico's works 1911-41), but there was also a growing interest
in the Neapolitan philosopher in the surrounding decades: R.
G. Collingwood's translation of Croce's *Philosophy of Giambattista Vico* appeared in 1913; C. E. Vaughan's *Studies in the
History of Political Philosophy, Before and After Rousseau,* which
contains a lengthy chapter on Vico, appeared in 1925; and H.
P. Adams's *The Life and Writings of Giambattista Vico* appeared
in 1935. Also available was Robert Flint's *Vico* (1884) and a
number of discussions of Vico's political, legal, and aesthetic
ideas, including D. C. Heron's *Introduction to the History of
Jurisprudence* (1860) and George Sorel's "Etude sur Vico" in
Le Devenir Social (1896). Since O'Hagan studied law at McGill
University in the late 1920s, it is possible that his preliminary
or even primary interest in Vico was as a philosopher of law.
This would not be inconsistent with the emphasis on crimes
and remedies in *Tay John* and, indeed, it highlights the extent
to which the novel deals with the interconnectedness of legal
and cultural matters.

Part 1: Legend

In the first part of *Tay John*, O'Hagan's account of the Shuswap
band who look for leadership to the man whom they call

---

4   For these and other details of O'Hagan's life, I am grateful to Geoff Han-
     cock's entry in the *Oxford Companion to Canadian Literature,* as well as
     to the note on "The Author" in the 1989 NCL reprint of *Tay John* and to
     the "Chronology" in Fee's *Silence Made Visible.*

"Kumkleseem, for his yellow head" (40) coincides closely with Vico's "age of the gods." "In this age," writes Flint,

> man ... was rude, fierce, emotional; endowed with a strong sense of the presence of the divine, although incapable of conceiving of it except as in visible things and forms; and gifted with an unregulated but vigorous and creative imagination. It was the age in which the family was instituted, in which language originated, in which myths were produced, and in which the chief rudiments of civilisation were brought to light. ... Unable as yet to distinguish otherwise than most vaguely between the physical and the spiritual, or between things and thoughts, men in the primeval age regarded the phases and aspects of nature as themselves divine existences or divine actions, and conceived of the creations of their own imaginations as corporeal animated realities. (218)

As depicted by O'Hagan with the help of various authorities and compendia, including *The Golden Bough* and, as he acknowledges, Diamond Jenness's *Indians of Canada*,[5] the Shuswaps are certainly "endowed with [the] strong sense of

---

5   O'Hagan acknowledges Jenness's work in the prefatory note to *Tay John*. As Fee point out, "O'Hagan's sources for much of the first part of Tay John's story [are] the Tsimshian myth 'The Dead Woman's Son' [in Jenness 197-9], which he uses with little revision, and the legend of Tête Jaune, which named Tête Jaune Cache and Yellowhead Pass" (13). For the latter, O'Hagan may have relied on the oral sources mentioned in his prefatory note, but Fee also suggests a written source in John Grierson MacGregor's *Overland by the Yellowhead*, 1, 26-27 and Ralph Maud uncovers borrowings from James Teit's *The Thompson Indians of British Columbia* 323-4. O'Hagan seems to have drawn either directly or indirectly on several sections of *The Golden Bough*, including Fraser's discussion of *"The Soul as a Shadow and a Reflection"* (250-5; which contains a reference to the Shuswaps), his chapter on "The Worship of Trees" (144-58), and his comments on the "magical qualities of stones" (43-44) and the use of "homeopathic magic to heal and prevent sickness" (20-22).

the divine" that characterizes the "age of the gods." "Believ[ing]
that the world [is] made of things they [cannot] touch or see"
(29),[6] they regard all animals as possessed of a "spirit" that
must be honored and placated for hunts to be successful.
Kumkleseem perceives an "owl [as] the soul of a departed
woman" (49), and, after his visionary sojourn at the head of
the "dark river," he is informed by Squeleken, "the oldest ... and
... most wise" of the "old men," that "[t]he bear-spirit will be
[his] guardian spirit" and "talk" to [him] with a man's voice"
(49-50). When a member of the band is sick, "Kwakala, who
was the farthest on in his magic" (38), makes a "likeness of
the sickness and burn[s] it" (34). Anxious and curious in the
face of natural phenomena that all people of the "age of the
gods" believe to be divine, the Shuswaps find "satisfaction in
divination ... [and] mythology," regarding dreams and visions
"as indications of the will of the Deity" (Flint 219), and the
arrival of Kumkleseem as the fulfilment of "their belief that
one day a leader would come among them—a tall man ...
with yellow hair, and lead them back over the mountains to
their cousins, the Salish tribes along the coast, from whom
in the first place they stemmed" (21-22). That the journey to
"the great green meadow" in the mountains (62) which partly
fulfils this prophecy entails the death of three members of the
band ("[t]hree times they stayed to mourn. Three more graves
they left behind them") is but one of the many instances of

---

6   Both Fee (11) and Arnold E. Davidson (33) call attention to the Platonic
    resonances of this belief, and its corollary "that behind the basket their
    hands made was the shape of the perfect basket which once made would
    endure forever and beyond the time when its semblance was broken and
    worn thin by use" (29). O'Hagan may also have had in mind the notion,
    traceable to Michelangelo and sometimes ascribed to Eskimo artists, that
    a sculptor merely makes manifest a shape that exists within a piece of
    stone.

the use of suggestive numbers (three, four, twelve) in the first part of the novel to imbue Shuswap culture with religious and mythical resonances.[7]

In a "revolt against ... [the] individualism" of the Reformation, Vico held that "the first stage in the 'long education of the human race'" occurred with "the birth of the religious instinct and, with it, the Family" (Vaughan 1: 252, 213). Civilization began when men, in fear of the "divinity" that they apprehended in thunder, took refuge in shelters with "certain women ... in religious and chaste carnal unions solemnized marriages ... begat certain children and so founded families" (Vico 9). In accordance with Vico's view of mankind's fundamentally "civic" nature (Vaughan 1: 252), the Shuswaps regard "We" as the "greatest magic" (44), and, as the interloper Red Rorty discovers to his great cost after raping Swamas's wife Hanni, they hold that "a woman ha[s] one man and a man one woman and no other" (27). The Viconian idea of the "monastic Family" (Vaughan 2: 213) and, with it, Vico's insistence that primitive people are "sociable," "religious, truthful, faithful," "temperate," "strong, industrious, and magnanimous" (424, 176), finds expression in the code of conduct by which the Shuswaps live: "it [is] bad to speak untruthfully, to steal, to be lazy, to lie with a woman till she ha[s] become [one's] own, or to boast if [one] is not a great man" (45). "We have our way with women that each man may know he lies with his own and not where another may lie," explains Tis-Kwinit; "[i]f the usage of time be not respected, and the mark of a man on a woman mean nothing, then each man must fight for his woman and the fathers of children will be nameless" (66). The torture and burning of Red Rorty by the women and children of the band is a manifestation of the

---

7   I am indebted for this insight to Bonnie Parkins.

"admixture of religion and cruelty" that Vico finds among cultures in the "age of the gods" (176-8).

The "mark" of betrothal to which Tis-Kwinit refers is earlier conferred upon Zohalat's daughter Shwat by the hunter Memhaias. After "paint[ing] on his back his dream-spirit—an eagle with a spear"—he "look[s] upon her," "touche[s] her breasts and point[s] an arrow against her belly," these being "signs" that she will "understand" (64). Like TisKwinit's "mark," Memhaias's spirit-painting and courtship "sign" accord with Vico's theory that in the "age of the gods" symbolic representation takes the form of "pantomimic signs, an imperfect form of language to which correspond[s] an imperfect form of writing, the sacred or hieroglyphic" (219). As Vico explains, the first language "was a divine mental language by mute religious acts or divine ceremonies, from which there survived in Roman law the *actus legitimi* which accompanied all ... civil transactions" (340). To express his competing attraction to Shwat, Tay John also employs a "language ... [of] natural signification," a "gesture" which has a "natural relation ... with ideas" (Vico 139): "where all who [are] watching might see, he lift[s] her skirt and rip[s] open her breech clout" (64). The fact that for less ceremonial occasions the Shuswaps use a "difficult and distinct" language that is "not ready with big words" (20-21) accords with Vico's view that all languages begin, as do children, with "monosyllables" (77), as, of course, does their naming of Tay John metonymically by the color of his hair, for, as Vico states, the use of metonymy in the "age of the gods" is "due to inability to abstract forms and qualities from subjects" (130).

In one of the several references to the New World in the *Scienza Nuova,* Vico observes that, had "they ... not been discovered by the Europeans," the "American Indians" would have continued to follow the same laws of social development as other cultures (414). With the removal of the Shuswaps to the high Rockies towards the end of the first part of *Tay John*, their gradual development through Vico's three stages once again becomes a possibility, albeit one that is scarcely sustained by the novel's emphasis on the westerly movement of European culture. For Tay John himself, however, the future is very different: the mysteriously delivered son of Hanni and Red Rorty, he has a partial affinity for Europeans that begins to manifest itself when he guides two prospectors to the "dark river" and receives in return a "rifle, ... bullets, [a] red coat," and "the new name of *Tête Jaune*" (55). With his insistence on being called by a white name that soon becomes corrupted to the nonmetonymic "Tay John" (55), he begins to stand apart from the Shuswaps both racially and ethically: "[h]is yellow hair marked his different birth. His rifle was his own and no man could touch it. His red coat was a sign of the white man's favour" (56). In Viconian terms, Tay John's emblematic "red coat" is also an "heroic blazoning" which, like a "family ... coat of arms," proclaims the identity and ownership of its wearer (340, 161-4) and, in so doing, indicates his movement from the "age of the gods" into the "age of the heroes." That movement occurs physically when, after a bloody fight with Memhaias which itself recalls Vico's notion that "duels" began in the "barbarous period" and continued under the "heroic commonwealth" (354), Tay John finds his isolation from the Shuswaps complete and attaches himself to the advancing European culture.

Part 2: Hearsay

Just as Red Rorty's tendency to see trees as men and his espousal of apocalyptic Christianity (14-19) makes him an appropriate presence in the first part of *Tay John*, so Jack Denham's aristocratic connections—his family owns "a great white house in the north of Ireland" (75)—make him an appropriate narrator for the portion of the novel that is homologous to the "age of the heroes." "Government," writes Flint of the "heroic age," "was aristocratic; law was based on the force of the heroes, who were, however, controlled by ... fear of the gods; in ceremonies, compacts, and judicial procedure, a scrupulous and religious regard was paid to particular words and formulae" (223). Flint also notes that, "while the mythological language of the divine age was largely retained" in the "age of the heroes," it was supplemented not only by "heraldic emblems and devices" but also by "metaphors and comparisons in ... articulated speech" (222). It is surely not fortuitous that most of the second part of *Tay John* consists of "articulated speech"—the "web of words" that is known in Edmonton as "Jackie's Tale" (77). In this context, "hearsay" is both a legal and a narratological term that nicely captures the split between language ("names") and reality ("things") which, according to Vico, came with the "abstract forms" of the "age of the heroes" (l30-1).

In his capacity as a surveyor for the Grand Trunk Pacific railway, Denham is a mapper and a namer who continually reveals his awareness of the power and limitations of words. "I found myself saying 'Yellowhead,'" he says of his first encounter with Tay John, "'Yellowhead.' I had to give him a name so that I could help him—morally, you know. I had to align him with the human race. Without a name no man is an individual, no individual wholly a man" (86-87). Denham is also much given to similes and metaphors: "[a] new mountain valley leads a man on like that—like a woman he has never touched" (80), he says at one point, and at another, "[Tay John] waited ... immobile as—well, immobile as an idol" (106). When Denham first sights Tay John across a stream that has "teeth in it" (like an animal or a saw), he senses that this "tall ... Indian ... [with] ... full ... thick ... yellow" hair is more than he seems: "there was something, it is hard to say, something abstract about him—as though he were a symbol of some sort or other. He seemed to stand for something. [H]is muscles across his body ... represented strength in the abstract" (83). As if elaborating Flint's comment that in the "heroic age ... types of character were personified as individuals—e.g., ... heroism in Hercules, and poetry in Homer" (223)—Denham conceives Tay John as a "type" of physical strength and himself as merely the teller of tales told by "innumerable others" (114). (Vico, it may be recalled, initiated the hypothesis that "[t]he great representative and type of a heroic poet"—Homer—was not an "individual genius" but the name appended to the collected wisdom and mythology of a "marvellous age" [Flint 222, and see Vico 301-32].) After the resonantly Herculean[8] Tay John kills the bear that he has been fighting across the stream from Denham, he follows what the reader knows to be Shuswap custom by placing its severed head in the "crotch of a tree" (89). Not only does Denham fail to appreciate the placatory significance of this act, but he also interprets the preceding struggle abstractly or, to use two of Frye's terms for the dominant mode of "verbal expression" in the "heroic age," allegorically or analogically *(Great Code* 5-8): "man had been created anew before my eyes. Like birth itself it was a struggle against the powers of darkness, and Man had won" (88). It is entirely consistent with the correspondence between the second part of *Tay John* and the "age of the heroes" that although Denham recognizes nothing spiritual about the hoot of an owl (90), he determinedly casts Tay John himself in the "heroic mould," seeing in him "some hint of a destiny ... that ... ma[kes] him stand ... taller and his yellow hair ... shine brighter" (101).

---

8   The Tay John of "Hearsay" can be aligned with other Herculean heroes in Canadian writing; see my discussion of this heroic type in *The Gay] Grey Moose* 217-33.

An increasingly obvious pattern of allusions to Arthurian legend amplifies the heroic and aristocratic resonances of the second part of the novel. Above Colin McLeod's bed in the cabin where much of the action of "Hearsay" takes place hangs "a large print of a girl, veiled in mists of modesty, who was always about to step into a fresh and bubbling pool, by whose sides the grass was forever green, the trees eternally in leaf, and the sky above steadfastly blue" (96). Very likely a reproduction of a mythological scene by an artist such as Poussin or Burne-Jones, this print is treated as if real by the representationally naïve Tay John (who sometimes "stands in front of [it] ... saying nothing, just staring, and run[ning] his fingers over it" [100]), but to the reader, as to McLeod, it fits neatly into the Arthurian pattern that gathers momentum when Tay John spots the piratical Timberlake's "cream-coloured" "sorrel mare" standing in "new green grass" and, Denham imagines, sees her not just "as more than a horse" but as the horse "on which he would ride to his destiny like a warrior to the wars" (102-3, 106). After failing to win the mare in a card draw,[9] Tay John again reveals his naïve literalism *and* the physical violence of the "age of the heroes" by obeying the biblical injunction that "[i]f a hand offend you cut it off" (109). Predictably, this gruesome act of self-mutilation prompts Timberlake to bequeath the mare to Tay John. As a "possession" *per se* and as the possession that draws him down from the high country to the "eastern slopes of the [Athabasca] valley" (113, 118), Timberlake's mare is both an instance and the agent of Tay John's movement across the rubicon—Denham's saw-toothed creek and, later, the Athabasca River—between the "age of the gods" and the "age of the heroes." Little wonder that when Tay John nearly drowns in the

---

9   See the *Scienza Nuova* 205 and 343 for Vico's remarks on the contractual nature ("pacts") of "heroic jurisprudence."

Athabasca while "hanging on to his horse's tail," the incident prompts an allusion to Arthurian legend: on seeing Tay John's "hand lifted" and shining in the "moonlight," recalls a witness, "[he] would not have been surprised ... if out of it a sword had been brandished before [his] eyes" (124, 125).

That witness is, of course, Arthur Alderson, the English engineer whose restless wife Julia fulfils the Arthurian pattern intimated by McLeod's print and Timberlake's mare by playing Guinevere to Tay John's Lancelot. When a startlingly "transform[ed]" Tay John reappears at McLeod's cabin wearing a "black high-crowned Stetson" and riding a "pinto ... with ... white-rimmed eyes, and arched neck" (119), he resembles both a medieval knight and an American cowboy. With her "white horse," her "high-heeled riding boots," and her aristocratically "purple bow" and "purple haze of ... perfume" (120-1, 129), Julia Alderson similarly combines the two heroic types of the cowgirl and the medieval lady. Not surprisingly, she is soon labelled a "'United Stater'" (121) and later reminds the men at McLeod's cabin of "pictures from old books of castles and knights with banners ... a wandering and abandoned Lady Godiva" (142).

These heroic associations are made explicit after Julia returns from spending a night on the mountain with Tay John and before she makes the accusation that he has "imposed himself on [her]" (145). The response of Arthur and her admirer Ed to this charge is predictably irate, but against their vengeful impetuosity calmer heads prevail. "The people to handle this ... are the police, the North-West Mounted," says the Aldersons' cook Charlie, who later expresses privately his belief that the lack of any sign of violent struggle ("there wasn't a mark on her") does not support Julia's accusation of rape (146). Moreover, Charlie is "impressed by the fact that as the days [go] on it [is] Alderson, more than Julia, who desire[s] to bring Tay John to what he call[s] 'justice'" (147). Nevertheless, two Mounties—Tatlow and Porter—bring Tay John down to face his accusers in a scene that resembles a more formal legal proceeding: Tatlow, playing the role of judge, sits at a table scattered with papers; Porter, "Tay John's advocate" (151), stands by the side of the accused; Julia reluctantly makes a statement and Tay John steps forward to assert his integrity (154). After the hearing, Alderson apologizes to Tay John, but Tay John pushes him aside and, discarding his emblematic "black Stetson," rides "into the mist and distance" (156). All this is very different from Red Rorty's treatment by the Shuswaps, and it accords closely with Vico's definition of "heroic juris-prudence" as a cautious process involving "the use of certain proper words" and "taking care or making sure" (343). As Den-ham puts it at the beginning of Part 3: "Tay John had met the new—the world of authority and discipline moving with the railway into the mountains" (161).

Part 3: Evidence—Without a Finding

In Vico's scheme, the "age of men" encompasses both the "ma-turity" and the "decadence" of human culture: at its close the historical cycle completes itself and ushers in "the ... new divine times" (398-9). Not only does the Viconian idea of *corsi* and *recorsi* help to account for Denham's suggestion that in meeting "the new" Tay John has encountered "the memory of an earlier authority and discipline" but it may also lie behind his ensuing assertion that "there is nothing new nothing really new in the sense of arrival in the world unless an odd meteor here and there. ... To-day was implicit in time's beginning. All that is, was" (161). Moreover, the markedly neoplatonic quality of Denham's subsequent meditation on human life—"[s]ometimes when we are older there is a glimpse. It appears

we are returning. We have made the circle" (162)—may also
derive partly from Vico, for, as Adams points out, the Viconian assumption that "[t]hroughout the ... universe there is
a perpetual tendency to return to its divine source" owes a
considerable debt to Ficino, Pico della Mirandola, and other
proponents of "the neoplatonic doctrine of emanation" (34-35).
"Men walk upon the earth in light, trailing their shadows that
are the day's memories of the night," intones Denham; "[o]ur
life, our brief eternity, our to-day is but the twilight between
our yesterday and our to-morrow" (162).[10]

    What, then, are the characteristics of the "age of men" that
signal the achieved maturity and incipient "dissolution" of a
culture? Perhaps the most direct approach to this question
is through Vico's argument that, "as myths fade away and are
forgotten" in the "age of men," the religious instinct that had
been present at the inception of the historical cycle is both
"purified" in its dedication to "diffusing morality" and fatally
weakened by "scepticism, and ... philosophy" (Flint 224). That
natural phenomena have relatively few mythological over-
tones in O'Hagan's equivalent of the "age of men" becomes clear
soon after Denham resumes his narration in Part 3: a "splash"
in Yellowhead Lake is caused merely by a "beaver's tail" or a
jumping fish, and "the hoot of [a] great horned owl" has much
the same status as a "shout" or a "man's laugh" from the nearby
village or the brothel across the water (165). The task of keeping
men from this brothel—of "diffusing morality"—falls to Red
Rorty's younger brother, a Roman Catholic priest whose very
name—Thomas—indicates the dubious nature of his religious
faith. "He was a man of faiths, this Father Rorty," explains Denham; "[h]e could not believe that his brother was still alive, yet

<hr/>

10 Of course there are also echoes here of Wordsworth's "Intimations" Ode.

he had faith that he might be" (186). An aesthete who quotes Keats (188), enthuses over sunsets (187), and holds that "[w]ithout the Cross our Saviour's life would not be beautiful" (188), Father Rorty is a "realist" and a "material[ist]" (184, 211) who is prone to hysteria (208) and cupidity (213). In a self-conscious and masochistic imitation of the crucifixion, he ascends one of the mountains near Yellowhead Lake, ties himself naked to a "school-marm tree," and, forgetting that the "rain [will] shrink the ropes till he [cannot] escape" (222) dies with "[f]roth on his lips" (221).[11] Taken together, two of Denham's comments on Father Rorty's death—"[P]riestly arrogance could go no further" and "[O]ur fathers worshipped trees. I think I understand" (218-9)—resonate with the Viconian idea of a return to "barbaric times" at the conclusion of an historical cycle (398). The fact that before indulging in his self-serving *imitatio Christi* Father Rorty writes a long letter confessing a Pauline and Augustinian inner conflict of "flesh" and "spirit" (210-16) also gathers significance from Vico's theory that the language of the "age of men" is both epistolary ("for men at a distance to communicate") and alphabetical (as in "Dobble ... [with] two *b's* in it").[12]

The recipient of this letter and the object of Rorty's attempt to reconcile sacred and profane love is Ardith Aeriola, a woman of central European origin who exercises an almost

11 It is worth noting that, while Father Rorty deliberately imitates Christ, Red Rorty's resemblance to St. Sebastian (27-28) is fortuitous, and a further instance of the religious and mythical associations that O'Hagan exploits in Part 1. Whereas Father Rorty's death is a manifestation of the "barbarism of reflection" that characterizes the terminal phases of the "age of men," Red Rorty's death occurs in the context of "a generous savagery, against which one could defend oneself or take flight or be on one's guard" (424).

12 See also the "crudely painted black letters" and "words, spelled out in red" of Dobble's sign (175) and the "large" and "small" letters of the promotional leaflet in his office (228).

universal appeal to men on the frontier because, by Denham's analysis, she represents in "idealised" form "all that they ha[ve] left behind" (195, 204). Part of Denham's explanation of the appeal of this *fin-de-siecle allumeuse* could stand as a gloss on the third part of the novel: "I remembered ... that woman was the death of heroes and the destruction of heroes' work—but heroes, those vulnerable men, are gone from the earth, and woman's power therefore no longer what it was" (192; but, perhaps, in the process of becoming so again). Although capable of being "idealised," Ardith Aeriola does not suggest "symbolic" or "abstract" qualities as did Tay John and even Julia Alderson in Part 2; on the contrary, she is perceived as an individual but representative woman—a physically passionate (200), somewhat cruel (201), and moderately talented (196) everywoman in an "age of men." "When you met her you felt you had found something. Reality of some sort ... She was a figure. She made her place. She stood for something— ... like a woman on a barricade thrown across the street. ... Here was woman" (197-9). Consistent with the democratic age that he, too, now inhabits, Tay John is "not quite so tall" as Denham remembers, and he now has "a thin line of black" in his hair which not only demystifies his yellow head but also associates him with the black-haired Ardith Aeriola (207, 242). When the two are together, Tay John is "a man no better nor worse than the others, but different" (253). Once regarded as divine, then perceived as heroic, he is now seen as merely human.[13]

The most striking manifestation of the decay and artificiality of the "age of men" in "Evidence—Without a Finding" is also the "low mimetic" equivalent of Tay John's luminously

---

13 His hair now leaves a "dark stain of oil" on "the collar of his buckskin
    shirt" and, manifesting the artificiality of the "age of men," "a steel hook
    attached to a pad of leather" has been "fitted to his forearm" (205).

yellow hair: the "immense gold cap" that glitters in the mouth
of Ardith Aeriola's scheming consort, the demotically named
Alf Dobble (168). A literary descendant of Stephen Leacock's
unscrupulously entrepreneurial Josh Smith,[14] Dobble is regarded with distaste and condescension by Denham. "Somewhat the picture of a villain—but not quite," his other "teeth
[are] large, long, ... [and] rather browned with tobacco," and
the "grey ends of his "brown moustache ... droop ... as low as
his chin," as if mimicking the physical difficulty that prompts
him to purchase an "Aphrodine Girdle" (168, 227-8, 233). It is
entirely consistent with the correspondence between Vico's
"age of men" and "Evidence—Without a Finding" that Dobble
considers himself "a man who knows other men—who knows
himself" and takes pride in taking "a realistic view of all things,
[and] their significance" (170, 224). It is also consistent with this
correspondence that Dobble has created a parodic fiefdom in
the Rockies (a "castle built of logs in the wilderness" [192]), and
that Denham's view of his *ersatz* "Lucerne" and its belligerent
inhabitants is heavily ironical, for, as Vico famously observes,
irony is not possible until "falsehood" begins to wear "the
mask of truth" during the "age of men" (131). Frye's inclusion
of deceptive advertising and bawdy humor among the characteristic productions of the "ironic mode" (*Anatomy* 43-49)
helps to explain the presence of both in the third part of *Tay
John*. Dobble's "Aphrodine Girdle" reveals him to be a victim
as well as a practitioner of "publicity" (224, 228), and Denham,
not previously given to reporting such matters, repeats several

---

14 The sign on Smith's hostelry in the opening chapter of *Sunshine Sketches
of a Little Town* reads "Jos. SMITH, PROP" (6). The equivalent sign in *Tay
John* carries the inscription "Alf Dobble ... Proprietor" (175). Leacock be-
friended O'Hagan at McGill and helped him to "obtain employment with
the Canadian Pacific Railroad recruiting farm labourers from England"
("The Author," *Tay John*).

scatological insults uttered by Dobble and his men. Dobble's remark that "railway officials have their brains in their bowels" sticks in his memory (181, 191), and he also recalls the story that Ardith Aeriola gave up a career as a music-hall singer after "[s]omeone shouted at her, 'Lady, yer cawn't sing with yer buttocks'" (196). Such remarks accord with Vico's distinction between the poetic and noble languages of the preceding ages and the "vulgar" speech of the "age of men" (144, 147, 342).

As an occasion for the exercise of law, Dobble's verbal and physical assault on Ardith Aeriola in the "big hall" at "Lucerne" (238-9) is parallel to Red Rorty's rape of Hanni in Part 1 and Julia Alderson's accusation of Tay John in Part 3. By comparison with "divine law" and "heroic jurisprudence," contends Vico, justice in the "age of men" is relatively "mild" (94): at its best, it "looks to the truth of the facts themselves and benignly bends the rule of the law to all the requirements of the equity of the causes" (343-4). When Dobble is discovered after the incident in the "big hall" "under some bushes" "badly beaten" and perhaps suffering from "nervous shock" (250), it is "generally agreed" by those who hear the story in Edmonton that he "[h]as got what was coming to him" (247). This consensus may explain the reluctance of the Mounties to pursue and charge Tay John and Ardith Aeriola as seems to be required by Dobble's accusations (254). More obviously a benign bending of the "rule of the law" is Sergeant Flaherty's later decision to "wink ... his eye" at Tay John's possession of caribou "meat ... out of season" on the principle that, while he cannot be "granted the freedom of the Indian in his hunting" because he is not part of "a recognised band," he can "hardly be bound to the restrictions of the white man. He had to live, was how Flaherty saw it" (255-6).

Less disposed to appreciate "the equity of the causes" is Jay Wiggins, the police Inspector whom Denham encounters in an office lined with "blue-backed reports," where he sits with his "head bowed [and his] hands clasped upon the desk top, as if in reverence before the accumulated and recorded achievements of the Force" (248). Wiggins is by turns pedantically legalistic, prejudicially biased, and narrowly rationalistic: he toys with the legal distinction between "assault" and assault and battery; he blames the Dobble incident on Ardith Aeriola, whom he describes as a "tart," a "foreign woman," and a troublemaker who "draws men like a piece of bad meat draws flies"; and he concludes that "[t]he whole thing isn't logical" (250-1). These attitudes are consistent with Vico's "barbarism of reflection" (424), the rationalistic decay of human sympathy and natural justice that occurs at the close of the historical cycle. "Even where civil equality is universally and fully attained" in the "age of men," writes Flint, "there will be great inequality as regards wealth, and from that inequality will flow ... grievous ills, general discord and disorder" (224). The most obvious evidence of the "decadence [and] dissolution" of the "age of men" in *Tay John* is the collapse of Dobble's fortunes and, with them, his "Lucerne—in the Heart of the Rockies":

> [t]he buildings fell into disuse. Trappers, trainmen, and others filched the logs for needs in other places. The cabins disappeared bit by bit, one by one, as though slowly sinking into the ground. You might say that Dobble left barely a trace behind him. Perhaps his investments in the East had gone bad. (253)

When "the peoples are rotting in ... civil disease ..., then providence for their extreme ill has an extreme remedy at hand," writes Vico; "they shall turn their cities into forests and the forests into dens and lairs of men ... Thus providence brings back among them the piety, faith, and truth which are the natural foundations of justice as well as the graces and beauties of the eternal order of God" (423-4). It is the "untutored" wilderness (74)—the site of what Vico calls "the primitive simplicity of the first world of peoples" (424)—that provides the setting for the two encounters with Tay John and Ardith Aeriola with which the novel closes.

In his account of the first of these, Sergeant Flaherty notices, not only that the couple is living in the Indian manner (255-8), but also that Ardith Aeriola is wearing a "silver cross" bequeathed to her by Father Rorty (257). Indeed, Flaherty's last sight of her is with her "hand upraised [and the] sun catching the silver cross" against a background consisting of a "smoking tepee," "wooded hills, and ... the great blue wall of the Rockies" (257). In addition to reporting that Ardith Aeriola appears pregnant (257-8), Flaherty records a further observation that is highly suggestive in the context of Vico's theory of *corsi* and *recorsi,* and suggestive, too, of a return to the mute language of gesture that characterizes the "age[s] of the gods": in answer to his question about whether she and Tay John will be "coming back," Ardith Aeriola takes a "few steps towards the river" and, "turn[ing] slowly," "trace[s] a circle with a neat moccasined foot through the grass" (256). The suggestion of a completed cycle and a new beginning is reinforced both by Ardith's spoken reply ("you tell them I'm not going back ... ever") and by her presumed pregnancy.

The second encounter with the couple in the "[w]ild country" comes from Blackie, a trapper "versed in the ritual and suffering of travel—man's form of worship of the vast round earth" (259). Already associated by these comments with old and "new divine times" (Vico 399), Blackie also has "the dark brow of a prophet" and, "[l]ike a prophet," speaks "in amazement" of "[a]lbino bears ... wolverines that c[an] outwit a man," and other "creatures" which can readily be seen as the products of an age of myth and imagination. There may even be Viconian resonances to the fact that Blackie's voice has "a resounding quality, like a voice out of a cave" (259), for, as observed earlier, Vico locates the origins of culture in the caves to which primitive men retreated when they were terrified by thunder. According to this "big man" from the still partly "unnamed" "country beyond the Jackpine" (258-9),[15] Tay John was pulling a loaded toboggan across a frozen lake when the two met, and his first words concerned the whereabouts of a doctor. On hearing that there is "no doctor around for a hundred miles, maybe more," "he sort o' caved-in" and, as if "havin' visions—or ... just plain crazy," informs Blackie that he is "going to a church ... over there behind the mountain" (261). As Tay John departs, Blackie sees to his horror that the "big load tied on th[e] toboggan" is a dead woman—Ardith Aeriola, Denham assumes—with "[o]ne eye ... open" and "snow in her mouth" (262). When Blackie recovers from his shock and, in an outpouring of human sympathy that is consistent with Vico's account of *recorsi,* decides to "see what he c[an] do to help," he picks up Tay John's "sled tracks" where they "enter ... the timber" and finds that, "in one place," the trail makes "a wide circle and return[s] to within a hundred yards of where it had been before" (262-3). After this final *recorso,* Tay John's trail indicates that he "climb[ed] slowly up the valley until he was well beyond the timber" and then headed towards one or other of "two passes" (263). According to Blackie—or,

---

15 See also Vico's description of the "true natural aristocracy" of Plato's commonwealth which, he holds, came into being when providence "ordained that men of gigantic stature, stronger than the rest, who were to wander on the mountain heights as do the beasts of stronger natures, should, at the first thunderclaps after the universal flood, take refuge in the caves of the mountains" (419). Blackie describes Tay John as "[a] tall fellow" who seems, by turns, "very big, shadowy like" and "no bigger than a little boy" (260). These different perceptions of Tay John accord with his final appearance at what may be the end of one cycle and beginning of another.

more accurately, Denham's version of Blackie's story—the snow had then begun to fall "in great wavering flakes without cessation,"[16] all but obliterating the sled tracks and leaving the trapper with "the feeling ... that Tay John hadn't gone over the pass at all. He had just walked down, the toboggan behind him, under the snow and into the ground" (263-4).

Has Tay John gone to his death in one of the passes, or has he returned to the earth from which he was believed by the Shuswaps to have emerged? If the woman on the toboggan was a dead and pregnant Ardith Aeriola, could her child miraculously rise from the grave? The answers to these questions will, of course, depend on the reader's attitude to the supernatural and the miraculous. Michael Ondaatje ends his seminal essay on *Tay John* by observing that Tay John "is vulnerable to fashion and progress and his only strength is the grain left in the memory and in the hope he will emerge in the future in different forms" ("O'Hagan" 31). Arnold E. Davidson observes near the end of his poststructuralist reading of the novel that "Tay John's descent into the earth to join in death a pregnant woman (his mistress/his mother) too obviously returns to the novel's beginning and the possibility of having it all to recount over again" (43). Margery Fee's brilliant analysis of the mythical components of the novel includes the observation that there are "powerful alternatives" to the "simple conclusion that Tay John has probably frozen to death.... Th[e] hint of a possible

---

16 In recalling the final paragraph of "The Dead" and *Dubliners,* this phrase and the snowfall that it describes suggest a debt and, perhaps, an allusion to Joyce's depiction of Ireland as a moribund culture that may (or may not) undergo a process of renovation. The "extended allusion" to Duncan Campbell Scott's "On the Way to the Mission" that Fee recognizes in Blackie's Story (16) also accords with the Viconian possibilities surrounding the conclusion of *Tay John* for strong suggestions of spirituality and rebirth surround Scott's murdered Indian and his dead wife.

return of the hero, of a cycle, is mythically irresistible" (16).
Perhaps it was especially irresistible when O'Hagan wrote
and published *Tay John* in the late 1930s, in the midst of the
Great Depression and on the brink of the Second World War.
Perhaps the concluding possibility of a Viconian return to the
"sociable ... religious, truthful, and faithful" "simplicity of the
first world of peoples" is O'Hagan's gently optimistic response to
the "civil disease," "private interests," "deep solitude," "obstinate
factions," "misbegotten subtleties," "base savagery," and "pre-
meditated malice" of the world around him (423-4). Perhaps
Tay John is set between 1880 and 1911—around the end of one
cycle *(siecle)* and the beginning of another—to reinforce this
optimistic possibility. Certainly many aspects of *Tay John,* not
least the Viconian patterns conjectured here, seem to reflect
and invite the idea that somehow, somewhere in the twentieth
century—perhaps at the beginning, perhaps near the middle,
perhaps at the end—one huge historical cycle is drawing to a
close and another is beginning to manifest itself. "So the people
waited, blind in time, not knowing what the days would bring,"
says the omniscient narrator near the end of the first part of
the novel. "And while they waited Tay John moved in and out
among them, always leaving, still always returning, making
great loops through the mountains, till the pattern of his travels
reached out from the village like the petals of a flower" (57).

Notes

I am grateful to several students and colleagues at the University of Western Ontario, especially Brock Eayrs, Bonnie Parkins,
Leon Surette, and J. M. Zezulka, for valuable discussions of
ideas contained in this paper, and to the Social Sciences and
Humanities Research Council of Canada for its support of my
scholarly activities.

Works Cited

Adams, H. P. *The Life and Writings of Giambattista Vico.* George Allen and Unwin, 1935.

Bahti, Timothy. "Vico and Frye: A Note." *New Vico Studies*, vol. 3, 1985, pp. 119-29.

Bentley, D. M. R. *The Gay]Grey Moose: Essays on the Ecologies and Mythologies of Canadian Poetry, 1690-1990,* U of Ottawa P, 1992.

Berlin, Isaiah. *Vico and Herder: Two Studies in the History of Ideas.* Hogarth P, 1976.

Brown, Norman O. *Closing Time.* Vintage, 1971.

Croce, Benedetto. *The Philosophy of Giambattista Vico.* Translated by R. G. Collingwood, Howard Latimer, 1913.

Davidson, Arnold E. "Silencing the Words in Howard O'Hagan's *Tay John.*" *Canadian Literature*, vol. 110, Fall 1986, pp. 30-44.

Fee, Margery. "Howard O'Hagan's *Tay John*: Making New World Myth." *Canadian Literature*, vol. 110, Fall 1986, pp. 8-27.

---, ed. *Silence Made Visible: Howard O'Hagan and* Tay John. ECW, 1992.

Flint, Robert. *Vico.* 1884. Philosophical Classics for English Readers. Philadelphia: Lippincott; Edinburgh: Blackwood, n.d.

Fraser, Sir James George. *The Golden Bough: A Study in Magic and Religion.* Abridged ed. 1922. Macmillan, 1971.

Frye, Northrop. *Anatomy of Criticism: Four Essays.* 1957. Princeton UP, 1973.

---. *The Great Code: The Bible and Literature.* Academic P, 1982.

Hancock, Geoff. "Howard O'Hagan." *The Oxford Companion to Canadian Literature*, edited by William Toye, Oxford UP, 1983, pp. 619-20.

Heron, D. C. *Introduction to the History of Jurisprudence.* London: Parker, 1860.

Jenness, Diamond. *The Indians of Canada*. 1932. U of Toronto P
    in association with the National Museum of Man and the
    Publishing Centre, Supply and Services, 1977.

Keith, W. J. *A Sense of Style: Studies in the Art of Fiction in English-
    Speaking Canada*. ECW, 1989.

Klein, A. M. *Literary Essays and Reviews*. Edited by Usher Caplan
    and M. W. Steinberg, U of Toronto P, 1987.

Leacock, Stephen. *Sunshine Sketches of a Little Town*. 1912. New
    Canadian Library, McClelland and Stewart, 1970.

MacGregor, John Grierson. *Overland by the Yellowhead*. Western
    Producer, 1974.

Maud, Ralph. "Ethnographic Notes on Howard O'Hagan's *Tay
    John*." Fee, *Silence*, 92-96.

O'Hagan, Howard. *Tay John*. 1939. McClelland and Stewart, 1989.

Ondaatje, Michael. "Afterword." O'Hagan, pp. 265-72.

---. O'Hagan's Rough-Edged Chronicle." *Canadian Literature*,
    vol. 61, Summer 1974, pp. 24-31.

Sorel, George. "Etude sur Vico." *Le Devenir Social*, vol. 9, Oct.
    1896), p. 787; vol. 10, Nov. 1896), pp. 906-1012; col. 11, Dec. 1896,
    pp. 1013-46.

Teit, James Alexander. *The Thompson Indians of British Columbia*.
    Edited by Franz Boas, New York: n.p., 1900.

Vaughan, C. E. *Studies in the History of Political Philosophy Before
    and After Rousseau*.

1925. Edited by A. G. Little. 2 vols., Russell, 1960.

Vico, Giambattista. *The New Science*. 1744. Translated by Thomas
    Goddard Bergin and Max Harold Fisch, Cornell UP, 1968.

White, Hayden. *Tropics of Discourse: Essays in Cultural Criticism*.
    Johns Hopkins UP, 1978.

The Declension of a Story
Narrative Structure in Howard O'Hagan's *Tay John*[1]

Kylee-Anne Hingston

When David Stouck states in his article "The Art of the Mountain Man Novel" that "actual exploits of mountain men had not been written down, but passed on by word of mouth so that they became the stuff of legends" (212), he implies that the process of storytelling is a development from circumstances or happenings, to oral tale, and then eventually to legend. He and many other critics of Howard O'Hagan's *Tay John* have seen the novel as portraying how story develops in this fashion. However, the section titles within the novel move from "Legend," to

1   In reprinting of this article, I want to acknowledge and apologize for its settler biases. My excuse is that I wrote this paper as a very early scholar, in the first years of my graduate education, before I had ever encountered critical race theory, Indigenous scholarship, or even heard the term "settler colonialism"—but this only explains and does not excuse its errors. I take this reprinting as an opportunity to make what small amends I can by referring to some of the relevant scholarship on settler appropriation of Indigenous stories. I thank the scholars, writers, and activists whose work has made me rethink this paper, O'Hagan's novel, and my role as a settler scholar on Treaty 6 lands: namely, Lenore Keeshig-Tobias, Lee Maracle, Eva Mackey, Margery Fee, and Stephanie Keane. I also thank the Indigenous Voices Team at the University of Saskatchewan's Gwenna Moss Centre for Teaching Effectiveness—Rose Roberts, Striker Calvez, and Maria Campbell—for helping me begin the ongoing work of Indigenizing my pedagogy and research.

"Hearsay" (one of the *OED* definitions of which is "oral tidings" or "tradition"), and then to "Evidence—Without a Finding." This seems to imply that O'Hagan actually believes that the process of storytelling is a degeneration from authoritative legend to inconclusive evidence. The novel itself also suggests that O'Hagan intended to represent storytelling not as a movement from a tangible reality or event to intangible mythic proportions, but rather as a declension from an elusive but indisputable legend to corporeal but uncertain facts. To O'Hagan, there is clearly a difference between telling a story and the story itself: to tell a story is to attempt to gain a hold, however tenuous, of an ethereal and absolute story, represented in *Tay John* by shadow, darkness, wilderness, and even by Tay John himself.

In the first section of the novel, "Legend," the narrator gives a Platonist explanation of Shuswap basket making: "[The Shuswaps] believed that the world was made of things they could not touch nor see, as they knew that behind the basket that their hands made was the shape of the perfect basket which once made would endure for ever and beyond the time when its semblance was broken and worn thin by use" (29). To *Tay John*'s version of the Shuswap people, a perfect and permanent Platonic form of the basket exists in "the shadow of what they could not yet discern" (29), and the physical baskets they make are imperfect and transient imitations or representations of the immutable form.[2] Plato also viewed

---

2 The novel's explanation is not, as far as I can find, grounded in Secwepemc customs or knowledge. As Sergiy Yakovenko points out, O'Hagan's knowledge about Indigenous culture primarily comes from "the 'White' anthropological sources such as Diamond Jenness's *The Indians of Canada* (1932)" (285). In the brief 8 pages of *The Indians of Canada* covering the Interior Salish peoples, basket-making is briefly mentioned for its "imbrication" of "geometric ... design," but that is all (357). Here and elsewhere in the novel, O'Hagan superimposes western mythology and philosophy over

art and storytelling in a similar manner: artists and poets are "imitators" who are "removed ... from the truth" (11-12). In the same way, O'Hagan intends the basket making to represent storytelling: the shadow's evidence, which is the basket or the tale, is a transmutable representation of the true form which exists, like legend, outside of the physical realm. And an ephemeral imitation is also all the evidence can be; it cannot ever be as pure as its form: "Each man sought the shadow beyond his work, and no man could reach it" (29-30). Telling a story, then, like making a basket, is a degenerative process and a removal from an authoritative origin.

However, many critics assume that in *Tay John* storytelling is a process in which simple events are altered through tale until they transmogrify into legend. In his paper entitled "Howard O'Hagan and 'The Rough-Edged Chronicle,'" Michael Ondaatje uses O'Hagan's depiction of the shout of Red Rorty to argue that the movement of the novel shows how legend grows from oral misrepresentations of events: "the paragraph [describing the shout] ends by moving from the clear image into something that is almost mystical" (Ondaatje 283). However, the description of Red Rorty's shouting actually supports the order in which the novel's sections are named:

> At other times he would shout when there was nothing to shout for, and would listen and smile when the mountains hurled his voice—rolled it from one rock wall to another, until it seemed he heard bands of men, loosed above him, calling one to another as they climbed farther and higher into the rock and ice. (14)

Indigenous culture, a common settler colonial literary move in which, as Margery Fee describes, the "heroic author takes over from the vanishing Indians to form a new indigenous mythology for the newcomers, who thus become indigenous themselves" (*Literary Land Claims* 6).

The movement of Rorty's yell develops from a mysterious, purposeless, and inarticulate origin into interpretable articulate calls removed from and yet attached to their source. This is actually the pattern the novel follows: shadow and darkness are the origin of Tay John, and people place a number of names upon him, which represent an aspect of him (his yellow hair), in order to interpret him; dusk gives land its being, and then man gives land its name in order to "keep it within the horizons" (80).

And naming, which Margery Fee has claimed is "analogous to myth-making" ("Howard O'Hagan's *Tay John*" 10), but which actually is analogous to storytelling in *Tay John* (see 167), is always, to O'Hagan, a decline from mythic or legendary power. Many critics have viewed Denham's explanation of the power of naming, "Put a name to it, put it on a map, and you've got it" (80), as investing a "higher truth" and "authority" into his own words and role as a narrator (Davidson 37) and as opposing his later statement that "to tell a story is to leave most of it untold" (Zichy, "Critics" 197-98). However, it is clear that this "getting" of the wilderness is a tenuous one. If the unnamed "is the darkness unveiled" (80), then to name wilderness is merely to place a veil upon it. The "magic" (80) that holds the land to its name is more like that of a street magician pulling a rabbit out of a hat than of gods creating or controlling worlds. Although the "few wisps of hair" from the mare's tail are Tay John's "title" to her, they do not actually keep the horse within his grasp (117), and neither does a name truly give one possession or comprehension of the land. Naming is always represented as degenerative: Denham, when he sees Tay John fighting the bear, gives the hero a name to "align him with the human race" (87). Thus, naming Tay John is a despiritualization and demythologization of him. Similarly, naming a country is a demystification and "humanization" of it (Keith,

"Growth" 82). Therefore, according to O'Hagan, storytelling is a humanization or despiritualization, as well as a weak articulation, of a legend.

While Arnold Davidson is aware that "the story declines from legend to hearsay" (37), he sees "legend" in *Tay John* as "the perpetual deferral of things hoped for as marked by the telling of that hope," and thus as being "grounded in nothing" (35). But Francis Zichy points out that "the authoritative narrative voice and historical and 'legendary' content [of Part I] suggest that it was certainly not O'Hagan's intention to do anything so paradoxical as to ground his novel in nothing" ("Critics" 192). However, Part I is not the only place in the novel where O'Hagan attempts to show that storytelling (and thus also his novel) is deeply rooted in some great intangible authority. Denham explains that Tay John's story "was a story which found its root in the memories of men, and its form, and a sequence to its incidents [and thus its empirical evidence] in their speech" (113-114). Denham also later calls the mind "the urn of blood and shadow, the place of silence behind our eyes, borne by each of us upon his shoulders like a penance for his days above ground" (153). This seems to suggest some universal subconscious in which all people are united in the shadow and darkness from which Tay John and the wilderness have sprung.

The passage of the novel that most forcefully repeats this suggestion is the one in which Denham uses the analogy of mountain-mining to express the nature of storytelling. He explains that to "tell a story is to leave most of it untold" because the "heart" of it, like that of a mountain, remains untouched by its telling, which "merely assault[s] the surrounding solitude" (167). Within this description, Denham states that every story has "its source in a past we cannot see, and its reverberations in a future still unlived," as does man, who is "the child of darkness, walking for a few minutes in unaccustomed light" (166). This is obviously meant to recall the legendary birth of Tay John from Part I, a legend of which Denham has no specific knowledge, and to foreshadow the end of Tay John and his story in which he supernaturally returns underground. Obviously, O'Hagan's purpose in this repetition is to emphasize the existence of an unknowable universal subconscious outside of the physical realm of evidence and storytelling from where stories and man are born and to which they return. When Denham says, "[Tay John's] story, such as it is, would have existed independently of me" (166), he is not implying that other narrators would propagate it regardless of him; he means that the story exists independently of any narrator. Yet, this "unknowable" and "unfathomable" darkness, which is the source of man and stories, is not exactly a "nihilistic void" as Stouck indicates (220). To call it such is to suggest that the shadowy home of story "has no real existence" or is "devoid of meaning" ("Nihilism"). Denham explains that a man's shadow is intended to be a reminder of the existence of the darkness which is his source: it is the "image of his end, sombre and obscure as his own beginning" (162). And, as J. Hillis Miller explains that meaning for Joseph Conrad's Marlow exists outside of his tale, saying that "[meaning] is a darkness, an absence, a haze invisible in itself" (26), so does meaning exist for O'Hagan and for Denham outside of the tale and within the shadow, darkness, and unnamed wilderness.

The major indication that O'Hagan intended to convey the idea that stories are born from an external non-physical realm lies in his description of the writing process of *Tay John*. In an interview with Keith Maillard, O'Hagan describes how he began *Tay John* as the diary of a man about whom he had read in Milton and Cheadle's *The Northwest Passage by Land*, and then changed the narration to that of an omniscient voice, which, by the fourth chapter, he felt was not sustainable

(23-24). He explains that the rest of the novel came to him through the disembodied voice of Jack Denham telling him the story; he then began to write the novel "as though [he] were just copying something down" (24-25). After hearing O'Hagan's explanation of writing *Tay John*, Maillard further explains the experience: "the story comes and it tells itself, and you feel almost like you're an empty vessel and the story is just pouring right through you .... It came from *somewhere else*" (25; emphasis added). O'Hagan agrees with Maillard's summation of creative writing as coming from a mysterious outside source, and says that "as crazy as this sounds, apocryphal I know, *it's so*" (24; emphasis added). O'Hagan's statement clearly shows his belief in the reality of an external and hidden origin of story; to ignore this and claim that O'Hagan intended *Tay John* to question "Truth" and "myth-making" (Fee, "Howard O'Hagan's *Tay John*" 10) is unfounded.

Although O'Hagan wrote much of Parts II and III of *Tay John* inspired by an almost supernatural outside source, the disembodied voice of narrator Jack Denham, W.J. Keith argues that O'Hagan's use of actual events in the novel supports the idea that the book is an expansion and growth of the ideas and incidents used. He writes that the various sources for *Tay John*, such as the headless man in Milton and Cheadle, the trapper known as Yellow Head, and Jenness's *The Indians of Canada*, the written source of the Tsimshian legend that becomes Tay John's birth story, are expanded by O'Hagan "into a larger whole" ("Growth" 79-80). However, when O'Hagan describes his borrowing of the Tsimshian legend to Maillard, he says, "happenings aren't copyrighted. It's only the writing that's patented. And it's my writing—it's not his writing" (28). This statement is partially a defence of his use of outside materials but it also indicates that he believes that the legend itself is the true source of story and that Jenness's and his own writings are merely the tangible, copyrightable, and degenerate evidence of it.[3]

That O'Hagan views his and Jenness's writings as merely versions of one legend shows that he likely did not intend the different versions of stories about Tay John in the novel to deny an immutable truth. Perhaps the intention of their inclusion was rather to question language's capacity to express the unknowable. Francis Zichy argues that the novel, particularly when rumours of Tay John's amputation become mixed with the tale of his bear fight, falsely (and unintentionally) causes critics to doubt the veracity of the "Legend" section, saying that the ambiguity shows "that the events of hearsay can be upgraded, or further corrupted, into legend with the passing of time" ("Critics" 195). Fee is one critic who doubts in this manner, saying that "Myth ... in O'Hagan's creation, is not immemorial, immutable, and universal, but flexible, time-bound, and appropriate to its setting" (23). Keith also contends that Denham's

---

3   In "The Magic of Others," Lenore Keeshig-Tobias argues that Canadian white writers "telling Native stories, writing Native stories" are "censoring the Native voice," "kill[ing] Natives softly with white metaphors and poetry, and trivializ[ing] Native gods"; she also notes that these writers "cry censorship and decry self-censorship" rather than "confront and deal with issues of appropriation" or "recognize the fact that [Natives] can tell [their] own stories and that there is protocol for the acquisition of stories and ... accept responsibility to and for the stories they tell" (174). O'Hagan's legalese defense, making *words* patented and *happenings* or *legend* as the non-copyrightable, avoids taking responsibility for stealing and transforming the Tsimshian legend—a legend already mediated to him through Jenness's anthropological reframing and retelling of it—into a settler-version of a Shuswap man's birth story. Moreover, since, as Fee notes, "cultural appropriation in settler colonies is driven by a need to cover up the theft of the land," O'Hagan's defense attempts to justify settler appropriation and reject Indigenous claims of ownership over story, correspondingly justifies "the most problematic form of appropriation, that of the land" ("The Trickster Moment" 24).

and McLeod's reactions to the Aldersons' new version, which he calls a "new legend," of Tay John's dismemberment shows that story "should grow and develop like an organism" ("Growth" 82). However, it is likely that O'Hagan intended the Aldersons' misinformation not to show the changeable nature of myth and story, but to further prove the ephemeral nature of tale-telling and the permanent one of legend. C. Kerényi, in the introduction to his book on *The Gods of the Greeks,* comments on the disparities between differing versions of Greek myths, writing, "in all … forms, developments and variations [there are] the same permanent and unmistakable basic story … [and] behind the variations can be recognised something that is common to them all: a story that was told in many fashions, yet remained the same" (9). Since O'Hagan gives a similar note to the end of "Montana Pete Goes Courting,"[4] as does Denham after he recites Father Rorty's letter,[5] O'Hagan likely intended readers to view the inconsistent versions of Tay John's story in a similar way, as changeable variations of a single "permanent and unmistakable basic story." Although the tale of Tay John itself modifies and does not always conform with empirical evidence of the events, it always reflects the immutable "essence" or "legend" of Tay John and carries what Denham calls "the remnants of his presence" (92).

This then seems to be how O'Hagan intended to portray stories in *Tay John*, as tangible mirrors or carriers (though not containers) of an elusive essence. Tay John himself is meant to represent the intangible essence of story. O'Hagan first establishes Tay John as a symbol for story within Part I through his

---

4   "The words, of course, in the foregoing tale are not exactly those of Montana Pete, but they give the effect of what he said" (O'Hagan, "Montana" 242).

5   "Some of the words, as I have repeated them, may be mine—the gist is his" (*Tay* 216).

supernatural birth from a grave. This "emergence" is repeated in Parts II and III in Denham's narrative: first, Denham depicts Tay John crawling from under the bear he had killed as "climbing out of the ground" (88), and later describes him as always giving the sense of "emergence—from the ground itself" (205). The idea of Tay John emanating a particular essence is also repeated: Denham says "there was something, it is hard to say, something of the abstract about him—as though he were a symbol of some sort or other" (83), and McLeod says that there is "Something working in the man. You can feel it when he is around. ... it's in his bearing, in just the way he carries himself" (99). Tay John's incommunicable "something" is further emphasized by his elusive physical body: when Tay John first appears, within one page his body shrinks to "only a few wisps of yellow hair," and then grows back again to normal size (38); when Denham sees Tay John at Lucerne, he thinks his hero is smaller than he remembers (204); and when Blackie sees him in the snow, Tay John at first appears very large, and then "no bigger than a little boy" (260-61). His elusive "something" is what causes the other people in the novel to try to impose a narrative upon Tay John, to give him a name in order "to keep [him] within the horizons" (80). However, the narratives fail to capture Tay John: "Evading definition, the soul of the being is always reached for but never caught, just as parts of a story can be assembled but its essence never contained" (Robinson 169).

In *The Indians of Canada*, which greatly informed O'Hagan's novel, Diamond Jenness writes that "when a people borrows folk-tales from surrounding peoples ... it cannot assimilate them if they differ radically from its own folk-tales, but modifies them to conform to ideas and patterns that are already familiar and imposes on them the individuality inherent in its own legends and traditions" (185). Thus, because Tay John is neither white nor Indigenous and is an unfamiliarity to both races, his essence is particularly hard for either his Shuswap community or the British, American, and Canadian colonists to understand or seize through narrative, which difficulty causes the people to superimpose familiar stories upon him. The Shuswaps of O'Hagan's novel attempt to make Tay John substantial and permanent by imposing the "Kumkan-Kleseem" story of a yellow-headed saviour upon him,[6] and by performing rituals, shaking rattles and singing to him (38), and sending him on a journey for visions (45). The colonists attempt to understand him through Arthurian legend: Alderson sees him as a lady of the lake (125), and Denham portrays him as a parodied Lancelot or Tristan in his relationships with Julia and Ardith.[7] However, neither the "Kumkleseem" narrative nor the "Arthurian" one, both of which intend to make Tay John a hero and saviour, are successful at binding him. He rejects the roles imposed upon him: he leaves the Shuswaps without leading them, he rejects Julia Alderson as a Guinevere, and he is chased away by the ineffectual Mr. Dobble. Paradoxically, yet logically, his refusal to be narrated is what makes him a particularly good represen-tation of O'Hagan's concept of story. Like the heart of the story, he remains "resistant to your siege" and "unfathomable" (167).

However, Margery Fee suggests that the purpose of using Greek, Arthurian, and Native legend to tell Tay John's story is to expose the man-made nature of myth: "O'Hagan therefore rigs up a new myth out of the pieces of old ones, revealing in the process how it's done" (10). She goes on to say that O'Hagan's "'enemy' in this novel, then, is not myth, but the belief in one

---

6   Of course, this Messianic Exodus story is one O'Hagan overtly borrows from Judeo-Christianity, as many critics' use of the term "Promised Land" when discussing it suggests.

7   Francis Zichy, in his paper "The 'Complex Fate' of the Canadian," further notes and analyzes the use of Arthurian legend in *Tay John*.

complete immutable myth: the Truth" (10). But O'Hagan's use of multiple myths is not to show that "myth has popular origin" (11), or to deny an immutable truth; rather, it is more likely to serve the purpose Keith suggests: to express and observe "mythic resonance" of the legends and of Tay John's story (*Style* 38).[8] Although the different stories transposed upon Tay John by the other characters and O'Hagan are inadequate to hold or fully explain him, O'Hagan intended them to reflect the essence of the hero, even as Tay John rejects or fulfills the heroic role.

Denham's admiration for the ability of words to similarly reflect the essence of what they signify runs counter to Davidson's argument that "words, in short, do not lead to any truths in or of the novel, and the text marks out a space of misnaming and misunderstanding" (30). Although this paper has argued that O'Hagan intended *Tay John* to reveal that words, tales, and evidence are degenerations from pure legend, it is in no way meant to imply that O'Hagan believes words are powerless. Keith's estimation of O'Hagan's view of words is closer to the truth, when he says that although "O'Hagan is skeptical of absolutes, or at least doubtful that human beings can make contact with them, there can be no doubt that he possessed not merely a firm respect for words and story but also a profound sense of 'mystery' behind the visible universe" (*Style* 38). O'Hagan's respect for words is particularly apparent in Denham's praise of the term "snow flies": "There's an expression for you, born in the country, born from the imagination of men and their feeling for the right word, the only word, to mirror clearly what they see!" (91). The key word in that passage is "mirror"; although the word

---

8 Of course, mapping European world understandings (Plato, Arthurian legend, Christology) over Tay John and Shuswaps further enact settler colonialism.

cannot capture or conjure snow, its capacity to mirror snow's presence is real and valuable. And although O'Hagan believes that the search for the right word or tale that will reach the "heart" of the story is ultimately elusive, he also believes it is inevitable and vital: as the novel's version of Shuswap people continue to seek the shadow behind their hands although it is unreachable (29-30), so too the mountain man will attempt to explicate "what he cannot understand" (114), the newspaper man will "set about to explain ... a happening beyond all their explanations" (193), and Denham will tell the tale of Tay John, "stretching [it] the length of Edmonton" (77). Perhaps the reason for telling a story is that to do so will at least give a reflection of it and will "relate it to the known world" (167): "Though the meaning is outside [of the tale], it may only be seen by way of the tale which brings it out" (Miller 26).

Although a number of critics have described *Tay John* as a work intended to deconstruct the concept of an immutable myth and the power of words or storytelling to create legend, O'Hagan obviously intended that his book portray storytelling and naming as a decline from legend which exists in an unknowable but permanent non-physical realm. Yet, although O'Hagan views storytelling as unable to capture the enduring legend and elusive heart of the story, he also intended *Tay John* to convey the ability of storytelling and words to reflect and "relate" the intangible to "the known world" (167). The contempt with which the narrators treat those who value the tangible evidence over the intangible legend, such as the Shuswaps, who are "told what to believe" (29),[9] and Father Rorty, who as "man of faith is always a material man" (211),

---

9   Again, this does not reflect the actual worldview of the Shuswap people, but rather the worldview O'Hagan gave them to serve his narrative purposes.

as well as those who rely solely upon the intangible, such as Mr. Dobble, to whom "illusions were more real ... than the dark pine-trees which gave logs for his buildings" (163), suggests that what O'Hagan was advocating in his book is a balance of the two: a belief in the existence of the intangible as well as a faith in the ability of the tangible to represent, however temporarily, the intangible. Unfortunately, the closest example given in *Tay John* of this balance is Denham, who, although he respects the power of words while recognizing their limitations, is a disreputable drunken voyeur with an inability to make up his mind between the two points of view. Nonetheless, by exposing both views, *Tay John* reveals the difference between storytelling and story, and illustrates the importance of both.

Works Cited

Davidson, Arnold E. "Silencing the Word in Howard O'Hagan's *Tay John*." *Canadian Literature*, vol. 110, 1986, pp. 30-44.

Fee, Margery. "Howard O'Hagan's *Tay John*: Making New World Myth." *Canadian Literature*, vol. 110, 8-27.

----. *Literary Land Claims: The "Indian Land Question" from Pontiac's War to Attawapiskat.* Wilfred Laurier UP, 2015.

----. "The Trickster Moment, Cultural Appropriation, and the Liberal Imagination in Canada." *Troubling Tricksters: Revisioning Critical Conversations*, edited by Deanna Reder and Linda M. Morra, Wilfrid Laurier UP, 2010, pp. 59-76. *ProQuest Ebook Central.*

"Hearsay." *The Oxford English Dictionary.* 2nd ed., 2005, U of Saskatchewan Lib. 8 April 2005, <http://www.oed.com.db.cyber.usask.ca/>.

Jenness, Diamond. *The Indians of Canada.* 1932. U of Toronto P, 1977.

Mackey, Eva. "Becoming Indigenous: Land, Belonging, and the Appropriation of Aboriginality in Canadian Nationalist

Narratives." *Social Analysis: The International Journal of Anthropology*, vol. 42, no. 2, July 1998, pp. 150-78.

Maracle, Lee. *My Conversations with Canadians*. Essays No. 4, Book Thug, 2017.

Miller, J. Hillis. *Fiction and Repetition: Seven English Novels*. Harvard UP, 1982.

Keane, Stephanie. *Getting Home from Work: Narrating Settler Home in British Columbia's Small Resource Communities*. 2016. UVic, PhD dissertation. *UVicSpace ETDs*.

Keeshig-Tobias, Lenore. "The Magic of Others." *Language in Her Eye: Views on Writing and Gender by Canadian Women Writing in English*, edited by Eleanor Wachtel, Sarah Sheard & Libby Scheier, Coach House Press, 1990, pp. 173-77.

Keith, W.J. "Howard O'Hagan." *A Sense of Style: Studies in the Art of Fiction in English-Speaking Canada*, ECW, 1989, pp. 23-39.

----. "Howard O'Hagan, *Tay John*, and the Growth of Story." *Silence Made Visible: Howard O'Hagan and* Tay John, edited by Margery Fee, ECW, 1992, pp. 73-84.

Kerényi, C. *The Gods of the Greeks*. 1951. Thames & Hudson, 1980.

"Nihilism." *The Oxford English Dictionary*. 2nd ed. 2005. U of Saskatchewan Lib. 8 April 2005, <http://www.oed.com.db.cyber.usask.ca/>.

O'Hagan, Howard. Interview with Keith Maillard. *Silence Made Visible: Howard O'Hagan and* Tay John, edited by Margery Fee, ECW, 1992, pp. 21-38.

----. *Tay John*. 1939. McClelland and Stewart, 1989.

----. "Montana Pete Goes Courting." *Wilderness Men*, Doubleday, 1958, pp. 223-244.

Ondaatje, Michael. "Howard O'Hagan and the 'Rough-Edged Chronicle.'" *The Canadian Novel in the Twentieth Century*, edited by Malcom Ross and George Woodcock, McClelland and Stewart, 1975, pp. 276-84.

Plato. "Selections from *The Republic Book X*." *Art and Interpretation*. Translated by Benjamin Jowett, edited by Eric Dayton, Broadview, 1998.

Robinson, Jack. "Myths of Dominance Versus Myths of Re-Creation in O'Hagan's *Tay John*." *Studies in Canadian Literature*, vol. 13 no. 2, 1988, pp. 166-74.

Stouck, David. "The Art of the Mountain Man Novel." *Western American Literature*, vol. 20, no. 3, 1985, pp. 211-22.

Yakovenko, Sergiy. "A Deceptive Initiation: An Ecological Paradigm in Howard O'Hagan's *Tay John*." *Le Simplegadi*, vol. 15, 2017, pp. 284-94.

Zichy, Francis. "Crypto-, Pseudo-, and Pre-Postmodernism: *Tay John, Lord Jim*, and the Critics." *Essays on Canadian Writing*, vol. 81, 2004, pp. 192-221.

Satirical Echoes
Re-Considering Howard O'Hagan's *Tay John* as Influenced by Joseph Conrad's *Heart of Darkness*[1]

JACK ROBINSON

The narrators of Howard O'Hagan's 1939 novel *Tay John* and of Joseph Conrad's 1899 novella *Heart of Darkness* are moral *provocateurs*, but they also participate in the ideology they attempt to expose and destroy: as Sandya Shetty summarizes the argument of Edward Said, "The critic of empire who functions from within the dominant culture must find it well nigh impossible to venture far beyond the very ideological barriers which he purports to dissolve" (Shetty 462). What applies to the narrators also applies to their authors. "As a creature of his time," Edward Said states, "Conrad could not grant the natives their freedom, despite his severe critique of the imperialism that enslaved them" (*C&I* 30). O'Hagan, coming forty years later, continues the discourse Conrad started on empire, gender, and otherness through what Michael Ondaatje calls "the very careful use of echoes—of phrases and images" (Afterword 203), several of which are rooted in *Heart of Darkness*. O'Hagan

---

1   Both Michael Ondaatje, in "O'Hagan's 'Rough-Edged Chronicle,'" p. 280, and Gary Geddes, in "The Writer that CanLit forgot" *Saturday Night*, November 1977, p. 86, note connections in imagery between *Tay John* and *Heart of Darkness*.

has a privilege that history denied to Conrad: he sees beyond the self-enclosed imperial world to evoke the otherness of the colonized, though only in flashes of insight limited by his own time. *Tay John* offers forward-looking glimpses of Indigenous values that have emerged as foundational to today's discourse on Indigeneity and delivers a warning about the problematic nature of cultural hybridity that is still relevant today but was unheard of in his time. This article renders what Edward Said defines as a "contrapuntal reading" of the two texts, first appreciating and articulating their internal complexities; second, reading from an external perspective in an effort, as Said describes it, "to draw out, extend, give emphasis and voice to what is silent or marginally present or ideologically represented" in the texts (C&I 66). In a contrapuntal reading, the exploration of the text's internal strategies takes precedence, as George M. Wilson puts it, because "the persuasiveness of commentary from an external standpoint depends upon giving full credit to the sophistication of the text" (Wilson 266).

Its unique narrative structure has preoccupied critics of *Tay John* from 1975 to the present, and especially during the flurry of critical attention that spanned the eighties and culminated in Margery Fee's 1992 collection of essays and research materials on the novel and the author. The authority of the narrative voice declines from the unqualified source of the "Legend" section to the "Hearsay" and "Evidence—Without a Finding" sections, where the veracity of narrator Jack Denham is saturated in textual ironies. In Arnold Davidson's 1986 article, he finds these ironies so profuse that "the text marks out a space of misnaming and misunderstanding" (Davidson 30). Davidson claims that the narrative engages in "endless deferrals" of certainty (43) until its meaning is "finally grounded in nothing" (35). In a 2004 article, Francis Zichy finds Davidson's conclusions too nihilistic ("Crypto" 192) and takes umbrage with the use of misleading labels, as when Margery Fee praises O'Hagan as an "avante-garde" novelist who flouts the tawdry realist conventions of his time ("Crypto" 194). Zichy points out that O'Hagan did not distance himself from contemporary Canadian realists, and that, in the international sphere, the realism of Flaubert and Henry James is far from unsophisticated ("Crypto" 194). In a 2005 article, Kylee-Anne Hingston follows Davidson, Fee, and others in focusing on the undecidability of narrative meaning. She argues that the novel shows the ability of storytelling and the word to "relate" the intangible to "the known world" (Hingston 188). In this sense, Hingston argues, the novel takes an approach that stresses balance regarding language, naming, and story: it "respects the power of words while recognizing their limitations" (Hingston 189).

From the outset, both novels were recognized as critiques of European colonialism. *Heart of Darkness* was published serially in *Blackwood's Magazine* in 1899 but not seriously reviewed until 1902. In that first serious review, Edward Garnett identifies the novella's satirical intent, concluding that it offers "an analysis of the deterioration of the white man's *morale*, when he is let loose from European restraint, and planted down in the tropics as an emissary of light armed to the teeth, to make trade profits out of the subject races" (Sherry qtd. in *HD* 99). Similarly, in his 1975 article that revived *Tay John* from the literary obscurity where it had lain for almost forty years, Michael Ondaatje draws attention to the novel's satire of the colonial society invading the Canadian Rockies circa 1880-1920: "The civilization growing up around Tay John is ludicrous in its self-importance" ("Chronicle" 280).

Wit, according to Matthew Hodgart, is the essence of literary satire, though Hodgart is careful to define wit not solely in its contemporary sense of the amusing display of language but in the context of its etymology. Hodgart comments that the word originally meant "mind" or "understanding" or even "wisdom"; and for Shakespeare, "cleverness" (Hodgart 111). But even for Shakespeare, the word was acquiring its modern meaning of "the power of giving pleasure by combining or contrasting ideas" or "the quality of speech or writing which can surprise and delight by its unexpectedness." In the seventeenth century, it was considered "the essential component of all poetry," and in its modern sense, "wit remains close to poetry." Hodgart concludes that the essential features of wit are "ingenious compression, a sudden revelation of hidden implications, and the linking together of two incongruous ideas" (Hodgart 111). The association with poetry is important, for both Conrad and O'Hagan are witty and lyrical authors; also crucial are the meanings of startling intellectual insight and verbal surprise or delight—qualities important in both novels.

Sardonic wit is the essence of Marlow's narrative voice, and its target is always "the merry dance of death and trade" called imperialism (*HD* 29). As soon as he begins his tale, he states that "The conquest of the earth, which mostly means taking it away from those who have a different complexion or slightly flatter noses than ourselves, is not a pretty thing when you look at it too much" (*HD* 21). While the African "savages" of the late nineteenth century worship their gods, Marlow finds the imperial project to be watched over by "a flabby, pretending, weak-eyed devil of rapacious and pitiless folly" (*HD* 31). Repeatedly, the agents of empire are called "pilgrims" (39, 41, 44, 57, 61, 68, etc.), the satirical irony being that they have come to worship greed, brutality, and raw power over others. The Eldorado Exploring Expedition, its name an allusion to Voltaire's satirical treatment of the lust for gold in his *Candide*, is a gang of thieves who embody the immorality of empire: their goal is "to tear treasure out of the bowels of the land ... with no more moral purpose at the back of it than there is in burglars breaking into a safe" (*HD* 46).

Marlow encounters the Chief of the inner station, Mr. Kurtz, as a voice of utter egotism, claiming that everything belongs to him (*HD* 63). His seventeen-page report is "eloquent" and inspiring to Marlow, conveying the image of colonization as an "august Benevolence," but this magnificent peroration is countered by Kurtz's scrawled conclusion: "Exterminate all the brutes" (*HD* 66). From the twenty-five-year-old Russian who embodies the amoral "spirit of adventure" (*HD* 71), Marlow learns that Kurtz had got the tribe to follow him by coming "with thunder and lightning" (*HD* 72), probably using superior European technology to convince these simple people that he was a god; then, he took them out on ivory-hunting expeditions, excavating vast quantities of what the traders call "fossil" ivory (*HD* 64) that had been buried for some time; ultimately, the chiefs of surrounding tribes "would crawl" as they came to visit him every day (HD 74). The African heads on stakes surrounding Kurtz's hut convince Marlow that he "lacked restraint" and was "hollow at the core" (*HD* 74). Kurtz affirms this verdict with his last words: "The horror! The horror!" (*HD* 86). Marlow interprets these words as a triumph of self-awareness but also as Kurtz's condemnation of himself and the imperial project he represents (*HD* 87). The brutality of imperialism in King Leopold II's Congo Free State was widely known to be the worst in Africa (*HD* 5). Patrick Brantlinger writes that there were at least nine possible historical models for Kurtz. Given the widespread brutality, he suggests that "*All* of the white officers in Leopold's empire were in essence Kurtzes" (Brantlinger 290).

O'Hagan's narrator, Jack Denham, is an Irish remittance man. Four times a year, when he receives his remittance from his wealthy family back in the county of Tyrone (*TJ* 55), he resides in a grand hotel in Edmonton. As a "remittance man," he has embarrassed his family by his profligate behavior in the past and has been paid to remain in the colony so that he will not embarrass them further. Denham is a man of restraint and respected practical accomplishments. He often hires out with outfits going west or north from Edmonton to the mountains; he is a "good man with horses and on the river." His words are heard with "tolerance and interest" by others because his "speech and life" are "close to events" (*TJ* 56). He always drinks just "two tall pale glasses of whiskey," living by the adage that one was "good for you, two were too many, and three were not enough": he jokes that he always takes "too many" (*TJ* 56). (The reader notices nonetheless that two tall glasses of whiskey contain a significant amount of alcohol.) Denham is witty, well-read, and contemplative. In contrast to the sternly job-focused Marlow, Denham takes a leisurely and speculative approach to life:

> He was a lanky man in his forties, who seemed older. He kept his brown beard tightly trimmed. Pouches hung heavily beneath his eyes so that the red of his lower eyelids showed, and someone said of him once, seeing him in his old tweed suit, that he resembled a somewhat thoughtful Saint Bernard dog. He walked along the wooden sidewalks, taller than average, a slouch hat over his eyes, moving at leisure through the world with a long careful stride, appearing to take a step only once in a while. (*TJ* 55)

The profit motive of capitalism is satirized by Denham in the character of Alf Dobble, an American entrepreneur who comes to the Canadian Rockies in 1911 to build a "*chalet*" (*TJ* 129) or the equivalent of a Swiss resort in the Alps, giving it the Swiss name of Lucerne (*TJ* 132). Dobble does not see the reality of the wilderness any more than do the sailors on the French ship that Marlow observes pointlessly shelling a continent (*HD* 29). While the French sailors are driven by fear of

the unknown (the savage, the wild), Dobble floats on a cloud
of capitalist abstractions. He sees nature as material to be
re-shaped: "He was staring up at the Seven Sisters, regarding them as though they too might come within his plans of
revision" (*TJ* 134). He is enthralled by image and name: "Publicity is the word, Mr. Denham" (*TJ* 170). His business offer to
Denham is that Denham could be the manager of Lucerne:
he has the right "bearing" to be there to greet the tourists,
or, as Dobble puts it, to "meet the world." Denham wittily declines such an exalted position: he points out that "meeting
the world" is "St. Peter's job": "And he meets them only one
at a time when they're pretty well tired out from the climb"
(*TJ* 129). The sensible Denham is appalled that Dobble has
risked so much when he possesses so little knowledge of the
actual terrain on which he plans to build: he has not had the
foresight to explore the country around Jasper in winter, so
he has no knowledge of the harshness of Canadian winters
and the difficulties the mountains pose for construction (125).
The relationship between Denham and Dobble is a battle of
egos: in a moment when words fail him, Denham expresses
his frustration with the grandiose ambitions of Dobble by
swelling his chest (of which he is quite proud) and popping his
vest buttons in Dobble's face (131). Possession is a key word in
Denham's satirical lexicon: "Possession is a great surrender,"
he states, echoing Dante's "Possession is one with loss": "The
more a man has, the more surely he is owned by what he has"
(83). This verdict applies to Dobble's absurd hopes for great
wealth and fame. Like Marlow, Denham is an outsider who
stakes his life on self-possession.

    As Francis Zichy points out, Denham has an "intimate
acquaintance with Catholicism" ("Fate" 214), and his satirical
treatment of key Catholic ideas is central to the novel's critique
of imperialism. The binary of body versus soul is represented

in Father Rorty's allusion to St. Augustine's statement in his *Confessions* that "the flesh lusteth against the spirit, and the spirit lusteth against the flesh" (*TJ* 160). The critique of the binary comes in Father Rorty's conclusion that it is unnatural to "deny the balance that life imposes upon us" (160). One can almost hear Denham's voice in Father Rorty's conclusion, and indeed, the letter containing these comments has been read, destroyed, and then reconstructed by Denham (*TJ* 147). Father Rorty's faith is tested when he is tempted by Ardith Aeriola; to replenish his faith, he lashes himself to a Y-shaped tree to experience for one night the agony that Christ felt on the Cross (*TJ* 166). Accidentally, rain shrinks the rope bindings; he cannot untie them and dies of exposure. Father Rorty promises to lend Denham his book *The Imitation of Christ*, the classic of Christian devotional literature. He quotes from it this passage: "he that knoweth himself becometh vile to himself" (*TJ* 161). Denham has no wish to hate himself, and the idea of imitating Christ strikes Denham as a delusion born of pride. He condemns the Church's self-serving and humanly destructive binary of heaven versus hell: "Hell will have its priests intoning masses, promising another heaven, dooming us, by that promise, to further hells" (*TJ* 140).

Empiricism and rationality are also the explicit butts of Denham's satirical attacks. RCMP inspector Jay Wiggins's investigation into Tay John's scuffle with Alf Dobble and his men, and into the whereabouts of Tay John and Ardith Aeriola, trails off into uncertainty. When Denham visits his office in Edmonton, Wiggins is presented in a satirical light, as he sits, "head bowed, hands clasped upon the desk-top, as if in reverence before the accumulated and recorded achievements of the Force" (*TJ* 188). Wiggins concludes that "The whole thing isn't logical" (*TJ* 192), but his logic is actually founded not on evidence but on social prejudice: he will not exert too much

effort in the matter because Ardith is a "bit of a tart" and one
of "these foreign women" who "are always making trouble,"
while Tay John is "a half-breed fellow with yellow hair" (*TJ*
190-191). His implied reason not to pursue the investigation is
that the subjects of his search are socially marginal: they don't
matter. Denham expresses his cynicism about empirical truth
and about the social prejudice underlying it by idealizing the
pair's uncommon "obedience to impulse" or their ability to be
present in the moment (*TJ* 192).

Irony is the main tool of satire, writes Alvin B. Kernan,
because of its ability to expose the discrepancy between what
is claimed and the truth: "Irony is the perfect rhetorical device
for catching the pretense which reveals itself as sham, since
its two terms permit the poet to create both the pretense and
the truth at once" (Kernan 33). Pope puts the same emphasis
on satire's function of exposing pretension: "in all ages, all vain
pretenders, were they ever so poor or ever so dull, have been
constantly the topicks of the most candid Satyrists" (qtd. in
Kernan 31). In fiction, irony is directed at the first-person narrator's inadequate version of reality. Sometimes the fictional
text provides no direct clue that readers should doubt the
perspective of the narrator in some way; sometimes a clue is
identifiable. In the case of Marlow, the clue is obvious: at the
end of his story, he lies, even though he insists that he has
a temperamental hatred of lies: "There is a taint of death, a
flavor of mortality in lies—which is exactly what I hate and
detest in the world" (*HD* 42). His story satirizes the "*pretending*, weak-eyed devil" of imperialism (*HD* 31) (my italics) that
is covered up by Kurtz's spoken and written eloquence, yet
Marlow's lie exposes him as a pretender himself. Marlow betrays the revelation Kurtz has imparted to him and his own
respect for it when he lies to Kurtz's Intended, saying that
Kurtz's last words were her name. It is a betrayal of what in

1899 was a ground-breaking critique of empire, and it calls into question Marlow's stances on gender and otherness. As Garrett Stewart puts it, "the political self-deception of Marlow serves to discredit him as a morally reliable narrator" (369).

Marlow's conventional view (for his time) of the status of women in society is surrounded with textual irony. When his story conveys the "ugly" truth that only strong men of the frontier can stomach, it invokes an ideology of separate, gendered spheres. As Johanna M. Smith argues, the woman's sphere is one of idealism or sentimental pretense: Kurtz's Intended sees him as an emissary of light, "weaning those ignorant millions from their horrid ways" (HD 92). In contrast, the male sphere is manly realism: as Marlow bluntly states, "the company was run for profit" (Smith 178). Confronted by the idealism of the Intended, Marlow dismisses half of humanity with his patronizing view that women are "out of it" and need to be kept "out of it" (*HD* 92). As Smith states, when Marlow pronounces the name of the Intended rather than Kurtz's truth, her name overlays for the reader what Kurtz said ("The horror! The horror!"). Marlow overlays the imperial obsession of profit with the icon of the female as "something you can set up, and bow down before, and offer a sacrifice to" (*HD* 21). Smith points out that this ideal is really a projection of patriarchal ideology: "While he appears to be bowing to *her,* he is in fact idolizing his own 'idea'—the 'something' he has 'set up' in her" (Smith 181).

Conrad may not have seen it in this way: he may have seen Marlow's lie as an insignificant or "white" lie. Conrad may have been unable to see outside of patriarchy, as he was unable to see outside of imperialism. Under the heading of a "contrapuntal reading," it is vital to reach outside of the author's worldview, just as Said does in his reading of Jane Austen's *Mansfield Park.* To the Bertrams and to Austen herself, the source of the family's fortunes in their plantations in Antigua is insignificant: they care only about the manners of their insular aristocratic English culture. Said reaches outside the author's vision to draw attention to a part of the text that is treated as marginal because of the unexamined ideology of imperialism (*C&I* 94). In the same way, it is crucial to reach beyond the narrator's and what may have been the author's perspective to place proper emphasis on Marlow's lie to the Intended: like the novel's satire of the pilgrims' idolization of theft by violence, it is an important critique of the ideology of the time.

On the frontier, both Marlow and Denham identify women with nature and sexuality: in both realms, women are portrayed as objects to be taken. When Kurtz's Intended holds out her arms in a gesture of farewell, she reminds Marlow of a similar gesture made by Kurtz's African mistress. This "wild and gorgeous apparition of a woman" is extravagantly adorned, wearing much ivory, no doubt bestowed by Kurtz. As she watches Kurtz being taken from her on Marlow's steamboat, a hush falls, and the wilderness regards her "as though it has been looking at the image of its own tenebrous and passionate soul" (*HD* 77). She stands "on the very brink of the stream" even when Marlow blows the shrill steamship whistle several times (a technique that is usually more effective than gunfire in frightening off the Africans). In the face of the "imbecile crowd" of pilgrims preparing to fire their rifles, she does not flinch, and it is likely that she is killed. Marlow's omission of this death from his tally of the deaths involved in his expedition up the Congo is significant. He counts only two male deaths, those of Kurtz and his African helmsman. His omission of this woman's death has three possible reasons: first, he did not see it clearly; second, it was the death of a woman and thus not important; third, it was the death of a woman identified with the wildness and darkness of Africa, and thus doubly not important. When Marlow insists that he "could see nothing more for smoke" (*HD* 84), the gap in the text suggests the limited viewpoint and perhaps the willful ignorance of the narrator and possibly the author.

Denham uses a simile that compares the attraction of untamed nature to the allure of female sensuality: he comments that "A new mountain valley leads a man on like that, like a woman he has never touched" (*TJ* 58). Denham's sexualization of Ardith is shockingly direct. Her unblinking black eyes and her pointing breasts stir desire in Denham, and of course her last name "Aeriola" is similar to "aureolae," or the dark skin around the nipples. Her self-awareness of her sexual presence gives her a certain arrogance (*TJ* 151). Julia Alderson is described by Denham as "small, young, not much more than a girl" (*TJ* 88), but her lack of womanly presence is made up for by her "heavy, musk-like perfume" (*TJ* 94) that creates a space between the wilderness men (*TJ* 89). After Julia leaves his cabin, McLeod feels the impulse to warn Tay John and tears down the large print of a white-skinned girl that Tay John had been fingering with desire. In depicting women as the objects of sexual desire for the frontier men, Denham expresses the raw ethos of the frontier, where brothels far outnumbered churches in every town. For Denham, women subdue men through their sexual power, through becoming the possessions that own their owners (as the young Julia Alderson is for her older and patronizing husband), or through domesticity. Dobble's men, when they see Ardith, pay mental homage to her as "the image of all that they had left behind" to come to the frontier (*TJ* 154). They have left behind the pleasures of hearth and home in pursuit of the freedom of the lone adventurer. In *Tay John*, the few women on the frontier do wish to take care of the mythic hero. Julia Alderson wants to bandage the "raw and red stump" of his removed hand (*TJ* 95); and after Tay John's fight with Dobble's men, his wounded head is described as "bound in white surrender" by Ardith Aeriola (*TJ* 184). Resisting the powers of women over them, the frontier men insist on the sanctity and separateness of their world. When a mountain man goes south to Edmonton, he goes "outside" (*TJ* 196). For Denham, women try to bring men down from their hegemony: thus, "women are the destruction of heroes' work" (*TJ* 145).

For Marlow, Africa is a vast stillness that gives no peace: it is "the stillness of an implacable force brooding over an inscrutable intention" (*HD* 49). Erupting from the bush in "intolerably excessive shrieking" so that it seems that "the mist itself had screamed" (*HD* 55), the Africans seem threatening and evil, or mysterious and inscrutable. E.M. Forster found such language "misty" (138), and F.R. Leavis, writing fifty years later, placed the novel in *The Great Tradition* of the finest written in English, while he concluded that phrases such as "unspeakable rites," "unspeakable secrets," and "monstrous passions" were needless adjectival constructs whose effect was "not to magnify but rather to muffle" the human potential for evil which they evoke (Leavis 179). Later critics have found that such impressionism is necessary because the horror Conrad addresses is indeed unspeakable. It could also be argued that such obscure symbolism springs partly from Marlow's ignorance of the Africans and their land. Marlow is only slightly different from those ordinary seamen mentioned by the fourth listener on the barge, in his introductory comments to Marlow's tale. This "outside" narrator remarks that most seamen lead "a sedentary life" by maintaining "a slightly disdainful ignorance" of the life they encounter on the shores they visit; on those rare occasions when they do go ashore, they uncover "the secret of a whole continent" in a casual stroll and generally find "the secret not worth knowing" (*HD* 119). Marlow is a practical steamship captain interested in completing an assigned task and in surviving in a situation that threatens his physical and mental health. Coming from Europe with a technology far more advanced than that of the African bush tribes he encounters, he regards his journey as one into the distant beginnings of human civilization and thus recognizes only a "distant kinship" with Africans.

Are narrator, novel, and author therefore racist, as Chinua Achebe claims in his influential 1975 speech? Since it is a speech, Achebe indulges in several rhetorical flourishes that do not support analysis: Marlow tosses out "bleeding-heart sentiments" (256); Conrad is a "thoroughgoing racist" (257); Conrad had an "inordinate love" of the word "nigger" (258); the novel is "an offensive and deplorable book" (259). Beyond these expressions of outrage, Achebe insists that any effort to draw a line between Conrad and Marlow is groundless because the text does not provide "an alternative frame of reference" other than Marlow's (Achebe 256). While the unspeakable speaker of Jonathan Swift's satirical essay "A Modest Proposal" does name the economic reforms that the author supported for colonial Ireland (Swift 353-354), literary texts are by no means required to provide such frames of reference. When an unreliable first-person narrator is involved, the text often merely suggests the inadequacies of the narrator's perspective; moreover, the "frame of reference" Achebe calls for does exist in Marlow's prefatory comment to his English listeners that their Caucasian ancestors were once the savages and their land the wilderness. Marlow asks his listeners to imagine the impressions of the Romans who came in their triremes to "run overland across the Gauls in a hurry" (*HD* 20). As they faced the wilderness, he says, the Romans must have felt themselves "in the midst of the incomprehensible" and been aware of "the fascination of the abomination" they saw in those white savages (*HD* 20). It is crucial to consider that Marlow does apply the damning word "abomination" equally to Caucasians and Africans. Achebe makes no mention of this point; rather, he condemns Conrad for not meeting Achebe's own 1975 standards of knowledge and etiquette for a discourse on race. He also neglects the evidence that Marlow does strive to identify with the Africans with whom he works. Achebe does not record Marlow's verdict that the loss of Kurtz was perhaps not worth the loss of his African helmsman: "I am not prepared to affirm that the fellow was exactly worth the life we lost in getting to him" (*HD* 67). Similarly, he fails to note Marlow's admiration for the self-restraint of the thirty-five cannibals on his boat (*HD* 57). There were 35 cannibals versus 5 Europeans—a proportion that, Brantlinger reports, was not uncommon in the Congolese-Arab war over the slave trade that occurred from 1891-1894 (in which both sides used cannibal soldiers), not long after Joseph Conrad had made his trip up the Congo in 1890 (Brantlinger 283). Marlow praises the cannibals for withstanding hunger (*HD* 57). If he had possessed more anthropological knowledge of African cannibal tribes, he would have known that they do not consume human flesh as daily fare for survival, but only in ritualized ceremonies, as Frances B. Singh points out (Singh 274); however, Marlow is not an anthropologist but a sailor, not a social scientist but a credible character in a novel.

Said points out that very little "was available for either Conrad or Marlow to see of the non-European at the time" (*C&I* 24). For narrator and author, "non-imperialist alternatives" were unimaginable and unthinkable (*C&I* 24). Nonetheless, because Conrad "*dates* imperialism, shows its contingency, records its illusions and tremendous violence and waste" (*C&I* 26), he unlocks the possibility of imagining a postcolonial Africa, though that potential would only become a reality well after Conrad's death in 1924 (*C&I* 29). O'Hagan's story, like Conrad's, does appeal to stereotypes of the author's time, as seen in the portrayal of a young Mountie, fresh out from

England, who is eager to search for Tay John: "chasing a half-breed hunter in the mountains" will be "like a story in *Chums*" (111), a boys' magazine about adventure in the colonies. S.R. McGillivray notes that stories in *Chums* were typically about "the lawless, savage anarchy of the wilderness" being brought to order by "white British civilization" (McGillivary 51). The typical *Chums* plot is subverted here: when Porter returns with Tay John, he has a new hero who has shown him how to see game in the wilderness: "the hidden was now revealed" (*TJ* 112). Both Conrad and O'Hagan purvey stereotypes: just as Africa had to remain wild and primitive for Conrad, the Indigenous for O'Hagan had to be hypermasculine and identified with nature.[2] *Tay John* does subvert the typical *Chums* plot, but it also appeals to readers like Porter: the novel is and is not like a story from *Chums*. At one point in the tale, when Tay John is coming into Jasper in the summers to work as a guide and packer, he undertakes to guide Ardith Aeriola and her maid over the high country to Mount Robson, but only on the condition that one "Jim Hawkins" comes along as cook (*TJ* 156). The name is an allusion to the boy-hero of Robert Louis Stevenson's 1882 novel *Treasure Island* and, as such, conveys

---

2   The critical discussion of these stereotypes of the Indigenous did not begin
     for at least another forty years. In a 2014 collection, *Masculindians: Con-
     versations about Indigenous Manhood,* edited by Sam McKegney, Mohawk
     scholar Taiaiake Alfred, in "Reimagining Warriorhood," pp. 76-86, states
     that images of the physically powerful and violent Indian warrior have
     the colonizing function of inventing a powerful opponent who must be
     constantly defeated. He states that the way to counter the stereotype of
     hypermasculinity is to "put the image of the Native male back into its
     proper context, which is the family" ("Re-Imagining" 79). In sticking to
     the stereotype of hypermasculinity in 1939, O'Hagan was harking back
     to the images of Indigenous masculinity established in James Fenimore
     Cooper's *Last of the Mohicans* and John Richardson's *Wacousta.*

O'Hagan's acknowledgement that his narrative participates in the genre of the boys' adventure story.

Streams separate Denham from Tay John's heroic battle with a female grizzly and Marlow from Kurtz's African mistress, who embodies the spirit of the continent (*HD* 84). The streams represent the ideology of a separation from nature and otherness that was endemic in the narrators' respective societies. Denham interprets the episode as "An epic battle: man against the wilderness" (63). He gives the tall yellow-haired Shuswap warrior the name of "Yellowhead" "to align him with the human race" (*TJ* 63).[3] The text contains two suggestions, however, that Denham's interpretation of the episode is perhaps impulsive and to be questioned in the context of the overall text. First, the narrator who introduces Denham at the start of the "Hearsay" section (just as an "outside" narrator introduces Marlow on the barge) describes Denham's story sardonically as "a faith—a gospel to be spread" and Denham as "its only apostle" (*TJ* 56). Denham's critique of Christianity, plus the overall text's critique of missionaries as tools of empire, suggests that any "gospel" or "apostle" is to be criticized in the context of this narrative. Second, much of the mythic stature of Tay John consists of his portrayal as an integral part of nature. Even in this scene, Tay John stands "with his feet planted on the ground ... as though he grasped it with them" (*TJ* 60-61). This is one of a series of ground images that continues throughout the novel. For Marlow, the African land is

---

3   W.J. Keith records that the fictional Tay John is based on a historical figure, a mixed-blood Iroquois named Pierre Bostonais who died in 1827 and whom O'Hagan transplants into the period of the building of the railways, 1880-1920. The existence of several place names bearing the name Yellowhead or Tête Jaune (Yellowhead freeway, Tête Jaune Cache, etc.) in the Jasper/Edmonton areas testifies to O'Hagan's awareness of how these names grow out of local history.

"something great and invincible, like evil or truth" that resists the "fantastic invasion" of the colonizers (*HD* 38). The land and its inhabitants remain unknown to Marlow; hence, he projects upon them a symbolic meaning determined by his cultural precept that human civilization must be pitted against nature, with the Africans aligned with nature.

The motifs of sight and naming are also treated ironically. Denham says that "it is only your vision" that holds a new mountain valley "within the known and created world" (*TJ* 59), yet in another passage, he calls this landscape "the country of illusion" because of its many visual and aural miscues (*TJ* 123): it is a place where the senses can't be trusted, or where the input from one is interpreted in the terms of another, as in Margery Fee's apt title *Silence Made Visible*. He then goes on to say that if you can name it, then "you've got it," whereas "the unnamed—it is the darkness unveiled" (*TJ* 59). The text treats naming as merely another delusory tool of civilization: when you have named it, you haven't got it: you've only got the arrogant illusion that you've got it. A case in point is the misnaming depicted in the "Legend" section, when Tay John goes into the land to fast for four days and to have a vision that will give him his spirit animal. He reports to the elders that he has seen several animals during the four days. Because the bear has strong symbolic meaning within the tribe, the elder Squeleken determines that the bear will be his guardian spirit, although part of Tay John's report suggests that he had a special sensitivity to the owl: "an owl, the soul of a departed woman, was in the tree above me, and my ears, become lonely, were tender to its message" (*TJ* 33). The text gives two further emphases to the image of the owl. First, the "Legend" section closes with this passage, after Tay John has left the tribe: "All that winter smoke rose from the new house built for Tay John. At night an owl perched by it and hooted" (*TJ* 49). Second, after Tay John has killed the grizzly and withdrawn into the woods, Denham comments that "An owl hooted somewhere close to me" (*TJ* 66). These passages suggest that the "soul of a departed woman" was that of his mother, calling him to be true to the legend of the boy born from his pregnant mother's grave.

Irony also informs the meta-narrative commentary in both texts. Every story waits, Denham says, "like a mountain in an untraveled land, for someone to come close, to gaze upon its contours, lay a name upon it, and relate it to the known world" (*TJ* 125). This makes telling and understanding stories seem easy enough, like the meaning of the yarns most seamen tell, as mentioned by the "outside" narrator who introduces Marlow: these tales have a "direct simplicity": their meaning "lies within the shell of a cracked nut" (*HD* 20). In Marlow's stories, however, the meaning is located outside the tale, like the mist that haloes the moon (20). Similarly, Denham states that a story is never fully told: when you have finished, a part of it remains untold. Just as he satirizes naming as a civilizing tool, he also exposes storytelling as another endeavor that can lead to the delusion that "you've got it." He does so through his choice of metaphors: storytelling is mining, surveying, laying siege to, making an assault on the mountain, he says (*TJ* 125-126). The paradox in these metaphors is that they name colonizing activities that define and extract and possess, but in the same passage Denham insists that storytelling is not an activity of owning and controlling. Denham chooses his metaphors from the invading culture of which he is a part but defends storytelling as a different sort of activity altogether—a matter of approaching the unknown and unknowable.

Satire produces uneasiness. The satirist depicts "a universe of unresolved problems," according to Patricia Meyer Spacks; moreover, "in the best satire he is likely to create level upon level of uneasiness" (Spacks 144). The levels of uneasiness pertain to the unresolved problems portrayed, and, in the cases of these two satires, to the uncertainty of the meaning conveyed. J. Hillis Miller argues that *Heart of Darkness* unveils western civilization as imperialism, the "reversal of idealism into savagery" ("Revisited" 218). Conrad's worldview in the novel is disturbing, Said argues, because nothing is stable but universal darkness:

> With Conrad, then, we are in a world being made and unmade more or less all the time. What appears stable and secure—the policeman at the corner, for instance—is only slightly more secure than the white men in the jungle, and requires the same continuous (but precarious) triumph over an all-pervading darkness, which by the end of the tale is shown to be the same in London and in Africa. (*C&I* 29)

Miller notes that this truth is represented as so layered and veiled that it becomes ultimately hidden or indecipherable. Miller argues that "an apocalypse is a narrative unveiling or revelation" ("Revisited" 207) but that Marlow's tale conveys the "dream-sensation ... of being captured by the incredible" ("Revisited" 211). In this story of a dream-sensation, the only revelation is the impossibility of revelation ("Revisited" 212), and nothing is unveiled but the act of unveiling ("Revisited" 215). As Miller argues in another place, there is always "a veil hiding something more truthful" ("Read" 102) because "the novel is ironic through and through" ("Read" 105), and the truth recedes beneath layers of irony. The apocalypse foretold is perpetually imminent, never quite yet: as Miller quips, referring to the title of Francis Ford Coppola's great film based on the novel, "Apocalypse is never now" ("Read" 218) but always about to arrive. Said recognizes that "Kurtz's heroic eloquence" is difficult to comprehend and evaluate: "what is it really? It is quite impossible to say. There can be no more accurate representation in fiction of the historic predicament of mind-tortured modern Europe" (*Autobiography* 113).

Denham interrogates the meaning of darkness more fully—though no more conclusively. The unnamed is "the darkness unveiled" (*TJ* 59), Denham says, and "light lives only in man's vision" (*TJ* 121), but while vision represents humanity's increasing knowledge, he warns that beyond our knowledge "is darkness still" (*TJ* 122), so we never conquer the unknown, any more than Marlow sees darkness as subject to human control: in Marlow's dream vision, humanity can never wring the darkness from the wilderness or the human heart; the best hope is that it may be kept at bay. What Denham says is also true for Marlow: all light springs from darkness since "darkness is the hub of light" (*TJ* 121). For both, human life is brief: Marlow says that humans "live in the flicker" of "a flash of lightning in the clouds" or of "a running blaze on a plain" (*HD* 20); Denham says that humans walk only "for a few short moments in unaccustomed light" before returning to the darkness, for man is "the child of darkness" (*TJ* 125). Man's shadow is "his dark garment," his "shroud," his reminder of his beginning and his end, and of his ignorance. There is, moreover, no truly new knowledge: "all that is, was" (*TJ* 121). As in *Heart of Darkness,* the wilderness represents the unknown and darkness (*TJ* 64), though Denham adds that birth too is "a struggle against the powers of darkness."

Apocalypse is implicit in *Heart of Darkness* but explicit in *Tay John,* where it appears in two passages. The first comes at the beginning of the "Hearsay" section and is delivered in the voice of the narrator who introduces Denham. Speaking in 1904, when the Grand Trunk Railway was first heard of in the region, the "outside" narrator delivers this lyrical sentence: "In small towns, set in half-circles of worship round railway stations, under a sun that labored across the sky all day, and set at day's end, great and red and bloated, as though slowly consumed by the fires of its own creating—farmers and settlers and ranchers met" (*TJ* 53-54). The sun consumed by its own creation symbolizes the end of that same civilization that is now arriving, worshipping its own technology. The second is stated by Jack Denham, as he stands with Father Rorty, watching some of Dobble's men paddle across a lake at dusk to visit some prostitutes:

> We watched the canoe go from us. The sun, low over the black rim of the western mountains, slanted on the lake waters until they became a carpet of creeping flame, failing as it advanced towards us, until at our feet only black water lapped, cold and spent and sobbing in the sandy runnel where the canoe's prow had rested. The canoe was wide, sat low in the water, two pairs of figures—four of Dobble's men—stooped monkishly against the centre thwarts, their backs to the west. The shape of the paddler in the stern rose above them, paddle flashing sword-like from the water and streams of water, blood-reddened against the sinking sun, running from its blade. For a long time we heard the tinkle of those falling paddle streams and the widening wake as a sigh upon the flaming waters. Then the four heads and the paddler's back and the canoe merged, blurred, became black and small and still, consumed before our eyes in the fiery expanse of lake and sky. As our vision faltered, the paddle flashed again, the lake's red bosom rose and swelled, and on it the black speck diminished to a quivering point of dissolution, hesitating one final moment at the fire-guarded gate of the world's end. Then we heard the canoe touch the other graveled shore. We heard men's voices, and before us the sunset rode triumphant on the waters. (141-142)

The apocalypse is associated with the relegation of women to the sphere of the sexual, with the sexualization of nature as feminine, and with the assault on both: the adverb "monkishly" is acerbic. The long history of female prostitution conjoins with the profit ethos of imperialism to imply that moral asperity is immanent.

Twinning is a technique of derision that O'Hagan borrows from Conrad. Unlike Conrad's use of doubles, which is serious in tone and prominent in his plots, his use of twinning pertains to minor characters such as the two women Marlow encounters in the office of the trading company before he embarks for the Congo. With symmetry that has a mocking effect, one is fat and the other slim, one old and the other young; they both knit black wool; the young one introduces the applicants to their interviewers, and the older one scrutinizes them "with unconcerned old eyes" (*HD* 24-25). Those who pass through are regarded as about to die, and more than half of them will; the two knitters are described as "guarding the door of Darkness" (*HD* 25). Similarly, the two Quebecois prospectors who introduce Tay John to white materialism are described as "tall men, with red faces, big hands, and big feet." They come forward "like twins who command the weather" (*TJ* 36), the satirical reference being to the two figures on a cuckoo clock—figures who, ironically, do not command but rather reflect the weather. The glee of these two men is mocked, showing that they are not self-possessed frontier men like Denham but rather are possessed by their desire for gold (*TJ* 37). O'Hagan extends this technique of twinning to major characters with the same sardonic effect. In the "Legend" section of *Tay John*, which falls outside Denham's ken (he is introduced only in the second "Hearsay" section and shows no knowledge of what happens in the novel's first section), the story of Red Rorty is told by a voice that comes from no specified source. "The source of the legend is never qualified" writes Michael Ondaatje ("Afterword" 201). The Rorty brothers are comic opposites: Red Rorty is appetitive and egotistical, while Father Rorty is repressed and intellectual, yet both are undone by the binary of flesh versus spirit, and both meet grim ends befitting the violent and often grotesque nature of frontier life.

Images of open mouths and misleading names represent the imperial lie in both novels. Marlow describes Kurtz's mouth: "I saw him open his mouth wide—it gave him a weirdly voracious aspect, as though he had wanted to swallow all the air, all the earth, all the men before him" (*HD* 76). The image conveys the truth Marlow has discovered beneath the lie of imperialism: the liberation of greed and the will to power without ethical bounds. The passage also specifies that the hunger is metaphorically a cannibal hunger: some African tribes are literally cannibals, but the European colonizers figuratively consume the colonized, as the English landlords do in Jonathan Swift's "A Modest Proposal." Similarly, a stone is put in the mouth of Red Rorty "as a word he tried to utter," and it is said that "the word has choked him" (*TJ* 16). The image exposes his boundless egotism. Concerning names, Marlow learns that the name Kurtz means "short" in German, yet the man lying on the stretcher "looked at least seven feet long": Marlow reflects with bitter irony that his name was "as true as everything else in his life" (*HD* 76). Similarly, Tay John, the child of Red Rorty and the Shuswap woman Hanni, assumes a name that symbolizes his cultural identity being altered in a colonial context. When he returns from his quest vision bringing sand laced with gold, two Quebecois prospectors rename him "Tête Jaune" or Yellowhead. He insists on changing his name from his Shuswap one of Kumkleseem. With the rifle, bullets, and red coat given him by the white men, and the new name, which his people pronounce as *Tay John,* he walks alone among them (*TJ* 38). He has adopted a name bestowed by the invading culture, and he becomes increasingly possessed by its possessions.

Self-doubt, fear, self-consciousness, and self-dramatization are aspects of the construction of the western self that Denham seeks to counter in promulgating his mythic tale of the heroic Tay John. When Denham sees Tay John fight the grizzly, he has his doubts about what he would have done if he were on the other side of the stream (*TJ* 56); in contrast, Denham observes that Tay John has "no doubts about himself" (*TJ* 57). Tay John is also fearless: he finds it incredible that Father Rorty fears his own body, and he struggles to articulate this strange idea to Denham: "I think he is afraid—of himself" (*TJ* 157). As Denham watches Tay John fight the grizzly bear, he expresses a western self-awareness of life as dramatic performance: "It seemed to me like a play being put on for my benefit, with the forest and mountains for backdrop, the gravel bar where this Yellowhead was for stage, and the deep river with its unceasing crescendo for the orchestra pit" (*TJ* 61). For Marlow too, his horrible experience is recounted with the westerner's awareness of theatrical performance: it seems like "some sordid farce acted in front of a sinister black cloth" (*HD* 28). In contrast, Tay John has no sense of self-dramatization, self-consciousness, or nervousness. When Julia Alderson asks the frontier men the tempting question of what they would do if this were their last day on earth (and any wish could be fulfilled), the other men seated around the campfire are evasive or defensive, but Tay John simply states, "I guess, I go hunting" (*TJ* 101). Similarly, at the trial for her rape, he stands "with his feet braced wide, as though he felt the roll of the earth beneath them" (*TJ* 115). It is Julia who paces as though "she could find no place to stand with ease" (*TJ* 115), and she eventually withdraws the charge.

Denham sees storytelling as a communal activity, as demonstrated in the narrative structure of the latter two thirds of *Tay John*. Denham relays portions of the tale from various secondary tellers, who contribute according to their different levels of information and insight. Amusingly, "down the line" Alderson has heard a story of Tay John "losing his hand in a fight with a grizzly bear"—an apocryphal conflation of key episodes in the hero's life (*TJ* 95). Denham passes on the stories of Alderson,

McLeod, Wiggins (relayed from Flaherty), and Blackie. He offers this commentary upon the way in which a backwoodsman takes up a story and transforms it: "His social function is to hand on what he has heard, with the twist his fancy has been able to add. He deals with things done—and with the shadows and the hopes of things waiting to be done. What he has not seen he deduces, and what he cannot understand he explains" (*TJ* 84). The tale will be altered, likely falsified. O'Hagan was aware of the achievements of classic English print literature (Conrad, Keats, etc.), but he also structures his novel as a communal folk art. The key value upheld by the text is community. The one generalizing reflection in the "Legend" section (of which Denham has no knowledge) celebrates community over individuality: "The boy says 'I'. The man says 'We'—and this word that the man speaks is the word of his greatest magic" (*TJ* 29). The ultimate narrative authority in the text is not Denham's voice but the communal voice of oral storytelling; that of the white wilderness men and the Shuswap. O'Hagan attributes to the Shuswap a Tsimshian myth that is recorded by anthropologist Diamond Jenness (Jenness 197-199) but was originally oral.

W.J. Keith notes that O'Hagan "showed the way toward including native legend" in Canadian fiction (83), which was indeed a pioneering narrative innovation in 1939, but Keith does not go further to inquire about how the text frames the Indigenous values contained in the Tsimshian legend. In *Tay John*, the Tsimshian tale of the boy who walks out of his pregnant mother's grave expresses the Indigenous acceptance of the cycle of life and the four stages of life symbolized by the four seasons; all of this is represented in many tribes by the medicine wheel.[4] O'Hagan uses the legend to give his narrative

---

4   Perhaps the best introduction to the general meanings of the medicine wheel is *The Sacred Tree: Reflections on Native American Spirituality,*

a circular structure. When Tay John and Ardith Aeriola are last sighted by Blackie, Tay John pushes her on a toboggan. Ardith is dead and pregnant; Tay John appears to walk down into the earth with her, bringing the legend full circle (*TJ* 199). The circle suggests a holistic and inclusive view of life, rather than a division of life into binaries and conflicting spheres (body/soul, male/female, colonizer/colonized). Weakened and knowing that her death is near, Ardith makes a gesture that may be read as a symbolic acceptance of her mortality: "She traced a circle with a neat moccasined foot through the grass" (*TJ* 194-195). Denham too associates approaching the end of life with the acceptance of the life cycle: "Sometimes when we are older there is a glimpse. It appears we are returning. We have made the circle" (*TJ* 122). The acceptance of the life cycle implies humility, which is contrasted with arrogance in Robert Bringhurst's distinction between "those who think they belong to the world and those who think the world belongs to them" (Bringhurst 241).[5]

As Said argues, the circularity of the plot of *Heart of Darkness*, with Marlow sitting cross-legged like a Buddha on a barge in the mouth of the Thames at the beginning and ending of the tale, may be read in two ways. First, it may suggest that the insularity of the imperial worldview is "not only aesthetically

---

fourth edition, by Phil Lane Jr., Judie Bopp, Michael Bopp, Lee Brown, and elders, 2012. With illustrations, it covers the four directions, four stages of life, and related cultural values.

5   In *The Knowledge Seeker: Embracing Indigenous Spirituality,* University of Regina Press, 2016, Cree-Saulteaux author Blair Stonechild establishes the Indigenous premise that "humans are not the centre of Creation" but are "among the most vulnerable" creatures (3). He then goes on to delineate the "inordinate amount of time" that Indigenous peoples spend in seeking spiritual experiences and to emphasize that "Indigenous peoples keep this ethical system alive through focus on ceremonial activity" (5).

but also mentally unassailable" (*C&I* 24). Second, the very artificiality of this circularity could imply a critique of the novel's
constructedness and suggest "the potential of a reality that
seemed inaccessible to imperialism" (*C&I* 29). In both novels,
the self-enclosed and self-referential nature of imperialism
is suggested by images of voice. Marlow finds Kurtz's voice
entrancing; at the same time, the man is little more than a
voice, and finally the voice of a horror. When Marlow himself is
tempted by madness, it is in the form of an immense jabber of
senseless voices (*HD* 64). In *Tay John,* whereas Father Rorty is
slight in stature and his voice is never more than a "whispered
hoarseness" (*TJ* 138), his brother is "tall, fair-haired and fair-
bearded" with a booming voice; he shouts for the sheer pleasure
of hearing his voice echo into the mountains (*TJ* 5). After he has
joined the Shuswaps and become known among them as a man
who speaks with "a great voice" (*TJ* 13), he seduces a woman
who is spoken for by another man and is killed by the tribe's
women. The Rorty brothers are of "those who think the world
belongs to them." The Shuswap, in contrast, are "peaceful and
not ready with big words" (*TJ* 10). Their deracinated leader, Tay
John, has barely a dozen words in the entire novel.

Glimpses and flashes of insight are paradigmatic means
of knowing in these impressionistic novels. Despite the "unreal" quality (*HD* 38) of the literal and moral fog (*HD* 58) he
confronts, Marlow sometimes gets "a flash of insight" (*HD* 54)
about it. Denham voices this same way of knowing: "Of what
was around me I caught only flashes here and there—as in a
thunderstorm when briefly under the lightning the countryside
is revealed" (*TJ* 179). Using this paradigm of knowing, the text
of *Tay John* offers glimpses into the world of the Indigenous.
Denham wonders about the cultural values of the Shuswap:
he sees Tay John adjusting to a new "world of authority and
discipline moving with the railway into the mountains," and

he wonders about "an earlier authority and discipline—that of the people among whom he was born, who lived beyond the mountains"⁶ (*TJ* 121). He wonders too about the hopes of the Shuswap: he sees Tay John's long yellow hair as a torch or a flame "to light the hopes of his people, whatever they may have been" (*TJ* 75). Denham's curiosity about Shuswap culture is an advance on Marlow's position of being too afraid or too judgmental or too busy to be curious about the culture of the Africans; of course, it is an advance made possible by O'Hagan's vantage point in history. In single images, *Tay John* hints at the indigenous acceptance of both the sexual and spiritual levels of relationship to the feminine. Tay John is drawn to white society "as the wild fowl are drawn to their flocks upon the breeding waters" (74). This image evokes the acceptance of sexuality and contrasts with the self-division between spirit and flesh imposed by the Catholic Church. When Arthur Alderson and Charlie save Tay John from drowning in a raging river, he is described as "stretched out straight, face buried in the sand, as if he were taking suck from the earth" (91). This image suggests the spiritual sustenance of and reverence for Mother Earth which informs indigenous spirituality and ceremony.⁷

---

6   Perhaps the best testimony about the "authority and discipline" of indigenous cultures, if one can generalize, is to be found in the "ethnographic novel" *Waterlily* by Ella Cara DeLoria. She was an "insider" in the sense that she retained her Dakota Sioux language and could interview elders about pre-contact tribal life; her novel is based on these interviews. She was also an "outsider" in that she used English well and did research for Franz Boas of Columbia University. In the novel, DeLoria covers the "order and discipline" of kinship obligations, child-rearing, sexual morality, marriage proposals, etc. First published after her death in 1955, the novel is now available in a new edition, University of Nebraska Press, 2016.

7   Throughout Richard Wagamese's *Embers: One Ojibway's Meditations*, Douglas & McIntyre, 2016, Creator is described as "she," and Wagamese takes spiritual advice from Old Woman.

Both Denham and Marlow sense that there is a spiritual relationship with the land that remains inaccessible to them: by default, it can only be called the unnamed, the mysterious, the incomprehensible, the inscrutable. Denham is cynical about revelations (*TJ* 56); at the same time, he is searching for one, and he finds it in his tale of Tay John. He stops short of propitiating the gods of the land, for the local gods are those of the indigenous people, as George Grant recognizes: "That conquering relation to place has left its mark within us. When we go into the Rockies we may have the sense that gods are there. But if so, they cannot manifest themselves to us as ours. They are the gods of another race, and we cannot know them because of what we are and what we did" (Grant 117). The colonizing society that has dispossessed indigenous peoples of their land has no right to and is unable to appropriate their gods. The same caution about over-reaching informs O'Hagan's depiction of story itself. Kylee-Anne Hingston's argument that "O'Hagan actually believes that the process of storytelling is a degeneration from authoritative legend to inconclusive evidence" (Hingston 181) needs to be amended with the stipulation that the legend or absolute story in question here is an Indigenous one.

Work is the ultimate value for the narrators of both novels. Marlow values "what is in the work—the chance to find yourself" (HD 44). In time, he ceases to see the land looking at him with "vengeful aspect" (*HD* 49)—apparently seeking some vengeance for this "phantom invasion" of colonizers—but not because he becomes more at peace with the land: he simply becomes too busy to pay attention. Marlow focuses on getting the job done and sticks to the colonizer's sphere of what Said calls "the authority and rectitude that come with greater power and development" (*C&I* 25). Denham and the frontier men respect a man who can handle himself in the woods, and Tay John is the backwoodsman *par excellence*; they respect him *because* they identify him with nature. Numerous instances tell them that Tay John is the individual who is truly "Indigenous" to the woods, while the white frontier men are the invaders. After Tay John's fight with the grizzly, Denham admits that "could I have spoken to him I believe I would have tried to excuse my presence there" (*TJ* 61). Alderson recalls that one glance from Tay John made him feel like "an interloper": "He—well he was something shaped by the river, by the hills around us to their own ends" (*TJ* 93). The difficulty for both Marlow and Denham is that they are complicit in the work of empire; Marlow directly as an employee of a Belgian trading company, and Denham indirectly as a man who hires himself out as a guide and packer for settler forays into the mountains. Denham is not able to recognize that Tay John's abilities as a wilderness man entail the indigenous belief in a spiritual relationship with the land. Denham observes Tay John leaving the head of the she-grizzly in the crotch of the tree (65) but is unaware that it is a cultural expression of respect for the spirit of the bear, just as contemporary indigenous hunters leave tobacco out of respect for the spirit of the animal they have killed.[8]

   While the text suggests several Indigenous values that have since been expressed fully by Indigenous authors, it also implies the colonial trap of cultural hybridity.[9] Preceding the

---

8   In Anishinaabe author Waubeshig Rice's novel *Moon of the Crusted Snow*, ECW Press, 2018, the young hunter and husband Evan, trying to live a traditional life on a northern Ontario reserve, says a prayer of thanks after killing a moose and leaves a tobacco offering (pp. 4-5).

9   In *The Sacred Hoop: Recovering the Indian in American Indian Traditions*, Beacon Press, 1992, Paula Gunn Allen asks the fundamental question that still plagues hybridity for Indigenous individuals: how does one participate in an Indigenous tradition that represents "the essential unity

Tsimshian legend of the boy being born from the grave of his pregnant mother is the underlying story of Tay John's egotistical missionary father, Red Rorty. Ironically, the authority of indigenous legend, which is absolute within Shuswap culture, is swept up in colonization. Tay John's hybrid nature and fate determine that he will become possessed by white possessions and that he will be drawn to a white woman, as his white father raped a Shuswap woman. As an indigenous warrior, he leads Ardith away from a society dominated by men like Dobble: as Denham puts it, "she hadn't fled from Dobble, or from fear of retribution because of Dobble, so much as she had fled from the life whose image he was" (*TJ* 192). Leslie Monkman interprets the partnership of Tay John and Ardith Aeriola as a withdrawal from materialism and a movement toward the spiritual values of Indigenous culture:

> But death comes to Tay John and Ardith only after they have retreated from the materialism and corruption of the white man's world, a world lacking both spiritual principles and, as the deaths of the Rorty brothers indicate, adequate spiritual guides. In returning to the landscape that provided a focus for the spiritual values and beliefs that sustained his mother's Shuswap culture, Tay John moves into an elemental and purer world. (Monkman 48)

That "elemental and purer world" is, however, compromised by cultural hybridity. Tay John's last words to Blackie explain that "I'm going to a church. There's a church over there behind the mountain" (*TJ* 198). Tay John's futile search is for

---

of a human being's psyche" while still confronting the "conflict, fragmentation, and destruction" that have damaged that psyche in colonial society? (81-82)

the sake of Ardith, so that she could have a Christian burial; thus, when last seen, the two have not escaped the pull of colonial religion, though they do complete the circular narrative pattern of the Tsimshian legend. The overall shape of the narrative imbricates Indigeneity and imperialism in the hero's tragic fate of cultural hybridity. In so doing, the text forecasts what would develop many years afterward: the theorizing of hybridity as a problematic political position in the context of colonial cultures.[10]

Tay John's severing of his own hand symbolizes his tortuous cultural hybridity. It is also noteworthy, and in accordance with the novel's critique of Christian psychology, that concepts of guilt or self-blame are seen in Tay John only in this Bible-inspired self-mutilation. Drunk in McLeod's cabin, he plays cards, betting his furs against Timberlake's mare; after losing, he takes an axe and chops off his left hand. In the midst of this painful and shocking scene, he is able to reveal his motivation: "If your hand offend you, cut it off" (*TJ* 81). Tay John has been reading McLeod's Bible, and his action is driven by what he misapprehends to be a sacred truth of white culture. Not being acquainted with verbal metaphor, he misinterprets the conceptual as literal. This lurid case of cross-cultural misunderstanding fueled by his use of alcohol marks his moving closer to white society. When he acquires a mechanical hand, he moves closer again. In Thomas Wharton's 1995 novel *Icefields*, he updates *Tay John* by inventing another satire of imperialism using the same setting of the Rockies in

10 In "Fictions of Mixed Origins: *Iracema, Tay John,* and Racial Hybridity in Brazil and Canada," *AmeriQuests,* 2013; 10 (1): pp. 1-9, Albert Braz concludes that *Tay John* dramatizes the "ostensible impossibility" of "ethnoracial hybridity" (7), as demonstrated by the hero's "utter solitude" and untimely demise (5).

the early twentieth century. The explorer Sexsmith discovers a young Snake woman, a shaman, who has the tracks of the rivers and streams on the palm of her left hand. Sexsmith evokes another image of a severed hand: *I imagine there are a few gold-seekers,* he sawed at his wrist with his pipe-stem, *who would do anything to get it* (Wharton 36) (italics part of the text). Wharton embeds in his text an acknowledgement of his debt to O'Hagan: one of the guides on the mountain trails is "the young O'Hagan" (Wharton 96).

Kenyan novelist and critic Leonard Kibera attests that "I study *Heart of Darkness* as a study of the West itself and not as a comment on Africa" (qtd. in Sarvan 285). Regarding their treatment of otherness, the forty-year gap between *Tay John* and *Heart of Darkness* allows O'Hagan insights that Conrad could not have imagined. O'Hagan completed a law degree at McGill university in Montreal but returned to the Rockies to work as a guide and trapper, like his narrator Denham, before moving on to a cosmopolitan life in Argentina, California, and Italy. Three of the nine sketches in his *Wilderness Men* are about indigenous figures. In a 1979 interview, O'Hagan stated that he had worked with mixed-blood indigenous men: "I've heard them maligned and I have found them to be impeccably honest all the way through" (Maillard 29). From this historical perspective, he also describes the term "half-breed" as "a horrible term" (29),[11] but this was, after all, eighty years after Conrad used "the n-word" in *Heart of Darkness*. As a child, Conrad suffered at the hands of Russian imperialism. He was born

---

11 In 1973, Maria Campbell published her memoir *Halfbreed* about growing up Metis in Saskatchewan. The memoir threw the prejudicial term in the faces of readers. It is also widely credited as constituting the inception of Indigenous literature in Canada in that it fostered a movement; this was 34 years after O'Hagan published *Tay John*.

into the Polish gentry in a western Russian province, and in 1863 his family was exiled to Vologda, where the harsh winters hastened the demise of both parents (*HD* 4). He struggled with seeing beyond imperialism and the dark vision of humanity it necessitated. In 1899, the year in which *Heart of Darkness* was published, he wrote to a friend that "I regard the future from the bottom of a very dark past" (qtd. in Ross 190).

In any discourse, it is important to accept the pastness of the past, to honour historical antecedents, and not to set up contemporary standards as absolute. History allowed Howard O'Hagan what it had not allowed Joseph Conrad: a few glimpses of the colonized cultures that would have to be rebuilt in the wake of European imperialism. Edward Said identifies the Eurocentric model for the humanities as one form of filial authority: "its authority comes not only from the orthodox canon of literary movements handed down through the generations, but also from the way this continuity reproduces the filial continuity of the chain of biological procreation" (*World* 22). He asks one question about the place of the intellectual in the world: should the intellectual's identity "involve something more than strengthening those aspects of the culture that require mere affirmation and orthodox compliancy from its members?" (*World* 24) One of his many responses to his own question is to celebrate authors like Vico and Swift who turned from the cultures to which they were filially bound by birth, nationality, and profession to make it their "whole enterprise" to resist the claims that their era made on them culturally and systemically (*World* 25). Joseph Conrad was an exile who felt deeply gratified to find a home in English culture; nonetheless, in *Heart of Darkness,* Conrad made it his effort to satirize European imperialism and, extrapolating from it, to confront the darkness of the human heart. O'Hagan found what Said calls "an affiliation" in the novel (and in Conrad) and expressed that affiliation in *Tay John*. The affiliation needs to be appreciated in detail with the *caveat* that, like us all, both authors were constrained by their respective times.

Works Cited

Achebe, Chinua. "An Image of Africa: Racism in Conrad's *Heart of Darkness*." *Heart of Darkness*, edited by Robert Kimbrough, third edition, W.W. Norton, 1988, pp. 251-261.

Brantlinger, Patrick. "*Heart of Darkness:* Anti-Imperialism, Racism, or Impressionism?" *Heart of Darkness*, edited by Ross C. Murfin, second edition, Bedford/St. Martin's, 1996, pp. 277-298.

Bringhurst, Robert. "The Persistence of Poetry and the Destruction of the World." *Essay Writing for Canadian Students*, edited by Roger Davis and Laura K. Davis, eighth edition, Pearson, 2016, pp. 241-245.

Conrad, Joseph. *Heart of Darkness*, edited by Ross C. Murfin, second edition, Bedford/St. Martin's, 1996, pp. 17-95.

Davidson, Arnold E. "Silencing the Word in Howard O'Hagan's *Tay John*." *Canadian Literature*, vol. 110, Fall 1986, pp. 30-44.

Forster, E.M. *Abinger Harvest*, Edwin Arnold, 1936.

Grant, George, *Technology and Empire*, Anansi, 1969.

Hingston, Kylee-Anne. "The Declension of Story: Narrative Structure in Howard O'Hagan's *Tay John*." *Studies in Canadian Literature/Etudes en Litterature Canadienne*, 2005, vol. 30, no. 2, pp. 181-192.

Hodgart, Matthew. *Satire*. World University Library, McGraw-Hill, 1969.

Jenness, Diamond. *The Indians of Canada*. U of Toronto P, 1977.

Keith, W.J. "Howard O'Hagan, *Tay John*, and the Growth of Story." *Silence Made Visible: Howard O'Hagan and* Tay John," edited by Margery Fee, ECW Press, 1992, pp. 73-84.

Kernan, Alvin B. "The Role of Irony in Satire." *Satire*, edited by Laura K. Egendorf, Greenhaven Press, 2002, pp. 29-37.

Leavis, F.R. *The Great Tradition*. New York UP, 1963.

Maillard, Keith. "An Interview with Howard O'Hagan." *Silence Made Visible: Howard O'Hagan and Tay John,* edited by Margery Fee, ECW Press, 1992, pp. 21-38.

Miller, J. Hillis. "Should we Read *Heart of Darkness*?" *Reading Conrad,* edited by John G. Peters & Jakob Lothe, Ohio State UP, pp. 88-121.

Miller, J. Hillis. "*Heart of Darkness* Revisited." *Heart of Darkness,* edited by Ross C. Murfin, second edition, Bedford/St. Martin's, 1996, pp. 206-220.

Monkman, Leslie. *A Native Heritage: Images of the Indian in English-Canadian Literature*. U of Toronto P, 1981.

Ondaatje, Michael. "Howard O'Hagan and the 'Rough-Edged Chronicle.'" *The Canadian Novel in the Twentieth Century: Essays from Canadian Literature,* edited and with an Introduction by George Woodcock, McClelland & Stewart, 1975, pp. 276-284.

----. Afterword. *Tay John,* New Canadian Library, McClelland & Stewart, 2008, pp. 201-209.

O'Hagan, Howard. *Tay John*. Afterword by Michael Ondaatje, New Canadian Library, McClelland & Stewart, 2008.

Ross, Stephen. *Conrad and Empire*. U of Missouri P, 2004.

Said, Edward. *Joseph Conrad and the Fiction of Autobiography*. Foreword by Andrew N. Rubin, Columbia UP, 2008.

----. *Culture and Imperialis.,* Vintage Books, Random House, 1994.

----. *The World, the Text, and the Critic*. Harvard UP, 1983.

Sarvan, C.P. "Racism and the *Heart of Darkness*." *Heart of Darkness,* edited by Robert Kimbrough, third edition, W.W. Norton, 1988, pp. 280-285.

Shetty, Sandya. "*Heart of Darkness:* Out of Africa Some New Thing Never Comes." *Journal of Modern Literature,* vol. 15, 1989, pp. 461-474.

Singh, Frances B. "The Colonialistic Bias of *Heart of Darkness.*"
    Heart of Darkness, edited by Robert Kimbrough, third edition,
    W.W. Norton, 1988, pp. 268-280.

Smith, Johanna M. "'Too Beautiful Altogether': Ideologies of Gen-
    der and Empire in *Heart of Darkness." Heart of Darkness,* edited
    by Ross C. Murfin, second edition, Bedford/St. Martin's, 1996,
    pp. 169-184.

Spacks, Patricia Meyer. "Satire Causes Feelings of Uneasiness."
    Satire, Greenhaven Press, 2002, pp. 143-152.

Stewart, Garrett. "Lying as Dying in *Heart of Darkness." Heart of
    Darkness,* edited by Robert Kimbrough, third edition, W.W.
    Norton, 1988, pp. 358-374.

Swift, Jonathan. "A Modest Proposal." *Essay Writing for Canadian
    Students,* edited by Roger Davis and Laura K. Davis, eighth
    edition, Pearson, 2016, pp. 348-355.

Wharton, Thomas. *Icefields.* NeWest Press, 1995.

Wilson, George. "Edward Said on Contrapuntal Reading." *Philosophy
    and Literature,* vol. 18, 1994, pp. 265-273.

Zichy, Francis. "Crypto-, Pseudo-, and Pre-Postmodernism: *Tay
    John, Lord Jim,* and the Critics." *Essays on Canadian Writing,*
    vol. 81, Winter 2004, pp. 192-221.

----. "The 'Complex Fate' of the Canadian in Howard O'Hagan's
    Tay John." Essays on Canadian Writing, vol. 79, Spring 2003,
    pp. 199-225.

Fantasy and Sovereignty
in Howard O'Hagan's *Tay John*
A Postcolonial Reading[1]

Sergiy Yakovenko

Howard O'Hagan's *Tay John* begins with a catchy and entertaining story of the eccentric Red Rorty, a failed Christian preacher, who, having slept with a married Shuswap woman, receives a humiliating death at the hands of the tribe's women and children. The reader is nudged to assume that Red Rorty and the Indigenous woman Hanni, who dies in pregnancy, are the parents of Kumkleseem, later rechristened by some Quebecois gold prospectors as "Tête Jaune," which is then anglicized to "Yellowhead." He crawls out of his mother's grave, goes through "sustained ceremonies of rebirth and renaming" (Davidson 33), receives his guardian spirit as a result of initiation, gets acquainted with the culture and the lures of the colonial world, and, as a young man, assumes his legendary role of a messianic leader for his people. The first section of the novel—"Legend"—ends with Tay John's mysterious disappearance from

---

1   A shorter and modified version of this argument is forthcoming in *Nature: Points of Access* (edited by Alain Beauclair and Josh Toth, Lexington Books); it has an ecocritical focus and considers the original Hegelian, rather than the Adornoian, concept of the lordship-bondage mechanics.

his winter dwelling, and thus his ostensible withdrawal from a tribal definition of leadership that means an absolute sacrifice of the individual for the collective.

As the "Legend's" undefined and omniscient narrator hands the story over to the taleteller Jack Denham after a brief introduction at the start of the second section, "Hearsay"—never to claim the story back again—the text keeps the reader in a state of suspense: How is Tay John going to resurface in Jackie's tale? Is Jackie's account of him going to make a sharp contrast with the quasi-biblical, slightly ironic, yet largely impartial and dispassionate narrative of the "Legend"? Denham comes from Britain to the "colonies" as a remittance man and intertwines periods of idle profligacy with hiring out as a wilderness guide. O'Hagan uses him, perhaps, as the typical philosophizing "amateur" colonist, one of "us," his readers, who are supposed to get a little amused with his funny appearance and his drinking credo, but whose world we largely share and whose vision we generally trust. The effect of this change in perspective is our anticipation of rediscovery of the protagonist and his story—"as if it were beginning again in another world" (Pivato 186): Tay John's personality, only surmised in the "legendary" part of the story as a lapse of life in a sequence of mythical events, should now come into the open in a live and concrete perception, experienced subjectively but tangibly. The first encounter between Tay John and Denham, however, despite the vividness of descriptions and characterization, reveals little more of the protagonist than the legend, and presents him as a fictitious actor on Jackie's ostentatious ideological stage.

From the moment the omniscient narrator of the first part cedes the story of Tay John to Denham, the latter—as a witness himself and an interpreter of the tales of others—takes the reader on a journey from his bombastic portrayal of Tay

John's fight with a grizzly, through the lures and perils of the protagonist's life on the fringes on the colonial society, to his reported demise and metaphorical return "into the ground" (*Tay John* 200). The "Denham" parts of *Tay John* are grounded in the narrator's psychology, as Francis Zichy observes in his 2003 article (201), but even more so in the narrator's relationship with the image of the protagonist that Denham puts forward and maintains throughout his tale. I contend that the initial scene of Tay John's combat with a grizzly is important as a momentum that propels the whole narrative because in the conclusion of this first episode, Denham is left not only with a self-imposed delusion of the epic quality of the event but also with the gaping void of a denied recognition. Orchestrated in the narrator's mind, the underlying symbolism of the scene can be projected onto the Hegelian Master-Slave dialectic, in whose framework, and according to Theodor Adorno and Max Horkheimer's explicative illustration, Denham can be compared with the Master figure of Odysseus as the first concertgoer, who is able to idly enjoy the seductive singing of the Sirens without risking his life and at the cost of the labour and impaired hearing of his crew. The Hegelian schema rests on the presumption that the Slave figure returns the gesture of recognition back to the Master, but in O'Hagan's novel it becomes aborted because Tay John refuses to return the gesture and, moreover, manages to maintain his own sovereignty in spite of all the failures that befall him. Contrapuntal comparisons with Conrad's Marlow, as well as with certain motifs in Jack London and Georges Bugnet, make it possible to lay out more precisely the ideological apparatus of appropriation that Denham employs with respect to Tay John, among which the sexualization of the wilderness, the Enlightenment supremacy of vision, language as a tool of colonization, and the juxtaposition of idea and instinct loom large enough to support the interpretations of the novel as an unmasking of Western arrogance. Tay John, emerging from the cyclic time-space and liberated from the collective identity of his Indigenous culture, figures as an inchoate modern self in pursuit of his individual happiness and destiny, and thus a novel's protagonist proper.

Wilderness Men and the Grizzly Bear

Narrator Jack Denham, as Zichy has noted ("The 'Complex Fate'" 202 etc.), does everything he can to avoid responsibility for a truthful account of Tay John's story, now by intimating his problems with alcohol, now by digressing into details about Dobble and Father Rorty, now by eloping with his own egotistic self to Edmonton during a turn of events that is critical for his protagonist. Of course, his situation allows him a greater mobility than Conrad's Marlow can afford in *Heart of Darkness*. While Marlow is confined by the inscrutable animosity of his immediate environment and by the strict limitations of his mission, Denham is mostly a free-floater, by no means restricted by space or time. As both are, however, not writers but yarn-spinners, or storytellers with inscribed-in-the-text audiences, their narrative situations are necessarily delimited by peculiar time-spaces that assume different predominant vectors: Marlow's of time—the span of one evening, and Denham's of space—"stretching his story the length of Edmonton" (*TJ* 56). In consequence, their yarns also gain two different qualities. Marlow's tale seems to comply with Wordsworth's requirement for poetry as "emotion recollected in tranquility" (Wordsworth 611): it arises in pensive silence when "the serenity became less brilliant but more profound" (*Heart of Darkness* 104). Denham spins his tale while following a friend "to his destination" after having had "two tall pale glasses of whisky" (*TJ* 56). As a result, Marlow's narrative is much more focused and as though executed in one emotional-stylistic key. Denham's narrative situation, however, is presented, as it seems, only for his story of "an adventure" (*TJ* 56) that introduces his first encounter with the enigmatic figure of the novel's protagonist, Tay John. Further ramification of the plot and the inclusion of other sub-narrators or witnesses make the initial narrative situation—that of "stretching his story the length of Edmonton" (*TJ* 56)—a rhetorical device akin to an invocation to the muses, which, nevertheless, emphasizes the importance and the emotional primacy of Denham's first meeting with Tay John. Jackie's account of this adventure offers a vivid picture of a Western self that is well set in a colonial ideological framework and deeply rooted in the mythology of modernity.

The lengthy and digressive depiction of the occurrence that was a matter of "split seconds" (*TJ* 78)—Tay John's bloody struggle with a grizzly bear—is called upon to render the sublimity and symbolic solemnity which Denham takes pains to invest it with. The narrator's main motivation is his fantasy of placing himself in the role of an Indigenous stranger, whose self-protecting combat with the grizzly is reimagined as an epic battle of man against the dark powers of nature. Robinson aptly observes that in "projecting his cultural values onto the stranger," "'Jackie's tale' gratifies his culture's vision of a polarized world in which heroes, victories, enemies, and ideals are perfectly clear" ("Myths of Dominance"). In Margery Fee's opinion, "Denham's projection clearly takes a literary form ... as well as fulfilling a psychological or moral need. His 'gospel' contains all the elements needed to reveal it as a wish fulfilment fantasy and a literary construct, as, indeed, does O'Hagan's novel at a more sophisticated level" (19).

The exposition leading to the adventure itself portrays Denham—to borrow Geoffrey Hartman's phrase—as a "halted traveler" (1) who puts forth great efforts to sell, or recalibrate, what for his ethos appears to be "almost … an adventure" as the most profound event for his aesthetic sensibility. Denham presents himself as an idling Sunday traveller on "a busman's holiday" (*TJ* 58): having left his survey team in camp, he was enticed by a lyrical lure of a "valley, with no name, a clear flow of water, clear and cold as spring water, coming from it through a lane of spruce-trees by our camp"—he just "wanted to see where it led to" (*TJ* 58). The power of emotions that Denham tries to convey in regard to the grizzly-human battle scene would hardly need a defence against any possible accusations of inflation, like the Wordsworthian "egotistical sublime," but the very stance O'Hagan's narrator assumes toward his ambience can arguably qualify him as a romantic stroller of the Lake School, and maybe even a kind of a Baudelairean flaneur of the Rockies. His reputation as a wilderness man would definitely prevent him from making a big deal out of the daffodils, but he certainly is something of a romantic "loner" (Keith 73), and in his tales, his powers of observation dominate over the crude sensation of an anecdote.

Denham's motivation, however, goes a little beyond a romantic stroller quest—it reflects a masculine desire for the erotically reimagined landscape: "A new mountain valley leads a man like that—like a woman he has never touched" (*TJ* 58). The next paragraph, which offers Denham's explanation of the invincible lure of the landscape, gains more if we continue reading it as a sexual metaphor for man's undying pursuit of a new erotic object:

> His [man's] experience tells him it will be much like others he knows—a canyon to go through, a meadowland or two, some forest, and its head up against a mountain wall or trickling from a grimy glacier. Yet still he goes up in hoping vaguely for some revelation, something he has never seen or felt before … (*TJ* 58)

In his discussion of the misogyny in *Tay John* as a "function of the taming of the natural world," Ronald Granofsky leans on Annette Kolodny's speculation in *The Lay of the Land* "that 'gendering the land as feminine' bespeaks 'a *need* to experience the land as a nurturing, giving maternal breast because of the threatening, alien, and potentially emasculating terror of the unknown'" (Granofsky 115). While the crux of the event that Denham makes central to his tale is, "as in Faulkner," "a result of the confrontation with the unknown wilderness" (Granofsky 15), the oedipal associations that Granofsky suggests through Kolodny's intuition do not seem to be the premise leading Denham to this experience. In fact, as Robinson shows in "Dismantling Sexual Dualities," the opposition of "maternal versus adult love" is just one of a few such dualities that pervade the novel, among which "the sexual duality of civilized versus natural" in this particular episode "is subjected to the same process of inversion and deconstruction": "The land is a darkly mysterious temptress for the questing westerners" (100). Carolyn Merchant reads the complex attitudes of Western culture toward the untamed American wilderness as a "recovery narrative" intended as remedy for humankind's eviction from the biblical Garden of Eden. In her opinion, "crucial to the structure of the recovery narrative is the role of gender encoded into the story" (Merchant 137). The remedial narrative necessarily mirrors the prelapsarian distribution of gender roles between a male, Adam, symbolic of "the original oneness," and a female, Eve, whose essence, harder to contain and more equivocal, trifurcates into the following major forms:

As original Eve, nature is virgin, pure, and light—land that is pristine or barren, but that has the potential for development. As fallen Eve, nature is disorderly and chaotic; a wilderness, wasteland, or desert requiring improvement; dark and witchlike, the victim and mouthpiece of Satan as serpent.

As mother Eve, nature is an improved garden, a nurturing earth bearing fruit, a ripened ovary, maturity. (137)

Contrary to Granofsky's suggestion, the mother Eve's image of nature does not ever seem to appeal to Denham's western ideals. His erotic appetite is certainly whetted by nothing else but the virginity of the landscape, "a country where no man has stepped before" (*TJ* 58-59), ensuring a perpetual object of desire whose full possession can never be accomplished. It is true, Denham's attitude has little in common with the colonial injunction of taming the wilderness and thus bringing it "into harmony with the Divine Order," which, according to Max Oelschlaeger, was "the governing medieval Christian perspective" (70). Denham's romance with the landscape is reminiscent of the much more forceful intercourse between the untamed wilderness and Roger, one of the two protagonists of Georges Bugnet's novel *The Forest* (*La forêt*, 1935), *Tay John*'s contemporary. A young French couple, Roger and Louise, move to Alberta to build a farmstead in the wilderness, but, infatuated with the virginity of the land and possessed by his affair with the landscape-mistress, Roger neglects his duties as a young husband and for a long time even fails to build a cabin, continuing to inhabit a tent—an extension of the wilderness. He takes a special pleasure in forcing himself into the thick of the forest, discovering its secret inhabitants whose privacy he is eager to violate. Although less entrepreneurial and vigorous, Denham shares with Roger if not the aesthetic then at least the erotic component of their infatuation, which, on occasion, borders on voyeurism.

Another aspect of the same motif that Jackie and Roger have in common is a symbolic appropriation of landscape by vision and language. Bedazzled by the beauty of his virgin mistress that is shaped in the pattern of his desire, Roger recklessly shares with his wife his passion for the other: "Look, over

there, to the northwest. You can see all *my land*. Last month,
when I came to visit it before registering it *in my name* at the
homestead office in Edmonton, it was *this view alone* that con-
vinced me ..." (Bugnet 18; emphasis added). Devoid of Roger's
proprietorial motivations, Denham exhibits a subtler—more
symbolical or even metaphysical—strain of his affair, more
overtly intimating his ties with the prelapsarian Edenic story:
in his pursuit of the virgin landscape, "he rounds a point or
pushes his head over a pass, feeling that a second before, that
had he come a second earlier, he would have surprised the
Creator at his work" (*TJ* 58). Denham clearly imagines himself
on an Adamic mission of naming the created world and thus
as though co-creating it, and presents this appropriation by
language as part of human nature: "It is physically exhausting
to look on unnamed country. A name is the magic to keep it
within the horizons" (*TJ* 59). By the Adamic agency of naming,
man (an unequivocally male representative of humankind)
linguistically assists God-the-Creator by keeping the creation
out of the surrounding and charging entropy. Denham majes-
tically proclaims, "The unnamed—it is the darkness unveiled"
(*TJ* 59). Therefore, naming is also called upon to stave off the
apocalypse, literally, "the unveiling," which J. Hillis Miller ties
with one of the main functions of Conrad's *Heart of Darkness*
(82). While Marlow in *Heart of Darkness* "comes back to civilization with nothing, nothing to witness to, nothing to reveal
but the process of unveiling that makes up the whole of the
narration" (Miller 83), Denham returns as a witness with a tale
about man's (Tay John's) victory over the powers of darkness
as uncontrolled, unhuman nature, which at some point is
described as "dark, black as the inside of a bear" (*TJ* 66).

The sense of vision is another faculty of the male appropriation of an appetitive object that makes—steeped deep
in Western tradition—an easy transition from eroticism to

metaphysics: "a country where no man has stepped before is new in the real sense of the word, as though it had just been made, and when you turn your back upon it you feel that it may drop back again into the dusk that gave it being. It is only our vision that holds it in the known and created world" (*TJ* 59). The "halted traveler" of the Romantic period, Wordsworth, as Frederick A. Pottle maintains, always needed imagination—in all the complexity of this Romantic concept—to sustain the metaphysical link between a natural object and his eye (283-86). Denham's Adamic vision, by contrast, is not complicated by any intermediaries: his optic sensibility draws on the Cartesian and Lockean "faith in the linkage between lucidity and rationality, which gave the Enlightenment its name" (Jay 85). Himself a rather noninvasive attendant of the capitalist and colonial ideas of progress and development, Denham turns out to be a part of what Merchant calls "a grand master narrative of Enlightenment"—"the recovery of the garden lost in the Fall—the bringing of light to the dark world of inchoate nature" (136, 137).

Martin Jay points out that the great faith that Enlightenment thinkers placed in the human faculty of vision meant that they altogether "distrusted the evidence of the competing major sense organ, the ear, which absorbed only unreliable 'hearsay'" (85). "Hearsay"—notably—is the title of the second section of *Tay John*, in which O'Hagan, who as a lawyer must have had a proclivity to mistrust this type of evidence, takes pains to compromise the reliability of his narrator in the latter's account of Tay John's story. The supremacy of vision for man's metaphysical task of "enlightening," or shedding the light of consciousness on the dark corners of creation, is slightly satirized in Jackie's narrative itself. When he returns late to his camp after witnessing Tay John's fight with the bear, "Night was about me like a covering from which I tried to escape" (*TJ* 66).

Under the circumstances, he resorts to his other sense—his tactile abilities: "My hands wandered far from me feeling my way. My fingers touched branches ... They were some company for me in the darkness" (*TJ* 66). The inclusion of this remark in the conclusion of the episode where darkness was defeated by "man" suggests Denham's self-irony. Besides that, there is always the motif of "a glass of whisky—whisky, another victory of man against the powers of darkness" (*TJ* 66).

Despite his tongue in cheek, O'Hagan can hardly dissuade the reader from taking seriously Denham's metaphysical speculations regarding man's primary vocation of "worlding" the world (to use Martin Heidegger's concept) by means of vision and language (Heidegger 1132). In this worlding, the positive faculty of vision is clearly juxtaposed with the suspicious and unreliable sense of hearing, which ultimately is figured in the negative or apophatic silence. In the virginity of the woods— of course, the virginity is always stipulated by the narrator's colonial pride, as the Rockies had for a long time been under the "naming" and "optic" powers of the Indigenous peoples— Denham thinks he "can *hear* the world being made." He adds that "anyway you can hear the silence" (*TJ* 59), which is one of the apophatic attributes of the Creator and a testimony to the negativity of hearing before man's vision appropriates the creation and gives it a name. Ultimately, vision can also be used to appropriate silence itself—as Denham vividly shows in one of his most lyrical passages about the flying snowflakes: "They were like immense moths winging down in the twilight, making the silence about me visible" (*TJ* 68).

O'Hagan's silence motif asks for an obvious parallel with "the white silence," so prominent in Jack London's narratives of the North and their mystical evocation of "the Young World" (London, "The Call of the Wild" 488). London's short story "The White Silence" seems to bring this image as close as possible to Denham's Edenic worlding ambitions: it is during "the passive phase of the White Silence" that "if ever, man walks alone with God" (London, "The White Silence" 438). However, God's proximity is assured neither by the prelapsarian Edenic nor by the lyrical snowfall silence—it is "the most tremendous, the most stupefying" trick wherewith nature "convinces man of his finity," which renders man "timid, affrighted of his own voice" (438). At the beginning of *White Fang*, London pictures the most sinister portrait of this silence: "There was a hint in it of laughter, but of a laughter more terrible than any sadness—a laughter that was mirthless as the smile of the sphinx, a laughter cold as the frost and partaking of the grimness of infallibility. It was the masterful and incommunicable wisdom of eternity laughing at the futility of life and the effort of life" (3). London's silence of the northern land falls under one of Edmund Burke's classes of the sublime, namely, "privations, such as darkness, vacuity, and silence, which are great because they are terrible" (Monk 34). O'Hagan, who shares with London a few themes and stylistic takes (both in *Tay John* and, especially, in his collection of stories *Wilderness Men*), nevertheless keeps his narrator Jackie Denham out of both the more common romantic sublime, which "suggested the association of God and wild nature" (Nash 46), and its London's variation (inhuman, apathetic, and implacable force of the wild), and rather renders Denham a more universal man of modernity who combines colonialism with the spirit of enlightenment.

A more detailed comparison between London and O'Hagan can be a fruitful study of its own, but for the sake of this particular analysis, suffice it to emphasize the key anthropological difference between London's characters and Denham as a "wilderness man": London's wilderness challenge, while exalting the courage and nobleness of human nature, neither separates humans from their environment nor gives them an edge on the evolutionary survival. Although London's northern tales' theme is often described as man pitted against the forces of nature, both humans and animals (usually dogs) are equal participants in the process of evolution and equally subject to the laws of survival. As Earl Wilcox points out, in London "man is merely a high-order animal, and his survival, his progress toward a higher state, is dependent upon his adaptability. In the northland, environmental and hereditary traits are more forcefully evident because of the heightened struggle" (183-84). Wilderness as man's object of struggle is also a part of Denham's fantasy, but his position—by all means more visionary and highfalutin—is characteristic of Western stances toward nature as something separate from the human, as an object of man's self-assertion and domination: "This was the sort of thing I had sometimes dreamed of—of meeting a bear one day close up, hand to hand so to speak, and doing it in. An epic battle: man against the wilderness" (*TJ* 62-63). As such, Denham's stance complies with what Oelschlaeger calls the "alchemy of modernism," which started in the Renaissance and prevails to this day: "Modernism thus underlies the emergence of a profound homocentrism, still dominant in the world, which may be characterized as *the ideology of the man infinite* or the rise of *Lord Man*, that is, a radical change in humankind's sense of relative proportions" (69). As a narrator, Jackie is not entirely devoid of what Keats called "negative capability," as he is not really persistent in imposing his own outlook on the events and people whose lives he becomes a part of. But in the account of his first semi-acquaintance with Tay John, Denham offers a ridiculously grandiloquent homocentric utterance that can hardly go along with his narrative situation as an inebriated anecdotalist escorting a friend to his house: "Like birth itself it was a struggle against the powers of darkness, and Man had won" (*TJ* 64). Among the first-person narrators, phrases of similar pomposity may be expected of the *Heart of Darkness* Marlow, but his narrative situation is much more conducive to meditation; stylistically, Denham's pomposity resembles rather London than Conrad, but London's high-flown pronouncements mostly issue from the third-person authorial narrator.

Denham and Marlow can be said to share some romantic fantasies: being virtually compatriots and contemporaries—Marlow an English captain and Denham a colonial remittance man from the north of Ireland—they are attracted to the darkness of the unknown and the unhuman, which they approach from the position of the "emissaries of light" (*Heart of Darkness* 113), and thus can be described as more or less sophisticated products of enlightenment. Marlow of *Heart of Darkness* admits that he has been lured by the blank spots on the map since he "was a little chap." Before he matured, however, ruthless colonial vigour had transformed the "white patch" on the map—central Africa—into "a place of darkness" (*Heart of Darkness* 108). Although at odds with the racism and cruelty of the West's "conquest of the earth," Marlow is rather slow at abandoning the enlightenment ideals: "What redeems it is the idea only. An idea at the back of it; not a sentimental pretence but an idea; and an unselfish belief in the idea—something you can set up, and bow down before, and offer a sacrifice to ..." (107). Similarly, introducing Jack Denham as one of the first surveyors of the Rockies, O'Hagan's third-person narrator includes him in the kind of "men carried on the wind of an idea." Those men "found themselves blown up a canyon where man had never been and words never lived before. Nameless river water tugged their saddle stirrups. In the winter silence was about them on the snow like a name each had heard whispered in his mother's womb" (*TJ* 54-55). In both cases, the European fantasy of geographical discovery, thickened in the image of the blank spots on the map or in the phrases like "unnamed country" (*TJ* 59), excludes any notion of a cultural equality between the enlightened Europeans and the Indigenous populations of those "virgin" lands. In *Heart of Darkness*, this blunder leads Marlow on an ominous journey toward a reluctant self-awareness; in *Tay John*, Denham seems too excited about his fantasy to deny himself a self-deceptive opportunity to make one Indigenous person—Tay John—a part of his dream.

Denham spots a yellow-haired mixed-blood stranger in a situation which he himself, ostensibly, has "dreamed of—of meeting a bear one day close up, hand to hand so to speak, and doing it in. An epic battle: man against the wilderness. And now I saw the battle taking form, but another man was in my place and with the river between us I could give no help" (*TJ* 62-63). Instead of fighting "an epic battle" himself, Denham is faced with a task much simpler and evidently more entertaining: to fulfill his dream, he must visualize and then describe the scene and its actor in a suitable fashion. Tay John's victory over the female grizzly becomes Denham's own triumph due to the latter's capacity for transposition or projection of himself upon the figure of the Indigenous stranger, who in the eyes of Denham must first qualify for his idea of "man."

In his account of the event, Denham cautiously leads his listener to the appropriate visualization—by noting the minute details of his own perception—of Tay John before the latter will be granted the status of epic hero. Denham begins almost exactly like Marlow in *Lord Jim*—by employing his own keenness of observation and intuitive knowledge of personality types. The objective for both Marlow and Denham is similar: to establish that the potentially dubious character is "of the right sort" and "one of us" (*Lord Jim* 49). The sympathetic description starts from the appearance: "I liked his appearance;

I knew his appearance; he came from the right place; he was one of us. He stood there for all the parentage of his kind ..." (*Lord Jim* 28). Jim's "ability in the abstract" (3-4) repeated three times on the initial pages of the novel, finds its stylistic echo is Denham's portrayal of Tay John:

> His brown skin glowed, and his muscles were a pattern of shadows across his chest and belly. Still, there was something, it is hard to say, something of the abstract about him—as though he were a symbol of some sort or other. He seemed to stand for something ... his muscles across his body—they weren't strength in the usual sense of being able to lift weights and that kind of thing. They represented strength in the abstract. Endurance, solitude—qualities that men search for. (*TJ* 60-61)

And now—for comparison—some scraps of Marlow's description of Jim:

> He stood there for all the parentage of his kind, for men and women by no means clever or amusing, but whose very existence is based upon honest faith, and upon the instinct of courage. I don't mean military courage, or civil courage, or any special kind of courage. I mean just that inborn ability to look temptations straight in the face—a readiness unintellectual enough, goodness knows, but without pose—a power of resistance, don't you see, ungracious if you like, but priceless—an unthinking and blessed stiffness before the outward and inward terrors, before the might of nature ... (*Lord Jim* 28)

Both narrators also underscore an unintellectual, innate, instinctual-inherited quality of their character-objects' sturdiness. In addition to Jim's "unintellectual" readiness, Marlow places him in opposition to the "emissaries of light" from *Heart of Darkness*, who are led and redeemed by an "idea": "Hang ideas! They are tramps, vagabonds, knocking at the back-door of your mind, each taking a little of your substance, each carrying away some crumb of that belief in a few simple notions you must cling to if you want to live decently and would like to die easy!" (*Lord Jim* 28). This juxtaposition between the man of ideas and the one of natural instincts is reflected in Denham's observations of Tay John: "He doubtless saw me before I saw him. He would have, that sort of fellow" (*TJ* 60). In his other surmise about Tay John's character, Denham denies him the ability to experience night dreams and establishes his own aesthetic, as it were, superiority as a bystander over Tay John's unmediated perception: "Yet I doubt if he, a man of his type, would ever have had a nightmare in his life. No, his sleep would be sleep—just sleep—like a deep shadow between each of his days. Nothing more than that. No place of vision … With me it was different. I was an onlooker. I saw what he didn't see." (*TJ* 57-58).

Master-Slave Dialectic

Only by dint of assigning certain functions between Tay John as an actor and himself as a spectator is Denham able to bridge the spatial and cultural divide that would otherwise prevent him from reconciling the two so remote perceptions of one event into one unified victory of "man" over "the powers of darkness": "He had won. *We* had won. That was how I felt" (*TJ* 64). The role Denham assumes in the process of this reconciliation, and the one he ascribes to Tay John, can make the narrator a perfect illustration of the Hegelian subject. Within the Hegelian Master-Slave dialectic of the self, the Master asserts his individuality by exercising his superiority over the Slave, whom he needs for an objective recognition of himself in the same way as the Spirit, or Idea, needs an extraneous physical object, or its own "other," to acquire a concrete form and thus be apprehended. For the realization of his Enlightenment Idea of conquering nature *qua* "the powers of darkness," Denham needs a concrete material thing (the bear), which becomes a resistant object of his desire, but being a Master-figure in his own orchestrated scenario of self, he loses his immediate touch with the material reality and leaves this function to the Slave, who therefore becomes a mediator and the Master's only possibility to get in touch with reality. Denham's problem as a spectator of the epic battle is his inability to fight himself, that is, to get an unmediated access to the materiality of the object, notwithstanding his uncanny proximity to the centre of the event. In several phrases, the narrator underscores both his nearness to the scene of the battle and the unbridgeable gap between the observer and the combatants, a natural obstacle that keeps Denham clear of the brutal embodiment of his dream:

> An adventure. A real one. Blood in it. It was a close call. I would have been in on it too? But there was the creek in the way ... and a man besides.
>
> It would have taken courage to cross that creek. I don't think it was possible to cross. I don't know now. Hard to tell. At the time, anyway, it was impossible. It wasn't wide. Twice as wide as a man, standing, might jump perhaps, but deep and swift. (*TJ* 57)

The rationalization of his passivity allows Denham to enjoy the bloody scene as an aesthetic performance of nature red in tooth and claw, in which his closeness to the stage guarantees the best viewer experience while securing his safety by the conventional gap between the actor and the audience: "Suddenly it seemed to me like a play being put on for my benefit, with the forest and mountains for backdrop, the gravel bar where this Yellowhead was for stage, and the deep river with its unceasing crescendo for the orchestra pit" (*TJ* 62). This scenario places Denham's tale in close proximity to Homer's story of Odysseus's encounter with the Sirens—the occurrence, which, according to Theodore Adorno and Max Horkheimer, signifies "the entanglement of myth, domination, and labour" (32).

To enjoy the sweet song of the Sirens and not to succumb to their mortal lure, Odysseus orders his sailors to tie him to the mast. For this reason, Odysseus as the Hegelian Master is the only one of his team who is able to experience the pleasure from listening to the seductive Sirens' song while avoiding the otherwise inevitable fee—his life: his companions, their ears plugged with wax at his behest, only pull the ship through, that is, provide the physical labour that is necessary for the Master to receive his pleasure. Thus by deceiving the natural deities, Odysseus reduces the lethal natural law to a purely aesthetic experience and becomes an onlooker rather than a participant in the implacable mechanics of the myth: the Sirens' "temptation is neutralized and becomes a mere object of contemplation—becomes art" (Adorno and Horkheimer 34). Denham, separated from the event of his life by the mountain brook, inevitably resembles Odysseus tied to the mast of his ship and physically unable to plunge into action. As a result, in Adorno and Horkheimer's words that hold true both for Odysseus and Denham, "The prisoner is present at a concert, an inactive eavesdropper like later concertgoers, and his spirited call for liberation fades like applause" (34). Confronted with the bear rather than inspired by the beauty of the Idea, Tay John—in Denham's schema—plays the role of the Slave getting away with his life and thereby resembles Odysseus's men, who "know only the song's danger but nothing of its beauty" (Adorno and Horkheimer 34).

To appropriate the fruits of the Slave's labour, that is, for Denham to participate in Tay John's victory over the bear, the Master must, as Alexandre Kojève puts it, "overcome" the slave "dialectically": "he must leave him life and consciousness, and destroy only his autonomy... In other words, he must enslave him" (14). Denham deprives Tay John of the capacity to realize the sublime magnanimity of the event, thus making himself an indispensable aesthetic and self-conscious counterpart of Tay John's heroism. An impressive bodily appearance and physical dexterity—the Slave's attributes—seem to be the only qualities Denham allows Tay John to contribute to "their" mutual victory. Therefore, the narrator gladly admits that his hero "did the one thing, the only thing he could have done, and did it well" (*TJ* 64). Comparing Adorno's interpretation of the master and slave dichotomy with the Hegelian original, Deborah Cook observes, "In Adorno's version of the master-slave dialectic, the slave will win her freedom not by viewing herself as completely distinct from nature (as her male masters have done), but by gaining a fuller appreciation of the extent to which she depends on nature as an embodied being" (89). While Denham allows Tay John this subordinate, feminized, and unsophisticated freedom, he reserves the narrator's sole right to conceptualize his hero's natural beauty: "He seemed to stand for something. He stood there with his feet planted apart upon the ground, as though he owned it, as though he grasped it with them. When he moved I would not have been surprised to have seen clumps of earth adhere to the soles of his moccasins ..." (*TJ* 60-61).

By acknowledging his hero's "strength in the abstract" (*TJ* 61), Denham credits himself for discerning its symbolism but at the same time recognizes—to use Jacques Lacan's concept—his own lack in the other as a metonymy of the wannabe of desire (Lacan 640), that is, his own physical impotence longing for a substitute body to make his dream come true. The Master simply does not possess the perfect body of the Slave, as is easily seen by contrasting Denham's description of Tay John with the authorial narrator's account of Denham himself: "It was in his face, too, long and keen as though shaped by the wind ..." (Tay John); "[Denham] was a lanky man in his forties, who seemed older ... Pouches hung heavily beneath his eyes so that the red of his lower eyelids showed ..." (*TJ* 61; 55). In his attempt to piece together the "we" of man as the victor in his strife with nature, Denham tries to mate "a bronze and golden statue planted among the grasses" (*TJ* 62) with himself as its sculptor, interpreter, and appreciator, and thus reaffirms Adorno's understanding of the Master-Slave allegory in terms of the negative dialectics, which "disclose[s] "the lack of identity between universal and particular, concept and object, even as it reveals their affinity" (Cook 158).

In spite of his desire to transform the sturdy stranger into the universal "man" whose manhood they could share, Denham is still uncomfortable with the crude wildness of Tay John's figure and its propinquity with the "unnamed country" that the narrator feels it is "physically exhausting to look on" (*TJ* 59). Therefore, continuing his Adamic vocation as an Enlightenment master of nature, Denham appropriates the stranger to the human race by naming him: "I found myself saying 'Yellowhead,' 'Yellowhead.' I had to give him a name so that I could help him—morally, you know. I had to align him with the human race. Without a name no man is an individual, no individual wholly a man" (*TJ* 63). Naming as a form of appropriation of things "wild" and unknown has been one of the habitual Western practices, and in this regard, Denham's wilderness unnamed is akin to the *Heart of Darkness* Marlow's "monstrous" and "unearthly" wilderness:

The earth seemed unearthly. We are accustomed to look upon the shackled form of a conquered monster, but there—there you could look at a thing monstrous and free. It was unearthly, and the men were—No, they were not inhuman. Well, you know, that was the worst of it—this suspicion of their not being inhuman. It would come slowly to one. They howled and leaped, and spun, and made horrid faces; but what thrilled you was just the thought of their humanity—like yours—the thought of your remote kinship with this wild and passionate uproar. Ugly. Yes, it was ugly enough; but if you were man enough you would admit to yourself that there was in you just the faintest trace of a response to the terrible frankness of that noise, a dim suspicion of there being a meaning in it which you—you so remote from the night of first ages—could comprehend. (*Heart of Darkness* 139)

Irrespective of the similarity in the theme and the narrators' problem with their objects, Marlow and Denham are on two different journeys. Marlow is on an inward-looking journey into the darkness of his own self, which he is horrified yet also thrilled to pick up from the outer darkness. He is descending the Congo River as though it were his ancestry line; he is not trying to impart his own "humanity" to the "savage" but discovers in that "savagery" is the truth which underlies his own human self. While Marlow acknowledges his affinity with the "wild" man in his "wildness," Denham must bring this wildness to submission, and only after naming, or taming, the wilderness and its human embodiment is he ready to admit it in his construct of subjectivity and self-consciousness. "Yellowhead" is a name that stems from the mere description, recurrent in Denham's introduction of the stranger who "wasn't all Indian. There was that yellow hair" (*TJ* 61). But to place his dream in reality and to include Tay John in the "we" of the victor, the narrator cannot be satisfied with the description alone: he must turn it into a proper name and by this magical trick make it a part of his own world. According to analytical philosophers such as Gottlob Frege and Bertrand Russell, proper names enable the passage between the language and reality and are a complete sign of the object, while the description refers to the qualities of the object but not to the object itself (Markowski 270-72). In turning a description of the dominant feature of Tay John's appearance (a distinctly racial feature—his yellow hair) into a proper name, Denham inscribes the stranger in the human race yet at the same time appropriates him for his own system of signification.

Denham's problem, however, is not easily resolved either by naming or by the mere division between the body and the intellect, or the statue and its sculptor. Denham, who, as a sovereign, laboriously endows Tay John with subjectivity in order to include him in his system of signification, does not, as it were, receive a confirmation of the receipt. Georges Bataille explains that our indifference to a passerby in the street is predicated upon his or her status as an object, but the situation changes when we "regard him as a *fellow human being*: this is true if I deny in him, at least in part, the objective character ... no longer seeing anything in him but the *subject*, with whom I *can*, with whom I *must* communicate" (*The Accursed Share* 244). As Hegel maintains, self-consciousness "exists for another self-consciousness; that is to say, it *is* only by being acknowledged or 'recognized'" (Hegel 86). In the strife that is the Master-Slave dialectic, the Master looks to deprive the Slave of his independent self-consciousness and make it a dependent one, but at the same time seeks to receive the Slave's recognition and service. Recognition is exactly what Denham's Slave figure, Tay John, unequivocally and repeatedly denies him. "He doubtless saw me before I saw him," notes the narrator. "He looked at me but gave no sign of recognition" (*TJ* 60). As Denham persists in appealing to Tay John's sense of fellowship by gestures and salutations, his feeling of shame rises proportionally to Tay John's refusal to respond to these appeals. Denham's overreaction evolves from his considering himself an intruder and from his accounting for the absurdity of the situation by attributing it to shame and to the universal need for remedial self-reassurance: "Then he looked directly at me ... I tell you, I was ashamed. I have no doubt he would have spoken to me had we met in the usual way" (*TJ* 61). The most perplexing for Denham is Tay John's slight of him in the very moment when the narrator is sure Yellowhead needs him to share "his moment of victory—when no man wishes to be alone" (*TJ* 64-65). As a result, Denham has to abandon all his self-reassurance and to pronounce a bewildering yet unequivocal verdict: "He disdained me, that fellow, absolutely" (*TJ* 65).

This lack of recognition proves the most challenging aspect of Denham's experience and may, at least partially, account for his description of the occurrence as "almost" an adventure. The feeling of the void left by Tay John's refusal to acknowledge Denham's share in the event is largely responsible for the narrator's whetted interest in Tay John's story, as well as for the halo of mystery around his figure that Denham's imagination preserves till the day the two meet again. Introduced to Tay John at Dobble's construction site, only near the end of the plot line, Denham dispels the mysterious aura and reports a few casual conversations with his former "hero"—"of horses, of grass, of his fight with the grizzly bear" (*TJ* 156), and of Ardith Aeriola and Father Rorty. One may wonder if the fulfillment of Denham's desire, the filling of the void left from the bear fight scene, explains the fact that the narrator abandons his hero in the critical moment, when Tay John leaves with Ardith after his brawl with Dobble and his men. Between the first fascination of the aborted Master-Slave dialectic and the final demystification of Tay John, there is no direct contact between the narrator and the character: Denham traces Tay John's story based on the accounts of others: Colin McLeod, Charlie the cook, Blackie (Pivato 186), even Alf Dobble, and "unnumbered others took it up and passed on" (*TJ* 84). For Denham, those tales about Tay John were only "the remnants of his presence" (*TJ* 68), unable to shake the narrator's first impression: "To me he was still the man on the lonely creek..." (*TJ* 74). When he can finally lay his eyes upon his hero in a casual situation, "Tay John was a man not quite tall as I remembered him from the afternoon in the valley above the Snake Indian country when he had outfought the grizzly bear" (*TJ* 155). It seems that Denham—and O'Hagan through his primary narrator—wants to show that the figure of Tay John is just one of the illusions—"in the country of illusion" (*TJ* 123)—shaped by the onlooker's or the tale-teller's or the listener's fancy.

The contrast between Tay John's attitudes, or stances, toward the narrator at the beginning and near the end of Denham's tale is as sharp as between "Legend" and the other two sections of the novel, "Hearsay" and "Evidence—Without a Finding." The story of the Shuswap people, which comprises the bulk of the "Legend," has no continuation in the subsequent parts of the novel. Deserting his tribe, Tay John, at the beginning of Denham's tale, an aloof loner yet still a spirit of his land and time (Braz 5), seems a figure of transition between the lost thread of the Shuswap story and the limited personal narrative of Jack Denham. But, irrespective of Denham's occasional arrogance, what cannot be taken away from him is his unbiased openness to his protagonist's character and motivations, a healthy sense of uncertainty that allows Tay John to be what he is, independently from the narrator's perceptions or limitations of his vision.

Tay John and the Mare

On a few occasions following the heroic fight with the bear, Denham's tale allows Tay John to refute and confirm the narrator's first impression of him, as comparable with Marlow's "first view of Jim" as "unconcerned and unapproachable" (*Lord Jim* 26). One of the most telling is the Timberlake mare episode, when Tay John, possessed by the desire to own the horse, cuts off his own hand in a drunken bout. Denham's account of this occurrence, which makes it sometimes difficult to distinguish between McLeod's tale (Denham does not witness the event himself) and Denham's commentary, is full of the narrator's surmises regarding Tay John's motivations. Having paid a tribute to the possibility of a romantic passion, Denham, who often takes pride in passing a skeptical psychological judgement, soon resorts to surmises that make Tay John's extraordinary fancy for the mare an indulgence in vanity: "Perhaps he remembered his village, where he came from beyond the mountains—and he returning with a horse beneath him. The Shuswaps, so far as I know, are not horsemen. On this horse he would be lifted above the others. They would look up to him. He saw the upturned faces" (*TJ* 76). The reader of the novel, who, unlike Denham, is familiar with the content of the "Legend," knows that Tay John used to have such admiration in the moment when he secretly left his people, along with his undisputed yet onerous leadership, in pursuit of his own liberated self. Not surprisingly, Tay John's further story disproves Denham's conjecture, offering no confirmation that Tay John intended to return to the Shuswap and show off on a horse. Already in the next chapter, however, when Denham again engages Tay John and his mare in speculations about the bondage of private property, the narrator slights his own surmises regarding his hero in an ironic reference to his own earlier guess: "And from the beginning it would seem the mare set out to introduce Tay John to her own people—to her own world" (*TJ* 83). Another instance when Tay John disproves the narrator's attempts to bring him down to the level of conceit and vanity is his discarding the black Stetson hat—his other proud possession—as a sign of his offended innocence, in the wake of the unfortunate accident with Julia Alderson. This episode, related to accusations of an alleged rape, also has roots in Denham's speculations about Tay John's motives: "In the dim light I dare say he could see the picture of that white-skinned girl above the head of McLeod's bed. That was something else he wanted, also, and with a horse beneath him and a road before him ... who knows?" (*TJ* 79). The episode ends with a semi-humorous scene that resembles a parody of the gospel story of four Roman soldiers casting lots and dividing Jesus's garments: Ed, Charlie, and Porter compete for Tay John's discarded Stenson hat, and McLeod accepts it from Porter's hands. The meaning of the scene is, again, two different surmises about Tay John's character: Porter, a young and inexperienced Mountie, gives the hat to McLeod and asks him to keep it for Tay John, while Tatlow, O'Hagan's most authoritative Mountie figure[2], guesses that Tay John will never come for it.

It is conceivable to view all Denham's efforts to trace back Tay John's story and to deduce his character after the bear episode as a continuation of the strife for recognition that started back then, in the middle of Denham's fantasy of the virginity of the wilderness and man's "struggle against the powers of darkness" (*TJ* 64). Jack Denham—O'Hagan's now

---

2   Sergeant Tatlow appears also in other O'Hagan's stories, such as "The Bride's Crossing."

passionate, now skeptical, now absconding narrator—tells his own clandestine or subconscious story of retribution under the guise of Tay John's story. His fantasy is predicated upon the trick of substitution, which we considered earlier as consistent with the Hegelian Master-Slave dialectic, and its almost bathetic failure is the result of Tay John's refusal to assume the role of the Slave.

The Master establishes his selfhood by means of receiving the Slave's recognition. This situation subjects the former to the following duality: on the one hand, he wants to preserve his sovereignly by receiving a full recognition from the other, while at the same time denying such recognition in return and reciprocating the other only with a partial recognition (as befits the Slave); on the other hand, by refusing to recognize the other on equal terms, the Master undermines the quality of the Slave's recognition and therefore also his own status as the Master. This duality may account for Denham's attempts to align the yellow-haired stranger with the human race by assigning him a name, Yellowhead—in order to receive a fuller recognition of his own status as the Master and the bearer of the great Enlightenment dream—man against the darkness of the wild. But Tay John's stubborn denial to provide such recognition can signify his lack of acquiescence, his refusal to assume the roles of the Slave and the actor in the onlooker's symbolic spectacle.

Recounting Tay John's story, McLeod describes a habit that in a remarkable way alludes to the bear fight scene in which Denham craves for but receives none of Tay John's recognition: "For one thing when he [Tay John] comes down here, he stands on the edge of the clearing and waits for me to come out and bring him over to the door. He never calls. He may be there hours sometimes, waiting, for all I know. But he always waits until his presence is recognized" (*TJ* 73). If we project this gesture on the Hegelian Master-Slave dialectic, Tay John requires a recognition that befits the Master, and definitely not the Slave. McLeod heard only some scraps of the "legend" that the reader of the novel is more intimately familiar with, but he knows that Tay John "was to be a great leader among" his people, and—as McLeod aptly observes—this sovereignty shows "in his bearing, in just the way he carries himself" (*TJ* 73). Admitting that McLeod and Tay John developed a friendship, Denham nevertheless appears to be torn in his perception and assessment of Tay John's status among the people of Western culture. The narrator diagnoses his protagonist as an individual who, having left his own world, failed to acquire or fully adapt to a new one:

> ... Tay John, the young man, born to be a leader among his own kind, who had turned from his fortune as another man might turn and walk out of the door of his house, and who, if he thought of it at all, perhaps thought that now he was a man unknown, the stream of whose life no longer flowed clear and sure, walled no longer by the faith of his people, but dammed into a pool and wasting its waters in muskegs and shallows. (*TJ* 74)

In this thought-provoking observation, Denham's metaphors ascribe to Tay John a quality of the modern self, which lives in the world where "all that is solid melts into air"—to use Marshall Berman's famous Marxian definition of modernity: by abandoning the secure world of sacred space and cyclic time, the traditional time-space of his community in which he had a defined status and role, Tay John faces "the thrill and the dread" of the modern world (Berman 13). "To be modern," says Berman, "is to find ourselves in an environment that promises us adventure, power, joy, growth, transformation of ourselves and the world—and, at the same time, that threatens to destroy everything we have, everything we know, everything we are" (15). However, what dramatizes Tay John's experience as a newcomer to the modern, or Western, world, is his interstitial position: in Denham's perception, Tay John is suspended between the two worlds, and his tragedy is that, having jettisoned his former self, he is not quite able to catch up with the new one: Tay John "moved now on the rim of the white man's world forming around him. He might never be able to enter it, but he was drawn to it, as the wild fowl are drawn to their flocks upon the breeding waters" (*TJ* 74).

In spite of his rationalizations, Denham is reluctant to abandon his romantic dream of Yellowhead—the figure of man pitted against the powers of darkness: "To me he was still the man on the lonely creek who had outfought the grizzly bear" (*TJ* 74). But maybe the contradiction, signaled by the word "still," between Denham's dream and common sense is only spurious, and precisely because Tay John is neither here nor there, Denham feels free to appropriate him for his own fantasy. Tay John's yellow hair becomes the material epitome of this Enlightenment abstraction, and Denham uses Conrad's metaphor of the torch for his own simile to signify a similar thing—the power of light against the powers of darkness, a battle for a vague benefit of humanity. The authorial narrator of *Heart of Darkness* mentions the heroes of the Thames "bearing the sword, and often the torch, messengers of the might within the land, bearers of a spark from the sacred fire" (104-105). Likewise, in Denham's high-flown portrayal, "it was more like a torch, that hair ... —a flame, anyway, to light the hopes of his people, whatever they may have been" (*TJ* 75). Those "hopes" are hopes "in the abstract," as it were, the hopes of an enlightened humanity, and Yellowhead, both a nickname and a figure of the torch, is too precious a symbol for Denham to abandon it easily.

Denham's account of Tay John oscillates between fascination and ambiguity, enthusiasm and apathy. Although the
narrator's fantasies die hard, he ultimately seems to admit the
discrepancy between the Yellowhead of the bear fight scene
and Tay John as a real individual. Ultimately disappointed
at Tay John's failure as a torch of hopes—either those of his
own people or those of Denham's Western fantasy, Denham
gradually loses interest in his hero as he discerns the latter's
desire to exercise the "unalienable rights" of the modern self,
which the United States Declaration of Independence aptly
phrases as "Life, Liberty, and the pursuit of Happiness." The
end of the novel, in Blackie's relation, shows the hero ema-
ciated and crazed, run down by his alliance with a woman,
Ardith Aeriola. It metaphorically sends Tay John back into the
ground where—according to the legend—he came from, and
thus apparently confirms Denham's earlier intuition of him as
a stream "wasting its waters in muskegs and shallows" (*TJ* 74).
Nevertheless, it is exactly this Tay John who becomes the protagonist of O'Hagan's novel —not the hero of Denham's fantasy,
but the one who, "contrary to tradition ... has stepped outside
the milieu of a domestic economy" of his Indigenous culture
and thus refused to turn his life into a continuing sacrifice as
"the magic self-surrender of the individual to the collective"
(Adorno and Horkheimer 61, 49).

O'Hagan's interest in his protagonist, as well as the success
of the novel as a whole, seems to be connected with the originary scene of desacralization, signified by Tay John's exodus
from the time-space of the legend—to arrive as "the surviving
individual ego," which Adorno and Horkheimer posit as a
prototype of a novelistic hero proper, as opposed to the hero
of epos and mythos (46). Tay John is called upon to pique the
reader's curiosity exactly where he fails to comply with Denham's fantasy and the symbolic role assigned to him within

any mythological domains—Indigenous or colonial. Instead of sacrificing his whole self to the collective, he is able to perform what René Girard would call a "sacrificial self-mutilation" (252) when following his singular fit of passion—to take possession of Timberlake's mare. Having failed to get hold of the horse in both a bargain and a card game, Tay John severs his hand "in one clean sweeping blow" (*TJ* 80). As a result, he ultimately gets his mare and gains reputation, but there is—both for the witnesses, McLeod and Timberlake, and for the reader—something more in this bout, what Bataille associates with "sacrifice" or "potlatch," "which by definition we cannot grasp—that we vainly call the poetry, the depth or the intimacy of passion" ("The Gift of Rivalry" 206). Tay John's action can be seen as one of the forms of potlatch, in which "a rival is challenged by a solemn destruction of riches," and which, according to Bataille and Marcel Mauss, is "little different from a sacrifice" (Bataille, "The Gift of Rivalry" 202). In potlatch, "*giving* must become *acquiring a power*" (203). The first words uttered by Tay John after the incident—quoted from the Gospel of Matthew, "If your hand offend you … cut it off "—indeed seem to signify Tay John's self-punishing despair and impotence,[3] but his next phrase unequivocally suggests a potlach spectacle, with its "connection between religious behaviours and economic ones" ("The Gift of Rivalry" 203): "'There', he said, "there … there is

---

3   A few scholars have attributed Tay John's purported literal understanding of the Gospel dictum as the main reason for his self-mutilating act (compare, for example, Jack Robinson's "Dismantling Sexual Dualities in O'Hagan's *Tay John*," p. 98, and D. M. R. Bentley's "The Wide Circle and Return: *Tay John* and Vico," *Dalhousie Review*, vol. 73, no. 1, p. 41). I am inclined to think that Tay John's next utterance—"'There,' he said, "there … there is something you *have* to take! … against your mare!'" (*TJ* 81)—explains his real motivation, that is, the potlatch gesture of rivalry, while the quote from the Gospel is a sort of "translation" into the sacral language of his audience.

something you *have* to take! ... against your mare!'" (*TJ* 81).
In potlach, which already "excludes bargaining," as Bataille
explains, "if he [the subject] destroys the object in front of
another person or if he gives it away, the one who gives has
actually acquired, in the other's eyes, the power of giving or
destroying" ("The Gift of Rivalry" 202, 203). Tay John is still
a modern self in the making, and, similar to Odysseus as an
emerging subject, "is still unreconciled to himself, still unsure."
"His affective forces (his mettle and his heart)," Adorno and
Horkheimer say, "still react independently to him" (47). What
he is certain to possess, however, is the sovereignty of the self
that does not rely on any backup in the guise of the collective,
the sacral, or the ideological.[4] He is the only self-sufficient
individual among the Alderson hunting party, as Julia's survey
game clearly shows. Like all men in the group, he is faced with
the question "what would you do on your last day of life?"
Given the unlimited opportunities, Tay John answers, "I guess,
I go hunting" (*TJ* 101), which means, as Julia understands it
too, that he lives a life that can be considered truly his own.
To obtain what he wants, Tay John sometimes works for the
surveyors or tourists, but he never serves them, from time to
time defying their expectations: "Tay John fired not a shot nor
lifted his hand to help with the work of making and breaking
camp. He was the guide" (*TJ* 98). His very posture is an ironic

---

4 In my interpretation of Tay John as a modern self in the making, I somewhat depart from Jack Robinson's view that the novel "denigrates" "the
   I" and affirms "the We" ("Dismantling Sexual Dualities in O'Hagan's *Tay
   John*," pp. 106-107). Margery Fee, on the contrary, proffers a purely literary
   function of the hero: "[Tay John] moves from myth, to epic romance, to
   realism; escapes irony by moving into comedy, and finally moves into
   myth again. But this myth is a peculiarly transitory myth, held in tension
   with all the major literary modes at once" ("Howard O'Hagan's *Tay John*:
   Making New World Myth," p. 14).

challenge to the ignorant mastership of the colonists in their certainty that "they were the first" in the country where "rivers were unnamed, the mountains unnamed." Although "they were the first," he still "rode before them and walked before them" (*TJ* 98). The sense of his own sovereignty, perhaps, also prevents him from returning Denham's gesture of recognition, which Tay John would have to reciprocate from the position of a nicknamed, symbolized, and appropriated figure standing for something in the abstract.

Conclusion

Tay John is not a typical novelistic protagonist: he does not change as a character, and if he surprises Denham and other "witnesses" or subjects of "hearsay" by his singular actions or reactions, he just shows something about himself that we feel he has had all along. Tay John's formative phase ends in the "legendary" part of the story. The result of his initiation, which should have changed him from the boy into the man, was—iron-ically—misinterpreted by the Shuswap elders as successful. "The boy says 'I.' The man says 'We'"—this form of transformation from the individual into the collective, when the new adult speaks "the word of his greatest magic" (*TJ* 29), is something Kumkleseem-Tay John has never really undergone. The description of the boy's stage can do the same justice to Tay John in his maturity: "The boy was a child with a child's spirit that moved and lived in a land of his own creation" (*TJ* 29). As such, Tay John could be a better fit for a picaresque story, and yet his function in O'Hagan's novel is far from being a centre of an adventure plot. His main characteristic is his constant withdrawal into his own privacy—like during his trip with the Alderson hunting party: "The farther they reached into the mountains the farther it seemed he withdrew from them" (*TJ* 98).

This ultimate privacy of the hero is the result of O'Hagan's narrative manipulations—from the implicit irony of the "Legend's" storyteller to the overdone unreliability of Jack Denham, who manages to reveal much more of himself than of the declared object of his tale. Tay John's exodus from the sacral time-space to the pursuit of his own happiness makes him both the modern self in the making and a dissenter who, even if subconsciously, resists the appropriation by Western ideologies and fantasies. Among those, Denham's Enlightenment-colonial fantasy of man's eternal battle with the dark powers of nature and of bringing the light of appellation into the dark corners of the world loom large as the most immediate intertextual background, which sends the reader now to Jack London, now to Joseph Conrad, to mention just the closest O'Hagan's predecessors. O'Hagan's main narrator, Denham—an investigator rather than a backwoodsman and a philosopher rather than a colonizer—symbolizes Tay John's fight with the grizzly as the originary scene of Enlightenment, in which the bear plays the part of nature's darkness and Tay John plays man as the winner. For the full success of the spectacle, however, Denham, the passive yet cheering onlooker, must first align the Indigenous stranger, Tay John, with the human race; that is, with himself as an enlightened westerner, and this game of substitution and transposition in Denham's creation of his own self inevitably makes the narrator the figure of the Master seeking to establish himself at the cost of the Slave, who deals with the physical reality of things but knows nothing of their true meaning. Nevertheless, both the sublime and the beautiful of an enlightened humankind, which Denham projects onto the Yellowhead figure, are crushed by Tay John's refusal to return the gaze of recognition to the fantasizing flaneur. This refusal of recognition is the inciting momentum of Denham's narrative that is largely responsible for making Tay John, rather than Denham's fantasy itself, its dominant object. The Master figure himself, as Denham lets the listeners to his tale discover, Tay John withholds his recognition from the reader, too, absconding into his privacy whenever we feel like recognizing him as one of us. Even through such an unreliable narrator as Denham, O'Hagan demonstrates a significant understanding of the conditions and attitudes of Indigenous people in Canada and their relations with settler societies.

Works Cited

Adorno, Theodor, and Max Horkheimer. *Dialectic of Enlightenment*. Translated by John Cumming, Verso, 1992.

Bataille, Georges. *The Accursed Share. Volume II: The History of Eroticism, Volume III: Sovereignty*. Zone Books, 1993.

----. "The Gift of Rivalry: 'Potlach'." *The Bataille Reader*, edited by Fred Botting and Scott Wilson, Blackwell, 1997, pp. 199-210.

Bentley, D. M. R. "The Wide Circle and Return: *Tay John* and Vico," *Dalhousie Review*, vol. 73, no. 1, pp. 34-53.

Berman, Marshall. *All That Is Solid Melts into Air: The Experience of Modernity*. Penguin, 1988.

Bloom, Harold, ed. *Romanticism and Consciousness: Essays in Criticism*. W. W. Norton & Company, 1970.

Braz, Albert. "Fictions of Mixed Origins: *Iracema, Tay John*, and Racial Hybridity in Brazil and Canada." *AmeriQuests,* vol. 10, no. 1, 2013, pp. 1-9.

Bugnet, Georges. *The Forest*. Translated by David Carpenter, U of Calgary P, 2003.

Cook, Deborah. *Adorno on Nature*. Acumen, 2011.

Conrad, Joseph. *Heart of Darkness and Other Tales*. Edited with an Introduction and Notes by Cedric Watts, Oxford, 2008.

----. *Lord Jim: A Tale*. Introduction and Notes by Susan Jones, Wordsworth Classics, 2002.

Davidson, Arnold E. "Silencing the Word in Howard O'Hagan's *Tay John." Canadian Literature*, vol. 110, Fall 1986, pp. 30-44.

Fee, Margery. "Howard O'Hagan's *Tay John*: Making New World Myth." *Canadian Literature*, vol. 110, Fall 1986, pp. 8-27.

----, ed. *Silence Made Visible: Howard O'Hagan and* Tay John. ECW Press, 1992.

Girard, René. *Evolution and Conversion: Dialogues on the Origins of Culture*. Interviewed by João Cezar de Castro Rocha, and Pierpaolo Antonello, T & T Clark, 2007.

Granofsky, Ronald. "The Country of Illusion: Vision, Change, and Misogyny in Howard O'Hagan's *Tay John*." Fee, *Silence Made Visible,* pp. 109-126.

Hartman, Geoffrey H. *Wordsworth's Poetry 1787-1814*. Yale UP, 1977.

Hegel, Georg W. F. *The Phenomenology of Spirit (The Phenomenology of Mind)*. Translated by J. B. Baillie, Digireads.com Publishing, 2009.

Heidegger, Martin. "Language." *The Norton Anthology of Theory and Criticism*, edited by Vincent B. Leitch, W. W. Norton & Company, 2001, pp. 1121-34.

Jay, Martin. *Downcast Eyes: The Denigration of Vision in Twentieth-Century French Thought*. U of California P, 1993.

Keith, W. J. "Howard O'Hagan, *Tay John,* and the Growth of Story." Fee, *Silence Made Visible,* pp. 73-84.

Kojève, Alexandre. *Introduction to the Reading of Hegel: Lectures on* The Phenomenology of Spirit. Edited by Allan Bloom, translated by James H. Nichols, Jr., Cornell UP, 1969.

Lacan, Jacques. *Écrits*. Translated by Bruce Fink, W. W. Norton & Company, 2006.

London, Jack. *Tales of the North*. Castle Books, 1979.

----. "The Call of the Wild." *Tales of the North*, pp. 443-488.

----. "The White Silence." *Tales of the North*, pp. 435-442.

----. "White Fang." *Tales of the North*, pp. 1-102.

Markowski, Michał Paweł. *Efekt inskrypcji: Jacques Derrida i literatura*. Studio Φ and Wydawnictwo Homini, 1997.

Merchant, Carolyn. "Reinventing Eden: Western Culture as a Recovery Narrative." *Uncommon Ground: Rethinking the Human Place in Nature*, edited by William Cronon, W. W. Norton & Company, 1996, pp. 132-159.

Miller, J. Hillis. *Reading Conrad*. Edited by John G. Peters and Jakob Lothe, The Ohio State UP, 2017.

Monk, Samuel H. "The Sublime: Burke's *Enquiry*." Bloom, pp. 24-41.

Oelschlaeger, Max. *The Idea of Wilderness: From Prehistory to the Age of Ecology*. Yale UP, 1991.

O'Hagan, Howard. *Tay John*. 1939. Afterword by Michael Ondaatje, New Canadian Library, McClelland & Stewart, 2008.

Nash, Roderick. *Wilderness and the American Mind*. Yale UP, 2001.

Pivato, Joseph. "Forest of Symbols: *Tay John* and *The Double Hook*." *Sheila Watson: Essays on Her Works*, edited by Joseph Pivato, Guernica, 2015, pp. 181-196.

Pottle, Frederick A. "The Eye and the Object in the Poetry of Wordsworth." Bloom, pp. 273-87.

Robinson, Jack. "Myths of Dominance Versus Myths of Re-Creation in O'Hagan's *Tay John*. *Studies in Canadian Literature/Etudes en Litterature Canadienne*, vol. 13, no. 2, 1988, https://journals.lib.unb.ca/index.php/scl/article/view/8084/9141

----. "Dismantling Sexual Dualities in O'Hagan's *Tay John*." *Alberta*, vol. 2, no.2, 1990, pp. 93-108.

Wilcox, Earl. "'The Kipling of the Clondike': Naturalism in London's Early Fiction." *Critical Insights: Jack London*, edited by Lawrence I. Berkove, Salem Press, 2011, pp. 180-195.

Wordsworth, William. "Preface to *Lyrical Ballads* (1802)." *William Wordsworth: The Major Works*, edited by Stephen Gill, Oxford UP, 2000, pp. 595-616.

Zichy, Francis. "Crypto-, Pseudo-, and Pre-Postmodernism: *Tay John, Lord Jim,* and the Critics." *Essays on Canadian Writing,* vol. 81, Winter 2004, pp. 192-221.

----. "The 'Complex Fate' of the Canadian in Howard O'Hagan's *Tay John." Essays on Canadian Writing,* vol. 79, Spring 2003, pp. 199-225.

The Constant Craving of Howard O'Hagan's Wilderness Women

RENÉE HULAN

When it appeared in 1977, the reception of Howard O'Hagan's *The School-Marm Tree* was lukewarm with some rather equivocal reviews and some unflattering comparisons to *Tay John*, the novel that was the target of an impressive reclamation project at the time. Highlights from the reviews are collected by Margery Fee in *Silence Made Visible: Howard O'Hagan and Tay John*. W. J. Keith judged *The School-Marm Tree* "a slighter achievement than *Tay John*," but a book that had something to offer—if read on its own terms (qtd in Fee 156). Gordon Powers declared it "hackneyed and meandering" and accused the author of combining "Harlequin romance and early Jack London" (qtd in Fee 154). Gordon Morash concentrated on the love story which he called "heavy with melodrama and very predictable" (qtd in Fee 156). On the other hand, *The School-Marm Tree* earned praise from Barbara Novak, who remarked that "O'Hagan's insight into the female experience is as rare, sensitive, and profound as is his understanding of nature" (qtd in Fee 155). Jane W. Hill wrote that "O'Hagan is especially fine in his understanding of women, their feelings and their place in this masculine world" (qtd in Fee 155), and P. K. Page admired it enough to write the introduction to the 1977 edition.

While some reviewers tended to read it as a love story that takes place in the Western mountains, others were careful to place it in wider social contexts shaped by class and gender.

As Page observes in her introduction, the story is one of "violence and yearning" (8). Selva, the novel's heroine, craves more than the circumscribed social world of the small western town can offer. In town, few choices apart from the greasy restaurant or domestic service are open to a penniless woman with no family. Trapped in domestic service, daydreaming of exotic places and seeking peace in the forest, Selva serves as an ideal reflector whose perspective gives rise to beautiful, sensitive passages depicting her home in the Yellowhead. After all, her name means forest in Spanish, the narrator explains, and the forest is where Selva was conceived. For Selva is a dreamer who fantasizes escape from the small town yet fears the wilderness, and her name, etymologically related to "sylvan" and "self," signals the story's focus on the heroine's subjectivity. Yet, Selva can never be truly "at home" in the mountains. In a novel whose symbolism is heavy, the meaning of names and the reflection of surfaces in symbolic settings seem to push this woman's story to the completion and resolution one expects in a romance novel. But then, a passage disrupts these expectations. Selva is alone with her lover Slim in the beaver meadow near a school-marm tree. They have made love. Before leaving, Selva takes a drink from the pool:

> He stood above her. She was helpless at his feet. If her face should sink lower, she thought, if he should bend over and close his fingers on her neck, press his shin across her legs behind her knees, she then could not move, nor see him, nor utter a word or a sound. And he would go away and leave her on her belly by the pool as though her thirst were beyond all quenching ... (23)

With a chill of recognition, one feels the total vulnerability of the woman who at once realizes the violent potential of her companion. Slim's violent nature is figured elsewhere in the description of his presence as a "moment's shadow" touching her cheek (16) and prefigured in the scene in which he tortures and kills a porcupine. In this passage, the familiar world takes on the meaningful strangeness of the *unheimlich*, when what "was intended to remain secret, hidden away, has come into the open" (Freud 132). The Freudian insight connects the feelings Selva has in the mountains, and her sudden uncanny feeling at the pool, to her self-knowledge. In "The Uncanny," Freud relates the experience to "the evolution of the sense of self, a regression to times when the ego had not yet clearly set itself off against the world outside or from others." Because she is a woman, Selva's identity is formed in relation to the lack posed by castration anxiety. Taken in the context of the images of severed parts that, as Ronald Granofsky remarks, signal Freud's theory of castration anxiety—Peter's severed tongue, the man with no legs—and the great sense of loss and nothingness Selva feels with regards to her mother's failed escape from motherhood and marriage and her father's absence (*SMT* 92), Selva's longing points to her position as a woman. In this uncanny moment, Selva apprehends her own being in what she is not as the repressed knowledge of the Other surfaces in her consciousness, or one might say in the language of O'Hagan's *Tay John*, as that knowledge is "unveiled" before her. Freud hypothesizes that such moments resonate with "remnants of animistic mental activity" that recall "the old *animistic* view of the universe" (147). The "presence in the mountains," the mysterious and mythic voices that critics have remarked in O'Hagan's work seem to resonate with these remnants. The particular sensitivity to the position of women that critics have noted in *The School-Marm Tree* can be read as a narrative exploration of the literary subjectivity of women that delves into the psychological complexity of *being* the Other in the Western novel, a genre in which women are always stereotypically cast as the civilizing presence against the male protagonist's flight towards individuality. Studying the position of women in O'Hagan's writing, however, offers an opportunity to re-examine his relationship to the modernist or postmodernist canons in light of the constant craving of his wilderness women.

The Dead Woman's Son: Reading *Tay John*

The 1974 New Canadian Library edition of Howard O'Hagan's best known novel *Tay John*, originally published in 1939, rekindled interest in "The Writer that CanLit Forgot," as Gary Geddes proclaimed a few years later. Talonbooks quickly published *The School-Marm Tree* in 1977 and reissued his 1963 collection *The Woman Who Got on at Jasper Station* (1977), followed by the 1958 *Wilderness Men* (1978). After Michael Ondaatje's afterword to the 1989 New Canadian Library edition, reading *Tay John* as a precursor to postmodern and post-colonial writing reshaped its critical reception, and O'Hagan's relative obscurity was cited in an inventive attempt to reclaim him as a precursor to the Canadian postmodern, an aesthetic that O'Hagan himself regarded with suspicion. As Margery Fee remarks, O'Hagan "rigs up a new myth out of the pieces of the old one, revealing in the process how it's done" (Fee 10). "Its New World flavour is lacking in nostalgia for the pure, the cultivated, and the European ... " (Fee 12) while "the historical and geographical detail unique to the Rocky Mountains region that marks *Tay John* as a new World parody of Old World pretensions to the universal" (Fee 9). Others have focused attention on the story's "untellable nature," the silences at its core. For these reasons, *Tay John* has been described as "Canada's first serious work of metafiction" (Geddes 84). In sharp contrast, Ella Tanner argues that a Platonic element "reveals a corresponding respect for language ... and ultimately, with the potential of language for disclosing, and perhaps even naming, the indwelling pattern of things" (11). What she suggests, convincingly I think, is that O'Hagan's concerns may be closer than critics have allowed to those of writers such as Alice Munro, writers interested in whatever hides beneath the surface of life. This interest in the hidden drew O'Hagan to people and stories that had been repressed.

In *Tay John*, O'Hagan appropriates or, as Mac Cassia puts it, "overwrites," the traditions and stories from the Tsimshian and Shuswap to imagine a mythic time for the North American West, thereby crossing the generic borders between wilderness storytelling and ethnography. Relying on ethnographic sources, especially *The Indians of Canada* by Diamond Jenness and Charles Hill-Tout, O'Hagan also drew on his own work as a mountaineer and guide. These experiences are often seen to ground his writing, as when Margery Fee asserts that the "choice of a Métis hero was based not so much on a romantic concept of the exotic other as on his own personal experience of discrimination, which came in part from having been treated like a servant by the tourists he guided" (11). The influence of storytelling on O'Hagan's style and the central authorizing role of experience forges a strong link between O'Hagan's wilderness stories and ethnographic accounts. The stories in his collection, *Wilderness Men*, for example, consciously integrate these literary forms. At the beginning of *Tay John*, O'Hagan acknowledges Jenness and Hill-Tout as well as his Métis friends Jonnie Moyé and Joe Sangré. It was Jenness's *The Indians of Canada* (1932) that provided O'Hagan with the legend of the fair-haired saviour of the Shuswap, a story that Cassia notes was neither "new world" myth "nor his to revise" (9). As Ralph Maud demonstrates, those passages that "deal most conspicuously" with Indigenous stories relied on these ethnographic sources as well and seem to confirm what can be intuited about the framing narrative in *Tay John*: that the omniscient narrator's "mysterious mythic voice" as some have described it, mimics the voice of the Indigenous storyteller recorded and translated by an ethnographer (95). Despite these influences, as Albert Braz asserts, Indigenous people do not have an actual voice in the novel, and the "fate of the progeny" of colonial sexual relations, Tay John's solitary life and eventual disappearance, demonstrates "the apparent impossibility of racial mixing in Canada" (1). The Indigenous storyteller, therefore, serves to voice a time immemorial, a mythic time that the modern characters try to control.

As Ella Tanner explains, the mystic side of O'Hagan's vision serves the "attempt to pin things down and through naming, to lay, as the surveyors do, a human map across the wild" (94). As the grizzly's death shows, the terms *uncanny* and *mystic* in *Tay John* are associated with the female, the thing that must be conquered by the masculine surveyors. *Tay John* gives accounts of a milieu that is characterized by a fear of women, and, as Granofsky also shows, the novel's structure relies on the binary opposition of masculine and feminine consistent with that fear. In the sections he narrates, Denham compares the mystery of the wilderness to the mysterious feminine. Rendering the landscape feminine, he remarks disdainfully that a "new mountain valley leads a man on like that—like a woman he has never touched" (*TJ* 80). The wilderness setting provides Tay John and Denham with a freedom to be masculine individuals through their struggle against the feminized wilderness. It has been noted by Tanner, Fee, and Francis Zichy that Tay John plays a role similar to that of Kurtz in *Heart of Darkness* by facilitating Denham's quest to dominate the tale. Denham, described as "a man of earth and common humanity yet isolated enough from his society to be individual too" (Tanner 96), seeks salvation through solitude, and his triumph is to "stand solitary, selfsustaining, unfathomable" (Tanner 20).

Many critics have noted how the wilderness novel's "deep strain of misogyny" (Stouck 217) surfaces in *Tay John* whether in Denham's comparison of "naming to rape" (Fee, *Silence* 11) or Jay Wiggins's comparison of Ardith to "bad meat" (Granofsky 115). Ronald Granofsky notes that this misogyny is always associated with characters from whom the author seems to distance himself (124), and Braz describes Tay John as "the product of a violent (but not necessarily unwelcome) sexual encounter" (4), the sort of encounter between white men and Indigenous women that characterizes colonization throughout the Americas. In light of O'Hagan's representation of women's experience in *The School-Marm Tree* (1977), including Rosie's story of rape, it is difficult to tag O'Hagan with the label "misogynist," though his character Denham certainly fits the description. If O'Hagan represents a literary West in which men's fantasies, as Annette Kolodny argues, have gained "the status of cultural myth," where women are an alien, civilizing presence and are "dispossessed of paradise" (12, 3), it is not because O'Hagan depicts the "honeysuckle vine trained round a cabin door" that Kolodny finds signalling the presence of women in early American literature (13).

While Robert Kroetsch focuses on "prairie fiction" in "The Fear of Women in Prairie Fiction: An Erotics of Space," and does not address O'Hagan's mountain wilderness specifically, the reading of rigid gender binaries with the West is telling. Kroetsch sets up a series of dichotomies: the house/horse, motion/stasis based on his assertion: "We conceive of external space as male, internal space as female" (73). In her response to the piece, Sandra Djwa takes issue with its metaphor of "making love in a new country" which "imposes a particular post-sixties view of sexuality and the creative process on novels that were written under quite different premises and published as long ago as 1918 and 1941" (84), rather than grappling with particular concerns of the early writers. The "muse" is the sexually available woman, and male creativity depends on the dominance of both women and the land. The way to respond to the mystery of the wilderness is by surveying, charting, mapping its territory, in some sense, defeating it just as Tay John defeats the female grizzly; for the men in the novel believe, as Denham claims: "Put a name to it, put it on a map, and you've got it. The unnamed—it is the darkness unveiled" (*TJ* 80). It is this unveiling that has been identified as postmodernist. For example, Fee observes that the novel has "more in common with Robert Kroetsch's *Gone Indian*" published in 1973 than it does with other books published in 1939. Kroetsch himself seems to concur when, in *The Lovely Treachery of Words* (1989), he explores *Tay John* as an example of the "unveiling" he believes to be characteristic of Canadian writing and Canadian *reading*, supporting his thesis that "Canadian literature, at its most radical, is the autobiography of a culture that tells its story by telling us repeatedly that it has no story to tell" (193). This particular vein in the criticism on *Tay John* usually focuses attention on "the untellable" nature of the story, the supposed silences at its core. Robert Kroetsch interprets the tale's "untellability" as an oppositional, revisionist narrative move, one intended to challenge various dominant narratives: "Recognizing as it does, through the fur trade of the western mountains, the metanarrative of empire, and recognizing through the processes of conversion the metanarrative of the Christian myth, it goes on to explore an acceptance of the 'hiddenness' of narrative in a manner that we now call, loosely, postmodern" (*Lovely* 182).

Kroetsch's equivocal use of the term seems to acknowledge the slipperiness of critical terminology and the problem arising from applying such terms to works written in one historical context but reclaimed by another. As W. J. Keith argues, O'Hagan carefully honed the storytelling form that is now the favoured device of ethnography, turning "yarn into serious art" (26). Keith analyses O'Hagan's writing within the tradition of tall tales told by actual mountain men, and argues that such stories "may be mysterious, even inexplicable, yet the possibility of their being true is almost always present. They are received, at any rate, with something close to Coleridge's willing suspension of disbelief" (25). Keith takes exception to the conclusion that, because *Tay John* challenges the myths at its own core by undermining their narratives, *Tay John* is "finally grounded in nothing" (35). For Keith, the real-life secrets of the wilderness men compelled them to tell tales, and it is for this reason that O'Hagan is "less concerned with clarifying the historical record" than with approximating the way the story is handed down (25). By having Denham and other storytellers reflect on the implications of the tales they tell, O'Hagan "nudges" readers to reflect on "style and meaning" (34) as he "emphasizes the articulateness" of these storytellers (32). Keith concludes that the "word" is not suspect as postmodernist readings assert; rather the meaning of the word is of great importance in the novel (37; see also Zichy; Hingston). For D. M. R. Bentley, what seems to be the highly original three-part narrative structure of *Tay John* actually reveals a debt to Giambattista Vico's theory of human history as the recurring cycle of three epochs: the age of the gods, the age of heroes, and the age of men (34-35), and he speculates that O'Hagan could have been introduced to the contemporary philosopher while studying at McGill. These influences, the art of "prim-itive" societies and modern European philosophy, point to the Modernist aesthetic shaping *Tay John*. Yet, as a writer of wilderness stories, O'Hagan was not embraced by Canadian modernism as he would be within the Canadian postmodern.

The reason O'Hagan was, for so long, the "writer that CanLit forgot," as Geddes put it, was attributed by postmodern writers and critics to the fact that O'Hagan was not received within the emerging Canadian modernism of the time. In an oblique comparison to *The Double Hook*, Michael Ondaatje names *Tay John* among those novels that signal a Canadian tradition that is "no longer a part of the realistic novel and no longer part of the European tradition" (272). Thus, Ondaatje describes and inscribes the genealogy of postmodernism explicated in Donna Palmeteer Pennee's pioneering work on the reception of *The Double Hook*. What *The Double Hook* offered critics was a starting point embedded in Modernism for the Canadian tradition, "a tradition under construction by such writer-critics as Ondaatje and Robert Kroetsch in search of traditions for their individual talents" ("Canadian Letters" 234). Because the "style and thematic" of *The Double Hook* "sacrifice historical, ethnic, and gendered specificity in the name of the redemption of the community," Pennee argues, it offered critics an ideal of the cosmopolitan Modernist literary culture for critics hoping to haul Canadian culture out of a perceived parochialism (*Femicide* 10). By including narrative femicide, *Tay John* conforms to the sacrificial mode of Modernism that Pennee explicates. In the final scene, both the woman and the Indigenized hero succumb as Tay John disappears dragging the pregnant and dead body of Ardith behind him. By associating *Tay John* with *The Double Hook*, Ondaatje was legitimizing O'Hagan's work as a Modernist forerunner to the Canadian postmodern and (perhaps unwittingly) supporting Pennee's insight.

In his interview with Keith Maillard, O'Hagan revealed his attitude toward postmodernism by comparing Michael Ondaatje's *Coming Through Slaughter* to modern poetry, which O'Hagan described as a "form of self-indulgence" (36). O'Hagan's scepticism, or his "lack of patience" as he puts it, suggest that it might be more worthwhile to discuss how his work stood apart from the modernist writing of his time, both in style and subject. O'Hagan's "fine" detailing of women's experience in *The School-Marm Tree* marked his difference from the Modernist mainstream that excluded women, and may account for his marginal place in early canons of Canadian Literature, even though *Tay John* conforms to the repression of otherness that Pennee identified in the Modernist aesthetic. What is compelling about O'Hagan's work is not its role as a possible precursor to the Canadian postmodern—though for these writers it clearly was that—but its various attempts to "unhide the hidden."

The Return of the Repressed: Reading *The School-Marm Tree*

The School-Marm Tree lacks femicide—the crucial component of literary modernism revealed in Pennee's work on *The Double Hook*. In *The School-Marm Tree,* O'Hagan does not kill Selva. Indeed, if there is a sacrifice that restores order it is that of the outsider, Peter Wrogg. Yet, Peter's death does not bring redemption; in fact, the requisite regeneration of society does not follow it. O'Hagan lets his heroine (and the other women) in the novel live. But what is even more compelling about this story is the fact that, not only does the author let her live, but he also refuses to have her punished. Not for enjoying her sexuality and attempting to defend her body against male sexual aggression; not for wanting a better life; not for transgressing boundaries of social class. Unlike other early twentieth-century heroines in her mundane circumstances—poor girls with few hopes, Gabrielle Roy's Florentine leaps to mind—Selva is not left abandoned and pregnant in a hypocritical and sexually repressed world. Even though it features the same dichotomy of illusion and reality, *The School-Marm Tree* is not a cautionary tale for girls with ideas above their station.

Although it was published much later, O'Hagan wrote *The School-Marm Tree* before the impact of the women's liberation movement had been fully felt. In it, one reads the typical frontier story of the individual frustrated by social roles and conventions; however, the freedom the frontier represents is not available to Selva, a woman, and her desire is represented in the school-marm tree, a tree that "resembled a gigantic human figure upflung against the twilight of the sky, enfolding the wind in its arms" (21). Scenes at the school-marm tree are tightly woven with other symbols. Trees are personified throughout: branches wave at her, beckon her (61). The wind that the school-marm tree enfolds in its arms bullies and pushes: "The wind propelled her, shoved her with masculine force, held her with the intimacy of possession" (26). And Slim is like the wind: "As with the winds, she fought against him and still yielded herself to him" (27). Selva's body is often described as a passive object buffeted by external forces like this. Even her body's own movements are often described as if some other force causes them (73). While this passivity reflects Selva's social position as determined by the intersection of class and gender, it is not her true character. When she defends herself against her employer's advances, and on the occasions when she stands up to Slim, a man whom she nevertheless fears, Selva demonstrates her ability to fight. The particular nature of her longing, which is often figured as a more general sense of "lack," is not chosen but ascribed to her along with her gender identity.

Margery Fee notes "the remarkable insight into women" in *The School-Marm Tree* (Fee 11) and remarks that "O'Hagan thought a lot more about race, place, and class than was typical of a person of his time" (9). He also thought about gender, and in ways that are rare. For what male writer has given the kind of chilling descriptions of Selva's feeling that men are always looking through her (102; 114; 150)? O'Hagan had little time for the masculine posing, the kind of "breast-beating" he associates with Hemingway. As he says in his interview with Keith Maillard, men like Hemingway "make a profession of being a man. I don't know. That seems to me what you more or less take for granted" (33). These comments suggest that "being a man" is a condition that is not dependent on the performance of masculinity typified by Hemingway's persona, the kind of masculinity that the novel critiques in its depiction of male violence and in its subversion of the Westward journey as the story of male individuation. In *The School-Marm Tree*, the male character whose quest leads West meets his own annihilation. This westering character is the Englishman, Peter Wrogg, whom Selva meets at the dance significantly on Empire Day. Peter speaks to Selva about the glamorous world of Montreal, assuring her that she could be part of that world by becoming a model in one of the department stores. As emissary of the East, Peter represents the glittering world displayed in the magazines she reads, and there are plenty of reasons to distrust him. She thinks about him with increasing frequency through the middle of the novel, imagining what he would see or think (Chapters 7, 8). Given the heavy symbolism throughout and the attention to clothing, the imperfect darn in his shirt gives the reader pause, suggesting he may not be all he seems. Clay's suspicion that Peter must have exaggerated his experience of mountain-climbing, and Peter's failure to defend himself against Slim, and his heavy drinking when he visits the chalet, foreshadow his eventual demise. Peter's failures, as much as the world he represents, awaken Selva's desire (203), and she struggles with the knowledge that she has been "moulding [him] to her desire" (196). Peter offers a way out to Selva, but, with his death, this escape route, like all others, is blocked. The East, Montreal in particular, may be the land of Selva's fantasies of a fine life, but the West is a place to inhabit. Selva finds freedom in the dark enclosure of the forest. Her ease with horses and cowboys and mountains unselfconsciously dissolves the opposition between them, for O'Hagan develops her love of the outdoors as important aspects of her character without suggesting that these facts make her exceptional *for a woman*. By eroding the stereotype of the westering character who lights out for the frontier and by representing the West as a home, O'Hagan reveals the instability of Western myths and of the East-West opposition on which they often hang.

In Selva, O'Hagan created a character who captured the tragic lives of women trapped by class and gender politics between the wars, their stories of social stigmatization, powerlessness, fear. For his wilderness women, physical and sexual harassment are facts of life. Like Mavis Gallant, writing in the same period, O'Hagan describes the experience of sexual harassment and assault before these terms appeared in common usage, and his characters respond to these unnamed violations in the ways available to them. When her employer Mr. Wamboldt tries to force himself on her, Selva defends herself by slapping him and barricading herself in her room, but she does not tell his wife, knowing that she will be "let go" in retaliation—as she soon is (72). She helplessly allows the man with no legs to force a kiss from her (83). Throughout the novel, race and class inflect gender to further subjugate all the women cast aside by the puritanical small town: Marie

Pierre, the blind 'Indian' woman who flees the abusive white man she lives with in Calling River (79); the doctor's invalid wife (84); Nancy Carstairs, the small town girl who wants desperately to be a new woman (98); Mrs. Otley, the charwoman; Miss Winters, "the old maid school teacher"; Mrs. Weaver, the enterprising widow. All struggle against the small town society and the limitations placed on women. When "Peter demur[s] about the idea of college" for a woman, the narrator reflects Selva's reaction: "Here again, as at the beer parlour where women had a separate entrance, and as at the campfire behind the chalet during the summer when the guides became silent at her approach because she was a woman, she was being excluded, if only by implication, from man's wider field of privilege" (186). Compared to the other women, Selva is the "exceptional woman," set apart from the other women in the novel by her looks and youth, her eventual ticket out of domestic service and the crabbed society of the frontier town, yet barred from male privilege.

While O'Hagan depicts the material conditions of these women's lives, their vulnerability to sexual harassment, social stigma, and male violence with convincing skill, the originality of his wilderness woman lies in the representation of a complex psychological struggle with an assigned female identity. A kind of sexual freedom, freedom from the consequences of sex, is available to Selva in this world that O'Hagan has created, yet the uncanny moment beside the pool indicates that contact with men comes either with the threat or the reality of violence. Coming upon Selva with Peter in the beaver meadow, Slim's violence becomes actual. Before Peter can protest, "with palm and then knuckles of his open hand, [Slim] had struck her twice across the face" (58). When Selva attempts to intervene, Slim slams his elbow into her throat so hard that she hits the school-marm tree and falls unconscious (59). In this world of male violence, consent is neither requested nor given, and the women seem to acquiesce to their lack of agency. In the first encounter with the guide Clay, a man who, in another scene, does take no for an answer (243), her vulnerability and her ability to choose are entwined:

> The tumult of the gallop, the pursuit, and at its end the fright of the approaching timber, had taken all strength from her. In its stead, the tender compliance of weakness was about her like a garment. She yielded herself, not to the man, but to the time, the moment, the place of brooding mountains of which he was a part …
>
> She would have said more but her throat was dry, her thoughts misted. She had no speech. She knew only that this which she had no power to resist—somewhere in the mad gallop along the ridge she had shed the power—was not what she had intended. (137)

This ambivalent scene comes before the reader learns what happened to Rosie. "Thunder reminds me of things I want to forget," Rosie says as she confides her story in Selva (143). A seventeen-year-old working in a restaurant in Red Deer, she was invited to go for a drive after work by a man from High River. When she meets him, there are three other men in the car. They force her to get in and later to drink whiskey until she passed out:

> She awoke in a field by the roadside. The thunder had awakened her or the rain and the hail on her upturned face. Her gingham dress was soaked …
>
> … 'I was sore. I was bleeding. It was the first time and I didn't even know which one or how many had done it. There were those four men, all with beard. It was like one face with four men behind it.' …

Rosie spoke dispassionately as though what she related had not happened to her at all but, perhaps, to a friend known to her grandmother in her grandmother's youth. Yet Selva felt her hurt, felt the outrage she could not express and rose with her from the field—the car had doubled back and left her less than a mile from town—rose with her and walked with her beneath the thunder and through the storm along the road and crouched with her by a hedge and took shelter with her for five minutes by a storekeeper's window before she crossed the street and groped her way through the back door of the hotel and up the stairway to her room. (144-145)

To endure the trauma, Rosie must dissociate from the events, leaving them for Selva to imagine. Selva's own sexual experiences seem to be free of shame or consequences, but she can feel another woman's "shame and pain, as if Rosie's experience were her own, were deep within" (144-45).

As Selva thinks over what Rosie has confided in her, she recalls crying after her own sexual encounter with Slim, which she remembers as a "struggle not so much with a man as with a force," but in Selva's case, her tears are for the disappointing experiences with Slim and an understanding that with Clay she "had experienced, if not all, at least what she had never known before" (146). With Clay, Selva is again acted upon as accepting her powerlessness yields to masochistic pleasure:

She waited, passive, blind as the moist earth which takes the plough. She waited for the Incorrigible, the Never-to-be-Denied, the Always-to-be-Conquered, the Victorious-in-Defeat now within the creamy narrows of her thighs.

"Easy," she whispered, "easy." Tossing her body, rolling her head from side to side, showing her gritted teeth, she said, "Hard, hard. Hurt me hard." (138)

As she waits in the snow for the men to come down the mountain, Selva realizes that "[s]he, a woman, hungered to be what she was not, to have what she could not have" (231). Selva's longing articulates her position as a woman in both post-war Western society and the imaginary West constructed in wilderness writing. Because there is no way of filling this imagined lack, there is no way to resolve her story. In the last scene of the novel, when Peter's revenant appears to her in a vision of the world he might have given her had he lived, she desperately entreats her lover: "Take me, Clay, take me. Take me, hold me. I'm cold and I am afraid" (245). There is no resolution to Selva's desire for another kind of life despite the purple prose of romance novels; instead, Selva is left lacking what she craves once again as "she reached for his lips to suck from them the breath that was mortal" (245). Selva's story has come full circle to the beaver meadow that is both home and distinctly *unheimlich*. When she responds to her own "living flesh" and chooses Clay's arm "solid with muscle" over the ghosts inhabiting her daydreams, she also asks if, from the home they will share, she will be able to hear the whistling of locomotives—a sign that her loneliness and longing for escape will not abate. Selva's craving is constant because O'Hagan cannot envision an end to her longing in this masculine world.

Works Cited

Bentley, D. M. R. "The Wide Circle and Return: *Tay John* and Vico." *Dalhousie Review*, vol. 73, no.1, 1993, pp. 34-53.

Braz, Albert. "Fictions of Mixed Origins: *Iracema*, *Tay John*, and Racial Hybridity in Brazil and Canada." *Ameriquests*, vol. 10, no. 1, 2013, pp. 1-9.

Cassia, Mac. Cultural Appropriation in O'Hagan's *Tay John*: 'New World' Mythos of the 'Postcolonial' Colonist. Unpublished thesis. University of the Fraser Valley, 2015.

Djwa, Sandra. "Response" to "The Fear of Women in Prairie Fiction" by Robert Kroetsch. *Crossing Frontiers: Papers on Canadian and American Western Literature*, edited by Dick Harrison, U of Alberta P, 1979, pp. 84-88.

Fee, Margery, ed. *Silence Made Visible: Howard O'Hagan and* Tay John. ECW Press, 1992.

Freud, Sigmund, "The Uncanny." 1919. *The Uncanny*, Translated by David McLintock, Penguin, 2003, pp. 121-162.

Geddes, Gary. "The Writer That CanLit Forgot." *Saturday Night*, vol. 92, no. 8, November 1977, pp. 84-92.

Granofsky, Ronald. "Country of Illusion: Vision, Change, and Misogyny in Howard O'Hagan's *Tay John*. Fee, pp. 109-127.

Hingston, Kylee-Anne. "The Declension of a Story: Narrative Structures in Howard O'Hagan's *Tay John.*" *Studies in Canadian Literature*, vol. 30, no. 2, 2005, pp. 181-192.

Kaltembeck, Michèle. "L'Expansion vers l'ouest dans *Tay John* de Howard O'Hagan." *Essays on Canadian Writing*, vol. 21, 1995, pp. 193-204.

Keith, W. J. *A Sense of Style: Studies in the Art of Fiction in English-Speaking Canada*. ECW Press, 1989.

Kolodny, Annette. *The Land Before Her: Fantasy and Experience of the American Frontiers, 1630-1860*. U of Carolina P, 1984.

Kroetsch, Robert. "The Fear of Women in Prairie Fiction: An Erotics of Space." *Crossing Frontiers: Papers on Canadian and American Western Literature*, edited by Dick Harrison, U of Alberta P, 1979, pp. 73-83.

Maillard, Keith. "Interview with Howard O'Hagan." Fee, pp. 21-38.

Maud, Ralph. "Ethnographic Notes on Howard O'Hagan's *Tay John.*" Fee, pp. 92-6.

O'Hagan, Howard. *The School-Marm Tree*. Talonbooks, 1977.

----. *Tay John*. 1939. McClelland, 1989.

----. *Wilderness Men*. 1958. Talonbooks, 1978.

Ondaatje, Michael. Afterword. *Tay John*. Toronto: McClelland, 1989, pp. 265-72.

----. "Howard O'Hagan and 'The Rough-Edged Chronicle'." *The Canadian Novel in the Twentieth Century*, edited by George Woodcock, New Canadian Library 115, McClelland, 1975, pp. 276-84.

Page, P. K. "Introduction." *The School-Marm Tree*. Talonbooks, 1977, pp. 7-10.

Pennee, Donna Palmateer. "Canadian Letters, Dead Referents: Reconsidering the Critical Construction of *The Double Hook*." *Essays on Canadian Writing*, vol. 51-52, 1993-1994, pp. 233-57.

----. *Femicide in the Critical Construction of* The Double Hook: *A Case Study in the Interrelations of Modernism, Literary Nationalism, and Cultural Maturity* Diss. McGill University 1994.

Stouck, David. "The Art of the Mountain Man Novel." *Western American Literature*, vol. 20, 1985, pp. 211-22.

Tanner, Ella. *Tay John and the Cyclical Quest: The Shape of Art and Vision in Howard O'Hagan*. ECW, 1990.

Zichy, Francis. "Crypto-, Pseudo-, and Pre-Postmodernism: *Tay John*, *Lord Jim*, and the Critics." *Essays on Canadian Writing*, vol. 81, 2004, pp. 192-221.

----. "The 'Complex Fate' of the Canadian in Howard O'Hagan's *Tay John*." *Essays on Canadian Writing*, vol. 79, 2003, pp. 199-225.

Myth Demystified
Realism and Settler Society
in Howard O'Hagan's *The School-Marm Tree*

CARL WATTS

As far as encyclopedia entries, survey courses, and compre-
hensive-exam reading lists are concerned, the name Howard
O'Hagan is mostly synonymous with *Tay John*. Since its publication in 1939, O'Hagan's sprawling novel of Western Canada's
mountains and myths has been assimilated to Canadian literary traditions including thematic criticism, postmodernism,
and the writerly yarn more generally.[1] Fittingly, much criticism
on *Tay John*, and on O'Hagan generally, takes an implicitly
poststructuralist approach, finding that the novel reworks the
almost universal binaries of myth—masculine and feminine,
human and non-human, light and darkness, settler and Indigenous—to account for Western Canada's cultural hybridity and
discourses of contestation. O'Hagan's short fiction, despite
having received less critical attention, treads similar ground.[2]

---

1   *Tay John*'s broad acceptance into the CanLit canon is perhaps best en-
    capsulated in the New Canadian Library's use for its edition of the novel
    an adapted version of Michael Ondaatje's 1974 essay, "O'Hagan's Rough-
    Edged Chronicle."

2   In addition to the novel discussed in this paper, O'Hagan produced two
    volumes of short fiction: *Wilderness Men* (1958) and *The Woman Who
    Got on at Jasper Station and Other Stories* (1963). The former provides

I want to suggest that the outlier in his oeuvre is his only other published novel, *The School-Marm Tree*. Coming years after O'Hagan's other writing, this late entry in the author's corpus occupies a strange position in Canadian literature, registering the unraveling of the country's realist mythologies as well as the incipient settler-colonial hegemony that was to follow the obscured modernism of early- and mid-century literature.

Based on a short story O'Hagan began expanding in the 1950s and yet not published until 1977,[3] the novel has received little critical notice. Contemporary reviews either faintly praised or else dismissed it as a more simplistic, amateurish, or even romantic treatment of O'Hagan's familiar themes. (Sheila Fischman's description of it in the *Montreal Star* as a "rather conventional love story" [39] is representative of the various formulations that appear in contemporary reviews, some of which I will discuss at greater length below.) Further complications are the novel's long gestation and the gradual consolidation of O'Hagan's literary reputation: given the decades-long gap between *Tay John*'s publication and the in many ways sudden appearance of *The School-Marm Tree*, the latter is discussed as either an endnote or a curious envoi—that is, on those few occasions it is mentioned at all.[4]

---

portraits of real-life figures of the Canadian west, including subsequently mythologized figures such as Albert Johnson (the Mad Trapper) and Archie Belaney (Grey Owl), and the latter consists of fairly conventional short stories that treat similar ground as *Tay John*.

3   As P. K. Page's introduction to the novel notes, the story appeared originally in *Story* magazine; O'Hagan began turning it into a novel in the 1950s while spending summers in Cowichan Bay (10).

4   A representative example is O'Hagan's entry in the Canadian Encyclopedia, which describes *Tay John* in detail and states that the author's short fiction "is also respected," only to conclude penultimately, "His novel *The School-Marm Tree* was published in 1977."

I seek to account for this neglect while also using the novel to augment narrowly poststructuralist interpretations of O'Hagan's other fiction. I build on Glenn Willmott's reading of *Tay John* in the context of romance and realism, arguing that *The School-Marm Tree*, in focusing almost wholly on white settler society, performs what Fredric Jameson identifies as realism's historical association with "the function of demystification" (*Antinomies of Realism* 22) and the concomitant dissolution that accompanies its establishment and codification as a genre or mode. *The School-Marm Tree* "demystifies" the process of myth-making at the heart of *Tay John*, examining the white settler subject as at once a recreation and deconstruction of the identities, relationships, and binaries identified in O'Hagan's previous novel, instead ironizing them in the form of inter-changeable characters instead of archetypes; instrumental rela-tionships that demonstrate a leveling out of the antagonisms of social class rather than participation in the problematic of the self-seeking individual; and descriptions of clothing and fashion that are foregrounded in order to portray the small regional and cultural differences that belie the comparative uniformity or totality of incipiently normative settler-colonialism (as opposed to depicting the individualism attributed to the frontier-era settler subject). The novel thus functions as a culmination of the work *Tay John* does in exploring and problematizing the binaries of myth; in the process, it registers both the growth of Canadian settler society as mainstream and normative as well as the narcissism of the white settler subject that enables and is intertwined with this process.

The School-Marm Tree tells the story of Selva Williams, who lives in Yellowhead—"a small town of not quite a thousand people" (16)—and is employed as a domestic worker in the home of the Wamboldts. Involved with a ranch worker named Slim Conway, she is subsequently attracted to Peter Wrogg, a comparatively urbane Englishman arriving from Montreal, who suggests the possibility of her becoming a model. The competition between the two men culminates in a fight in the beaver meadow, in which Slim is the victor and Wrogg is rendered temporarily speechless. Selva, having been assaulted by Mr. Wamboldt and subsequently dismissed, ventures into a beer parlour with the open-minded Edna Weaver and meets another rancher, Clay Mulloy, who gets her a position at a tourist-oriented chalet in the mountains. Clay impresses Selva with his history in Montreal (where he studied at McGill), and the equal-parts rugged and ambitious rancher invites her to join him in his plan to open his own resort in the distant Fry Pan Mountains. A New Zealander named Mr. Branchflower, whose "general bearing of aloofness," "intonations of ... voice," and "clipped phrases" remind Selva of Wrogg (159), appears at the chalet, coming across as savvier, sportier, and more goal-oriented version of the latter; the narrative at this point shifts to a second-person reflection, addressing and critiquing various characters associated with the chalet and describing an at times violent atmosphere of male homosociality. (This section builds on a preceding description of the rape of Selva's co-worker, Rosie.) The narrative continues with a dreamlike meeting between Selva and Wrogg, the latter having inquired about Selva on his way back through Yellowhead and then set out on his own for the chalet. Wrogg, the morning after descending into drunken reveries about his mother, goes riding with Selva and Clay; each man offers to take Selva away from Yellowhead, and, despite the animosity between them, the two go climbing together. Selva later encounters Clay in the foothills, and the latter reports that the inexperienced Wrogg has fallen and is trapped on a ledge further up the mountain. The book ends with another dreamlike sequence in which Selva, ill with pneumonia, perceives several characters collaborating to rescue Peter and then learns that the latter has died of his injuries.

Even this brief synopsis reveals several similarities between *Tay John* and O'Hagan's later novel. Aside from being set in the mountains of Western Canada, *The School-Marm Tree* features characters whose appearances and disappearances are shrouded in mystery and hearsay. Although Indigenous characters and themes are lacking, the story's settler characters enact similar themes of exploration along an expanding frontier, and their backstories are to some extent born of the various settler histories characterizing the Canadian West of the early- and mid-twentieth century. What is more, orally transmitted mythologies share some space in the novel with the comparatively verifiable (or just recorded) histories that compete with the former in much modern and postmodernist fiction. (This is evident in Selva's fraught backstory, in which her mother, "before her death, knew that she would leave the homestead and go away to make her living"—a prophecy that also finds expression in a Winnipeg address passed from mother to daughter, written on "a piece of mauve writing paper" [90].)

And yet, the myth-making and subtle interrogation of that process that occur in *Tay John*, and which have made the latter a productive object of study for thematic-critical and post-structuralist approaches, do not appear in quite the same form in *The School-Marm Tree*. Examples of the robust critical discussion of *Tay John* include the brief yet foundational study by Michael Ondaatje, which found a shying away from focus on a central protagonist and movement instead toward the "raw power of myth" (24) via its "very careful use of echoes" (25), or "variations [that] are always there setting up parallels"

(26).[5] Margery Fee sharpened these observations into a take on O'Hagan's simultaneous use and problematization of the binaries of myth, arguing that he inverts the common binary of light and darkness (9), for instance, as part of his larger project of dismantling Western systems of myth without destroying them—as "rig[ging] up a new myth out of the pieces of the old ones, revealing in the process how it's done" (10). Jack Robinson has further deconstructed O'Hagan's engagement with myth, finding that the novel undermines "the world-explaining myth of ideology itself" (166) and ultimately supports the "postmodernist assumption" that "all reality is fictive" (169); more recently, Kylee-Anne Hingston has found codified in the text itself a larger acknowledgement that the very process of storytelling is premised on "a degeneration from authoritative legend to inconclusive evidence," as O'Hagan was interested less in the inscription of intangible myth and more in exploring a narrative process of "declension from an elusive but indisputable legend to corporeal but uncertain facts" (181).[6] Critical engagement with the text focuses as much on the formal aspects of its storytelling as on its content.

So it is that *The School-Marm Tree*, despite the above similarities in theme and content, has not gotten this kind of

---

5 Ondaatje acknowledges the aspects of irony that exist in the novel, but he describes these as "directed not towards the source of the myth but to the story-teller's need for order" (29). His article thus at once preserves the structures of myth at the heart of thematic criticism and paves the way for understandings of the quintessentially Canadian genre of historiographic metafiction, which Linda Hutcheon famously regarded as an example of the postmodernist need to "trouble, to question, to make both problematic and provisional any such desire for order or truth through the powers of the human imagination" (2).

6 A focus on nuts-and-bolts narrative that has since been taken up by Kevin Roberts, who regards *Tay John* as "simultaneously creating and criticizing in legal terms the very existence of his mythical figure" (195).

sustained and nuanced attention. And, indeed, the reviews the novel receive anticipate this wider critical neglect.[7] John Thompson, writing for *The Globe and Mail*, described it as "quite unlike *Tay John*": "Both are set in the Rockies, but where the earlier work is mythic, *The School-Marm Tree* is realistic, ordinary in almost every way" (41). Barbara Novak claimed that the novel's "realistic, simple plot has more in common with the author's short stories" (B4). Many reviews dismiss its simplicity yet also frequently struggle to describe the latter. References to its simplicity, predictability, or romance crop up as frequently as do descriptions of its somehow more straightforward realism: Gordon Morash praised its "tightness of scenes and incidents" even as he ultimately dismissed the book for being "a love story that is heavy with melodrama and very predictable" (9); Gordon Powers relied on a similar duality, stating that the novel "curiously combines Harlequin romance and early Jack London" (and concluding that it was "hackneyed and meandering") (42); Jane W. Hill wrote that it was "only superficially a realistic, anecdotal account of what happened to whom," and that deeper down it was "an almost mythic tale, a fusion of events and the philosophic meaning of those events" (18). W.J. Keith noted that it "might be more accurately classified as a romance rather than as a novel," ultimately describing it as a "uniquely beautiful moral fable"; yet even this sympathetic review praises the novel for "reveal[ing] O'Hagan as a little less enigmatic than the wilderness and mountains about which he writes" (28).

---

7   This survey of contemporary opinion on the text is indebted to the compendium of reviews provided by Richard Arnold as part of his annotated bibliography that appears in Margery Fee's *Silence Made Visible: Howard O'Hagan and* Tay John (1992).

Such reviews do include a degree of attentiveness. Hill finds
that "O'Hagan is especially fine in his understanding of women,
their feelings and their place in this masculine world" (18), for
instance, and Novak also remarks that O'Hagan's "insight into
the female experience is as rare, sensitive, and profound as is
his understanding of nature" (B4). Such descriptions indicate
that even skeptical contemporary reviews identified an intricate, or at least functional, realism in the novel, as well as an
attention to the specificities of O'Hagan's cast of characters.
The coexistence of this strain with the more frequently remarked romance of the text brings to mind Glenn Willmott's
exploration of the nuanced position of realism within con-
ceptions of Canadian literature. Willmott argues in *Unreal
Country* that "the old antinomy" of realism and romance is
better understood as a "screen through which we may see their
necessary (if antagonistic) interaction and transfiguration"
relative to modernism. Romance and realism here function
as "inverted shells," with realism "turned inside out":

> The conventional function of realism, to register the interrela-
> tions and values of a given, secular world, or "what is," is eroded
> by the uneven and unstable, slash-and-burn transvaluations of
> a material life subject to the unpredictable synapses of global
> economy, media, and mobility. A self-ironicizing realism is now
> required in order to register these unevenly signifying events,
> which mark the shifting social limits and vectors of global flows
> themselves; it is required, however ephemerally and paradoxically
> self-consciously, as a provisional ground for the imagination "at
> large." (5)

Willmott discusses at length the common bildungsroman
structure of such novels; he regards *Tay John* as one such
"self-development" novel, in which "the mobility-restlessness

plot is unable to cast up a teleology that will make retrospec-
tive sense of it and so must end ... arbitrarily" (33).

Willmott does not engage directly with *The School-Marm
Tree*, but the novel for the most part fits such a pattern. Still,
its somewhat ambiguous conclusion holds out the possibility
of Selva's demise, which would make for a far from arbitrary
ending. Similarly, although *The School-Marm Tree*'s realism
is inverted and problematized, the novel is unique for the
doubling of its main characters and the interchangeability
of its minor ones—oftentimes, it reads as if it is parading
its structural shortfalls or inadequacies in an act of strange,
self-concerned myopia. If *Tay John* is constructed out of an
inverted complex of realism and romance that registers the
uncertainties of modernity, as Willmott has it, then O'Hagan's
later novel seems to redouble the self-ironizing function of
realism not as part of a modernist's registering of modernity, but rather as the author of *Tay John*'s unraveling of the
myth-making of that text. In other words, *The School-Marm
Tree* in many ways finishes the work *Tay John* starts.

Fredric Jameson has more recently probed the function
of realism, finding in the historical development of the mode
itself a self-ironizing quality similar to that which Willmott
identifies in modern Canadian literature. Hill's statement that
the novel was both "almost mythic" and "a fusion of events
and the philosophic meaning of those events" seems to register precisely Jameson's point that the very nature of realism
means that it interrogates and therefore cancels itself; that
is, realism's status as an "epistemological claim" that "mas-
querades as an aesthetic ideal" (26) and which, in its very
establishment, thus constitutes "its own inevitable undoing"
(28). Realism, in other words, is an inherently unstable venture that breaks down from its initial expression of alienated
bourgeois individual into disorganized, ill-defined affect, the

potentiality of which is increasingly distributed among and contained within realism's subgenres (the *bildungsroman*, the historical novel, the naturalist novel). And indeed, Colin Hill's recent look at what he calls "modern realism"—that is, early twentieth-century Canadian writers' "largely successful experiments to balance the objectivist stance of the traditional realist with the subjective perspectivism of the high-modernist form" (16)—identifies a perhaps more explicit, or at least more identifiably Canadian, variant of this subtle, inherent self-reflexivity as well as its evolution (or devolution) into the simultaneously less structured and yet blandly omnipresent narrativization Jameson finds encoded in the historical development of realism more generally.

Following these studies of realism, I want to suggest that *The School-Marm Tree* participates in a similar process of formal undoing, but that because of the more restricted, specifically Canadian milieu in which the novel takes place, what is registered is less Jameson's larger theory of quasi-realist subgenres and more the messy completion of settler colonialism, expressed formally as a revision of O'Hagan's own prior processes of myth-making. Just as Willmott identifies the potential and uniqueness of the modernism that obtains in inverted formations of realism and romance, and following which one could identify the development and subsequent dominance of a postmodern sensibility in Canadian fiction, so does *The School-Marm Tree* reveal a moment at which the unfinished individualist problematic of the modern novel dissolves into the newly epic predictability of an increasingly totalized settler-colonial world. The novel thus registers not the revised myths required to depict the unpredictability of a new country (that is, the task carried out by *Tay John*), but rather the growth of Canadian settler society as mainstream and normative, as well as the narcissism of the white settler subject that enables and is intertwined with the former process.

This phenomenon is initially most evident in the messy sprawl of the novel's characterizations. Early on, the novel presents characters as distinct in terms of class and yet, within such strata, as interchangeable on the level of behaviour and narrative. Evident even from the brief synopsis above, the novel revolves around paired or doubled characters—Slim and Clay, Wrogg and Branchflower, Edna and Rosie. Many minor characters are explicitly interchangeable: when Selva grows accustomed to her work at the chalet and comes to know the other ranchers by name, the final three of the four she lists are even named "Sam, Dick and Harry" (157); later, summer tourists are described as "no more than a succession of sunburned faces showing in the afternoon at the clearing's edge and of shoulders and bobbing heads on horseback leaving in the morning on the trail for town." The passage states explicitly that the uniqueness of individual profiles are themselves somehow finite, their variety predictable as opposed to infinite or unexpected: "Each face was strange and each in its strangeness was familiar. She had seen it, she had seen them all before" (169).

Such interchangeability is also evident in the reduction of narratologically important characters to the coincidences of linguistic play—as in the passage, "Don't call me Mrs. Weaver. Edna's the name. See, they go well together. Selva ... Edna" (94)—or imagery that captures the beginning of a process in which the individual dissolves gradually into the type, as in Rosie's retelling of her rape: "There were those four men, all with beards. It was like one face with four men behind it" (144-45). These swappable characters bring to mind Jean-Paul Sartre's work on the relationship between individuals and groups. The first volume of Sartre's *Critique of Dialectical Reason* includes a description of the evolution from clusters of individuals to basic group units and finally more abstract concepts of collective identity. He regards the "fused group" as emerging from real-time social processes of reciprocity and seriality, whereas the notions of collectivity that dominate in the identity politics of the present day—race, nation, ethnicity, markers based on gender or sexual orientation—are pledge-based and therefore comparatively abstract (419).

Sartre's ideas are relevant to *The School-Marm Tree* in that the novel offers a picture of his bizarre configuration of individual and group, self and other—again, some midpoint at which these distinctions visibly begin either to unravel (according to the architecture of realism) or to crystallize (following Sartre's narrative of individuality expanding gradually into societal complexity). This in-betweenness is evident in the half-heartedly instrumental relationships that obtain among many of the novel's main characters, such as that between Selva and Peter. During an early encounter, he says he didn't expect to find someone like her at a dance above a billiard hall:

> "Why not?" he echoed. "That's a hard question to answer. Perhaps because you reminded me of someone I know. A man's always looking for and finding the same woman, you know. She comes from a small town too. A place called Granby in the Eastern Townships in Quebec. She now works as a model in one of the women's shops in Montreal." (45)

And just as the working-class Selva functions as an almost interchangeable object of desire and beneficence, so too does Slim, and then Peter, and then Clay offer her a similarly attainable, similarly prestigious escape (into a better domestic work, a model in a department store, a junior business

partner, respectively). What results are neither individual-
istic characters serving a plot arc nor types that represent
any meaningfully differentiated group identities, whether
those be associated with the binaries of myth—man-woman,
settler-indigenous, human-animal—or the more specific
ethno-cultural or gender-sexual identities associated with
Canadian postmodernist or contemporary literatures that
were ascendant around the time of *The School-Marm Tree's*
1977 publication.

   This interchangeability is intertwined in other ways with
a larger failure on the part of characters to learn or progress.
One of Selva's reflections at first depicts her as a type stub-
bornly resistant to the narrative of *bildung* structuring the
modern Canadian novel (as Willmott conceives of it above)
and realism more generally: "She, Selva Williams, had not
altered. She was what she had always been" (96). "[A]nd yet,"
the passage continues, "since she had been out with Peter,
even Mr. Wamboldt had acted towards her as he had never
acted before. It was as though Peter had touched her and
revealed what until then lay hidden" (96). Still, the baldly instrumental nature of these relationships is evident, even as
their promise is never fulfilled: Selva admits she "was not in
love with Peter. She liked him and respected him because
he respected her and because doors that were closed to her
were open to him and his kind"; subsequently, she describes
him as "a frail vessel, but one strong enough to contain her
hopes for a while ..." (120). Similarly, Slim, after emerging the
victor from his physical confrontation with Peter in the beaver
meadow, is subsequently compared with Clay in a way that
skirts the distinction between differentiated character and
undistinguishable male foil:

   Slim had not made a scene, she decided, because Clay's
   bearing suggested an untapped strength. In appearance he

was not a big man—he had the large hands and small feet of a horseman and the narrow hips and tapered body that went with them. Yet he seemed big. It was as though he were a big man compressed into a smaller frame, as a coiled spring might be compressed. (130)

The subtle, shifting distinctions between large and small, outwardly and implicitly powerful, collapse the respective physical strength and bearing of the two men into distinctions so slight they function as almost arbitrary.

This dynamic is accompanied by O'Hagan's use of minor, flat characters less as plot devices or props and more as emanations of a particular occupation or social status that never quite fulfill the narratological role one could associate with such archetypes. Hank Barton, for example, is described as "the lean faced son of the bank—somehow she thought of him more as the son of the bank than as the progeny of its manager" (28). Shortly afterwards, we encounter "the western divisional manager of the railroad who had come from down the valley in his private car."; the doctor, "grey moustached, red cheeked, lifting his knee to slap it as he laughed at a joke told to him by Bill Wilkins who ran the outfit for which Slim worked as guide, packer and horsebreaker"; and, finally, the statement that

> These, and others like them, were older people, established people who did not work for wages, nor have one job today and another one tomorrow. They had made their compromises and stood by them. They sometimes addressed one another as "Mr." and "Mrs." and met with reserve and, on occasion, when unprepared, with dignity. (30)

Such descriptions register a vague sense of class conflict, but none of the figures in question (other than Slim) participate in any enactment of such drama that is meaningful on the level of challenging the precepts of that normative social system. Foregrounded instead are the titles of "Mr." and "Mrs.," which indicate the relationships among interchangeable, easily replicable components performing a middle-class ritual of shared individual dignity.

This simultaneously open-ended and yet foreclosed system of character development becomes comprehensible (and does work in explaining the other oddities in the novel's lengthy descriptions of fashion and physical appearance, as will be discussed below) in the context of the establishment of settler-colonialism. This unraveling of the standard significations of realism, visible in the doubled or interchangeable characters and meta-descriptions of material things, takes on significance beyond the text's self-reflexive undoing of realism when one considers these phenomena in the context of the settler-colonialism that has become normative in direct proportion to the receding of the quasi-mythical frontier depicted in *Tay John*. Eva Mackey has formulated a particularly useful and succinct way of understanding this construction in a Canadian context. She suggests that whiteness structures the "unmarked" group that forms the centre or "core" of Anglophone Canada's mainstream settler society (157). As part of the country's official multiculturalism, immigrants function as bearers of cultural difference that in their alterity sustain the notion of a whiteness as normative, or defined above all else by its ostensible embodiment of supposedly universal values like "rationality, efficiency, equality, and economic progress" (160)—supposedly unmarked values that are evident in the above series of interacting "Mr." and "Mrs." characters.

More recently, Audra Simpson has described settler-colonialism as a process of capital accumulation that is premised on dispossession—an ongoing, open-ended process that is "still happening in spaces seized away from people in ongoing projects to mask that seizure while attending to capital accumulation under another name" (440). What limited engagements with this past that do exist—Simpson deals specifically with recent Canadian leaders' apologies to Indigenous communities—construct acts of violence as having occurred in a past in which the perpetrators existed in a state of ignorance that, at the time of the apology, has been rectified, therefore establishing a history of semi-acknowledged violence and "keep-[ing] open the possibility of a prior sense of good" (438-39).

Simpson's formulation is relevant to *The School-Marm Tree* because the latter registers incipient mainstream settler-colonial society—that is, an inherently violent, exclusionary system whose human errors nevertheless indicate its ostensible beneficence—as normativizing itself discursively, much in the way realism (as Jameson has it) fulfills its own "epistemological claim," becomes normative, and dissolves into a disorganized registering of affects or else a proliferation of ever-more-particular subgenres. As the novel draws to a close, progress—or the navigation of the socio-economic antagonisms that are outlined but never treated at length—accordingly comes to be envisioned spatially: "When he [Clay] moved, it occurred to Selva, he moved in only one direction—forward. Peter moved forward, it seemed, only that he might take another step back" (202); "Peter was up there. She was up there for Peter was part of herself. He was that part of her which had climbed the highest—and now he must return to her again" (232). Such passages are instances of the collapse of metaphor beyond past metonymy and into the still more literal, with characters either leading an expedition or else staggering, climbing shambolically up and then down. In this whimsical rehearsal of tropes of social advancement and self-discovery, more collective markings of difference—age and nationality in addition to class—also fit in this spatialized settler system in which both individuals and groups (including social classes) are construed as aimlessly picaresque and yet existing without the structuring principle of the individual journey. When Clay states, "I was about eleven then and we were living in one of those little towns on Vancouver Island where Englishmen go to retire when they're no more use in this world. Moss grows well down there" (209-10), he expresses less class antagonism than his experience of a space formerly marked as such but that now functions as an undifferentiated field of settler existence to which both he and said Englishmen have access.

In addition to this oddly replicable and yet constrained character development, the novel's engagements with materialism and narcissism of small cultural or regional differences functioning as inquiries into the (incipiently normative) settler subject itself are opposed to the larger, previously dominant systems of myth that structure *Tay John*. The frequent and lengthy descriptions of clothing and related consumer products that appear in *The School-Marm Tree* add to this unravelling of realist mechanisms such as supposedly transparent and objective description. Often, such passages provide detailed descriptions of not only clothing itself, but also its representation in magazines or in-store displays. On the very first page of the novel, Selva looks at a fashion magazine while she waits for Slim. The magazine advertises "dreams … for those who had money to buy them," but this simplistic critique of advertising is immediately supplemented with Selva's projection of herself into a detailed universe of luxury, adventure, and almost magical-realist detail:

> In the glossy pages where they were displayed, Selva sat with dapper men and women at tables in exotic climes. She stood in a one-piece swimsuit on a sandy shore as green waves broke and

washed at her feet. On the desert, wearing jodhpurs, she galloped on a painted horse through the sagebrush. Again, as she posed in doorways in a new blue frock or ascended an unending series of marble steps, the sun of California shone upon her tawny hair and laid the black velvet of a shadow for her to tread upon. (15-16)

In addition to its intricate description of vivid, gaudy colours, this passage exists at a still further remove from the gradual shift away from an organized telling and towards a disorganized, affect-laden showing that Jameson identifies in realism generally. In depicting Selva's looking at a magazine, the passage in a sense describes the act of describing, with the vague, foreclosed process of personal growth or social advancement dispersed among the representation of the mechanics of advertising.

Later, when Selva is preparing to embark on her ostensible escape from Yellowhead, mid-twentieth-century advertising's vague associations of particular products and fashions with social mobility structure her actions:[8] "She had wanted jodphurs [*sic*] such as she had seen advertised in the fashion magazines where men and sun-browned girls stood beside horses, but unable to buy them in Yellowhead, instead had bought a pair of grey, tight fitting, ship-cord trousers such as the men wore" (132). Even the gruff Slim, the small-town counterpart to the bigger dreams offered by Peter and Clay, is depicted in the opening pages as being "firm" in his request for the pink as opposed to grey version of a particular shirt, his demands requiring the clerk to take the last remaining

8   Faye Hammill and Michelle Smith have identified in several so-called "middlebrow" magazines published in Canada between 1925 and 1960 a tendency to circulate "fantasies of travel" in which connections are made between "geographical mobility and upward mobility," with readers of said magazines being given "an opportunity to acquire knowledge and prestige as well as to experience pleasure and luxury" (1).

one from the store window, "temporarily spoiling the display."
And yet, even this early characterization of Slim as obstinate
and demanding fails to mark him out as an individual—Selva
is later informed by the clerk that "the selection was limited
because there had been a run on pink shirts"; "It always happened that way during the month of May" (16).

The novel's stranger moments combine these qualities in
a way that further dissolves the antinomies of either myth or
realism proper in a totality of settler-colonial social relations
and the concomitant minor or arbitrary differences of the "local colour" that obtains in the novel's settings and characters.
The mundane quirks of bodily appearance show themselves at
once as cartoonishly vivid and worthy of commentary as are
the above fashions and yet as fuel for meaningless social gaffes
that themselves further dissolve the alternately doubled and
subverted class hierarchies. Take, for instance, this ostensibly
class-inflected exchange between Rosie and Peter:

> "But then I would have remembered you anyway."
>
> "Really?"
>
> "Yes, because your eyebrows aren't neighbours."
>
> Peter glanced at Selva in astonishment. Then, holding his
> face in profile at Rosie, regarding her warily as he might a strange
> form of life seen for the first time through the bars at the zoo.
>
> "I mean," Rosie said, "that your right eyebrow rides higher
> than your left one and it's curved and your left one is straight."
>
> Peter did not take offence. "I am probably a very curious
> appearing fellow," he said. (187)

A scene one might reasonably expect to revolve around
social class expresses instead a puzzled fixation on the arbitrary oddities of personal appearance. (What makes less
"sense" than the accident of a human face's asymmetricity?)

Even the human-animal binaries of *Tay John* are at times reduced into the absurdity of the socially awkward turned phrase, like when Rosie reprimands Clay over a plate of ginger snaps—"You've had your tea. Those are for the people"— and the latter responds, "What the Hell do you think I am—a kangaroo?" (153). At once a bizarre joke and an absurdist collapsing of socio-economic difference into the differences between human and (exotic, cartoonish, or geographically distant) animal, Clay's retort registers not only a devolution from telling to showing but also the arbitrary significations and comparisons left behind when class, regional, and cultural oppositions exist in a predictable and resolved state.

It is in a similar confusion of arbitrary difference and meaningful character trait that the novel's self-reflexive depictions of materialism and consumption dovetail with the pat narcissisms of regional difference. Fairly early on, the text depicts a vast swath of the Anglo-settler world, its cities, towns, regions, and family units at once visible in their distinctness and yet also in their quaint interchangeability:

With the feel of the flannel in her fingers, a great hunger came upon her, for the cloth itself, for the way of life it represented, for the man within it. He was pink and clean. He stood secure above the town, removed from its necessities. Tomorrow, the day after, he would be gone. She would see him no more. He was a man of business and affairs, his roots in the East, in England. He moved in the world at large. In Vancouver on the Coast, in Montreal, other people would be waiting for him, other girls, other afternoons. ... And even now Slim might be knocking on the backdoor of the Wamboldts' house. (50)[9]

---

9   The at once abrupt, exotic, and entirely familiar intrusion of the New Zealander Mr. Branchflower later in the text adds to the totality of this picture of Anglo-settler societies.

The slipperiness of individual and local difference at times coalesces with the linguistic play that earlier on marks Selva and Edna as logical counterparts, like when Selva's monologue embodies Peter's mother and her selection of female objects: "And now this last time, you ran away again into the mountains and you brought back with you this girl with the tawny hair, the long legs, the rude, western accent—or is it that she lacks an accent? Now she too has gone and you have come back to me" (197). As the novel draws to a close, the purposeless, back-and-forth movements of its characters resemble a dance in the enclosed field of incipient settler-colonial totality.

It is thus that the oddly predictable and yet oddly revised mountains of *Tay John* reappear in O'Hagan's "other" novel and its decades-long gestation. Indeed, *The School-Marm Tree* at once expands and restricts the sweeping temporal, spatial, and discursive ambitions of *Tay John*, instead interrogating its own craft and portraying its transatlantic settler universe as largely devoid of the mystery that has made O'Hagan's masterwork such an enduring object of analysis. Its fine-tuning of the themes and techniques of that iconic novel functions as a streamlining of O'Hagan's own realist impulses; the novel fits with Willmott's inverted shells of realism and romance, but, coming decades after the obscured modernism unpacked in *Unreal Country*, it shows us some version of the potential or immanent totality that was coming to envelop and smooth out O'Hagan's beloved Western Canadian hinterland and the shifting, hybrid cultures and individuals inhabiting it. *The School-Marm Tree* therefore may not be quite the achievement that is *Tay John*, but it is nevertheless an intricate, self-reflexive entry in Canada's rich tradition of modern-ish realism.

Works Cited

Arnold, Richard. "Howard O'Hagan: An Annotated Bibliography."
    Fee, pp. 127-59.

Fee, Margery. "Howard O'Hagan's *Tay John*: Making New World
    Myth." *Canadian Literature*, vol. 110, 1986, pp. 8-29.

Fee, Margery, ed. *Silence Made Visible: Howard O'Hagan and* Tay
    John. ECW P, 1992.

Fischman, Sheila. "A Mountain Celebration." Review of *The School-
    Marm Tree* and *The Woman Who Got on at Jasper Station*, by
    Howard O'Hagan. *Montreal Star*, 11 Mar. 1978, p. 39.

Hammill, Faye, and Michelle Smith. *Magazines, Travel, and Mid-
    dlebrow Culture: Canadian Periodicals in English and French
    1925-1960*. U of Alberta P, 2015.

Hill, Colin. *Modern Realism in English-Canadian Fiction*. U of
    Toronto P, 2012.

Hill, Jane W. "The Man Who Digs Mountains." Review of *The
    School-Marm Tree* and *The Woman Who Got on at Jasper
    Station*, by Howard O'Hagan. *Books in Canada*, vol. 7, no. 4,
    Apr. 1978, pp. 18-19.

Hingston, Kylee-Anne. "The Declension of a Story: Narrative
    Structure in Howard O'Hagan's *Tay John*." *Studies in Canadian
    Literature*, vol. 30, no. 2, 2005, pp. 181-90.

Hutcheon, Linda. *The Canadian Postmodern: A Study of Contem-
    porary English-Canadian Fiction*. Oxford UP, 1988.

Jameson, Fredric. *The Antinomies of Realism*. Verso, 2013.

Keith, W.J. "Where Men and Mountains Meet." Review of *The
    School-Marm Tree* and *The Woman Who Got on at Jasper Sta-
    tion*, by Howard O'Hagan. *Canadian Forum*, vol. 58, no. 681,
    June-July 1978, pp. 27-28.

Mackey, Eva. *The House of Difference: Cultural Politics and National
    Identity in Canada*. U of Toronto P, 2002.

Mitchell, Ken. "Howard O'Hagan." *The Canadian Encyclopedia*, 3 April 2014, https://www.thecanadianencyclopedia.ca/en/article/howard-ohagan/.

Morash, Gordon. "Life, Death and Struggle." Review of *The School-Marm Tree* and *The Woman Who Got on at Jasper Station*, by Howard O'Hagan. *NeWest Review*, Apr. 1978, p. 9.

Novak, Barbara. Review of *The School-Marm Tree* and *The Woman Who Got on at Jasper Station*, by Howard O'Hagan. *London Free Press*, 25 Mar. 1978, p. B4.

O'Hagan, Howard. *The School-Marm Tree*. Talonbooks, 1977.

----. *Tay John*. Laidlaw and Laidlaw, 1939.

----. *Wilderness Men*. Doubleday, 1958.

----. *The Woman Who Got on at Jasper Station and Other Stories*. A Swallow, 1963.

Ondaatje, Michael. "O'Hagan's Rough-Edged Chronicle." *Canadian Literature*, vol. 61, Summer 1974, pp. 24-31.

Page, P.K. Introduction. *The School-Marm Tree*, by Howard O'Hagan, Talonbooks, 1977, pp. 7- 10.

Powers, Gordon. "Of Men vs. Mountains, Minus Machismo." Review of *The School-Marm Tree* and *The Woman Who Got on at Jasper Station*, by Howard O'Hagan. *Ottawa Citizen*, 11 Mar. 1978, p. 42.

Roberts, Kevin. "VOIR DIRE as Fictional Structural Procedure in *Tay John*." *Canadian Literature*, vol. 214, Autumn 2012, pp. 194-98.

Robinson, Jack. "Myths of Dominance versus Myths of Re-Creation in O'Hagan's *Tay John*." *Studies in Canadian Literature*, vol. 13, no. 2, 1988, pp. 166-74.

Sartre, Jean-Paul. *Theory of Practical Ensembles*. Translated by Alan Sheridan-Smith, edited by Jonathan Rée, NLB, 1976. Vol. 1 of *Critique of Dialectical Reason*.

Simpson, Audra. "Whither Settler Colonialism?" *Settler Colonial Studies*, vol. 6, no. 4, 2016, pp. 438-45.

Thompson, John. Review of *The School-Marm Tree* and *The Woman Who Got on at Jasper Station*, by Howard O'Hagan. *The Globe and Mail*, 4 Mar. 1978, p. 41.

Willmott, Glenn. *Unreal Country: Modernity in the Canadian Novel in English*. McGill-Queen's UP, 2002.

Legendary Loners and Lonely Acts
Civilization, Freedom, and Sovereignty in *Wilderness Men*

ALBERT BRAZ

> "The belief that it is possible to stand beyond the culture in some decisive way is commonly and easily held. In the modern world it is perhaps a necessary belief."
> —*Lionel Trilling*

Howard O'Hagan has become almost totally identified with a single book, his ground-breaking 1939 novel *Tay John*. However, he is also an accomplished creator of short fiction and, perhaps more importantly, of true-life stories or sketches. As befits someone who grew up in the foothills of the Rocky Mountains, O'Hagan is particularly adept at capturing the experiences of solitary men who attempt to evade or at least resist modern civilization by seeking refuge in the wilderness. His best-known sketches appear in his collection *Wilderness Men* and, while they tend to be interpreted as little more than blueprints for subsequent works of fiction, they shed much light both on O'Hagan's literary oeuvre and on his conception of the world. Almost all of them focus on the conflict between civilization and nature, dramatizing the pervasive human desire to escape organized society. Since they are chiefly located in Canada, a settler society still riven by the seemingly insurmountable divide between its Indigenous and non-Indigenous inhabitants, they also reveal a deep anxiety about the country's colonial roots.

The human relationship to nature is obviously a pivotal one, perhaps the quintessential human relationship. Harking back to the archetypal story of Cain and Abel, it pits the hunter against the agrarian (and later the industrial and post-industrial), a contest that seems to have been predestined to be won by the latter (Wiebe, "Louis Riel" 199). As Sigmund Freud notes, social and cultural progress has long been equated with the domination of nature by humans. "We recognize," writes the founder of psychoanalysis, "that countries have attained a high level of civilization if we find that in them everything which can assist the exploitation of the earth by man and in his protection against the forces of nature—everything, in short, which is of use to him—is attended to and effectively carried out" (*Civilization* 45). Freud is aware that such extensive control of nature by humans is not wholly positive, since the result is that "they would have no difficulty in exterminating one another to the last man" (112).[1] Still, he is perplexed that vast numbers of people have come to embrace the notion that "what we call our civilization is largely responsible for our misery, and that we should be much happier if we gave it up and returned to primitive conditions" (38). Nevertheless, this appears to be the reality. As Lionel Trilling asserts in the passage that serves as epigraph to this chapter, the conviction that one ought to transcend one's culture is not just a common belief but a "necessary" one (xii), as evident in the "hostility to civilization" that permeates so much of modern literature (3; see also 108 and 118).

---

1 Freud admits that, of course, "We shall never completely master nature; and our bodily organism, itself part of that nature, will always remain a transient structure with a limited capacity for adaptation and achievement" (*Civilization* 37).

O'Hagan is thus not anomalous among twentieth-century writers in fashioning a literary universe where people are driven by the desire to flee what they deem civilization. What is striking about him is that he is so knowledgeable of the wilderness in which they seek a haven, especially considering that he is such a worldly figure. In addition to earning a law degree at McGill University, O'Hagan travelled and worked around the world, from California and New York to Australia and Sicily. Thanks to the assistance of his former McGill economics professor Stephen Leacock, he was able to get a job as a publicist for the Canadian Pacific Railway, "recruiting farm labourers in England" (Geddes 86). After that, he joined the Ferrocarril Central Argentino (Central Argentine Railway), as "*Jefe de Publicidad*—'Chief of Publicity'" (O'Hagan, "Accepted" 50). Yet, imaginatively at least, he always returned to his beloved northern Rockies, producing a body of writing that has earned him the moniker of the "Mountain Man of Canadian Letters" (Geddes 84), an epithet that never seems more warranted than in his short nonfiction.

Wilderness Men was first published in the United States in 1958 and comprised sketches of "ten men," three Indigenous historical figures who clashed with Canadian law or their own communities—Almighty Voice, Simon Gunanoot, and Tzouhalem—and seven white "westward-seekers, who sought out the West and came to know it" (O'Hagan, *Wilderness* 1958: 5).[2] When the collection was reprinted in Canada in 1978, it included all the original texts except "Montana Pete Goes Courting," likely because by then O'Hagan had fictionalized some of the material in his short stories "The Tepee" and "The

---

2   To avoid confusion, the few references to the first edition of O'Hagan's collection are followed by the date of publication, *Wilderness*1958; references to the 1978 edition appear simply as *Wilderness*.

White Horse" (Keith 76). The same happened in 1993 when *Wilderness Men* was published jointly with *The Woman Who Got on at Jasper Station and Other Stories* as *Trees Are Lonely Company*. Given that O'Hagan eventually elected to limit his collection to sketches of "nine men" (*Wilderness* 5), and for the sake of accessibility, I will focus mainly on the texts included in his 1978 Canadian edition.

Both O'Hagan's fiction and nonfiction have been characterized as "tales of hearsay" (Geddes 86), being purportedly based on stories that O'Hagan first heard from veteran mountain guides and trappers. However, the sketches that make up *Wilderness Men* differ in crucial ways. Besides the fact that some deal with Indigenous individuals and others with people of European descent, some are the result of extensive research while others are based on the author's personal experiences. For instance, in the foreword to the 1978 edition, O'Hagan acknowledges that he "knew" the subjects of both the opening and closing pieces and that the only reason he used "the third person was ... to preserve the same point of view throughout the book" (*Wilderness* 6). The first sketch is particularly effective. Titled "The Black Ghost" and set in 1920, it relates the story of a seventy-five-year-old trapper named "Old" MacNamara,[3] who lives in a small cabin on Yellowhead Lake, on the British Columbia side of the Rockies some 30 kilometres west of Jasper. Long used to living in isolation, MacNamara cannot reconcile himself to the fact that "his little paradise" has been invaded by competing railways (10). Indeed,

---

3   In the sketch, O'Hagan mythifies the identity of "Old" MacNamara by stating that if "he had a proper first name he took it with him to the grave" (*Wilderness* 9). However, in an interview years later, O'Hagan casually identifies the trapper as "Daniel MacNamara" (O'Hagan and Maillard 30), underscoring the constructedness of his nonfiction.

that his way of life may be coming to an end, a predicament with which O'Hagan clearly empathizes.

Because of the collapse of the price of furs with the arrival of the railway on the Rockies, MacNamara is forced to do odd jobs for the doctor in the closest town, which leads him to meet the latter's son, "a seventeen-year-old youth locally called 'Slim' who was home from his studies at McGill" (12). Slim (O'Hagan) discovers MacNamara "to be an artist in words" and, despite vehement opposition by his parents, accepts the old man's invitation to go to his Yellowhead Lake cabin to watch the annual caribou migration (12). During his visit, Slim is told two stories that affect him profoundly.[4] The first is about his host's encounter with what he labels "the Thing." MacNamara tells Slim about an odd experience on a creek near Mount Robson. Even though certain that he was the only person in the whole valley, MacNamara is "roused by a sigh, a sob, and then a crashing in the bush," followed by "a beastlike smell" (14). He senses a presence in the forest, but he cannot see anything. For the first time in his life, he feels utterly alone and petrified, so he empties his rifle's "magazine into 'the Thing That Walked like a Man'" (15). As Slim remarks, "Atavistic man is forever seeking in the shadows that which he most fears to find" (17), underlining how dread of the unknown can rob even a seasoned denizen of the woods like MacNamara of perspective.

The other story that MacNamara shares with Slim involves what the old-timer terms "'the strangest hunt' of his life," an odyssey that "lasted without a break for almost three weeks"

---

4   One assumes that he was probably subjected to other stories, not likely all of them memorable. In "Montana Pete Goes Courting," O'Hagan writes: "The fiction that the backwoodsman is usually taciturn needs to be exploded. He is, in fact and with exceptions, an inveterate gossip and teller of tales. Were it not for this, his experiences would not have been so amply recorded" (*Wilderness* 1958: 227-28).

(18). At the beginning of his journey, MacNamara beats the "brains out" of a porcupine he comes across simply because trappers have a deep aversion to the spiny-coated rodents for destroying all their possessions, notably their foodstuffs (18). But this would turn out to be "the last [porcupine] he was to lift his hand to in anger" (19). Soon after, he spots the tracks of a wolverine who had unsuccessfully attempted to steal the cache of food MacNamara had hidden—but not before ripping his cabin apart while avoiding the many traps he set for it. No matter what MacNamara tries, the wolverine evades him. At one point, "the four-footed, evil-smelling marauder" not only manages to hurl his "whole winter's grubstake" on the snow but renders it inedible with its scent (22). Following two weeks of pursuing the wolverine, MacNamara is forced to concede defeat, that he is "pitted against an adversary with a mind as nimble as his and a body more agile than his own." This admission follows his discovery that sometimes, instead of "stalking the wolverine," it is the wolverine that is "stalking him" (24). Yet an extremely cold morning a few days later, MacNamara gets "a glimpse of the wolverine ... the first time he had seen one alive" in all his years in the mountains (24). So he immediately resumes his chase of his nemesis. But when he finally encounters the wolverine, he is dying, not because of anything MacNamara does, but due to a devastating attack by a porcupine. The lethal strike leaves the wolverine's "muzzle and face ... so barbed with porcupine quills that there, in the tree-shrouded dusk, he resembled the bristled horror of a childhood dream" (25), giving credence to O'Hagan's claim that if it were "not for the porcupine, the wolverine would be the ruler of the bush" (26; see also O'Hagan, *School-Marm* 229). MacNamara is so grateful to the porcupine that he undergoes what Slim calls a "conversion" (26) and, from then on, never harmed another member of the species.

The last sketch in the collection also involves an alliance between a human and a wild animal. "I Look Upward and See the Mountain"[5] chronicles the experiences of the Dutch-born painter Jan Van Empel in the Rockies in the late 1920s. By the time he arrived in Jasper from New York, where he had grown up and studied art, Van Empel was best-known for his Alaska landscapes. Yet, for O'Hagan, he was "as truly a wilderness man" as MacNamara and the other personages that populate his book, one whose "life was a quest for mountains" (175). That being said, O'Hagan remarks that the townspeople find Van Empel's presence in the community "at least 'peculiar,'" considering that he does not seem to work for a living and can go for days without leaving the shack he has rented, conjuring visions that he might be "a wizard ... brewing enchantments against those around him" (176). Such suspicions appear to be confirmed when Van Empel exhibits some of his paintings at the local drugstore, including one in which he "had put a tilted outhouse well into the foreground of a town scene, snow-covered mountains looming above" (177; see also *School-Marm* 38). Moreover, when Jasperites protest that most of the town's dwellings "now had septic tanks and that the showing of outhouses would offend summer tourists," Van Empel is unrepentant, responding that "the outhouse is there, so I paint it" (177). He further quips that if the local people show him how to paint a septic tank, he will do it too.

O'Hagan portrays Van Empel as one of "those pilgrims who, since the dawn of history, have come to the mountains to search for what they would never find" (180). Even though

---

5   In the 1958 edition of *Wilderness Men*, the sketch bears the slightly longer title of "'I Look Upward and See the Mountain against the Sky'" (245), with the title itself appearing in quotation marks, which explains the double set of quotation marks.

the painter knows that each person sees a mountain differently, he says that, as "an artist, I look for what is inside the mountain, something that is like a magnet and draws me to it. The mountain as a force, that is what I want people to feel when they look at what I have done" (181). The length to which Van Empel would go to know the mountains intimately, instead of just being content with photographs of the alpine scenery like tourists, is evident when he hitches a ride in the cabin of a locomotive to Mount Robson. He spends part of the trip sitting on a contraption above the cowcatcher, an experience that enables him to witness a grizzly racing against the train. This episode presages a closer encounter that he has later on with two other bears, as he inadvertently gets caught between a female grizzly and her cub. Because of his fascination with "places where man once had lived, but lived no more" (186), Van Empel decides to explore an abandoned cabin at the end of a clearing. But as he steps over the threshold, he senses that he is not alone and freezes. At first, all he can hear is the flowing water of a nearby river and what sounds "like a child's muted sob—a child incongruously lost in the forest and wanting his way home" (187)—but then he spots the grizzly. Faced with a rock wall at one end and unable to climb the high-branched trees, Van Empel feels that his only possible escape is by wading the river. But the bear would not allow him to move in that direction, even if she did not threaten him. Not only that, as he backs toward the mass of roots that has grown over a fallen balsam tree behind the cabin, the grizzly seems to be leading him. He soon discovers why, as her cub has become ensnared in the tree's roots and is unable to extricate himself. Under the vigilant eyes of the grizzly, always making sure that he never gets between her and her offspring, the "thoroughly frightened" Van Empel (187) gingerly proceeds to untangle the cub from the roots, until he runs off to rejoin his awaiting progenitor. As Van

Empel explains later, it was as if the grizzly "had herded him towards her young one with what vague hope in her animal mind only God would know" (188). Ironically, three years after surviving his fateful encounter with the grizzly and her cub in the wilds of the Canadian Rockies, Van Empel got killed as a result of a car accident in New Mexico, still searching for mountains. But the moral of the text seems to be that Van Empel and the grizzly establish "a community of interest" (188), a bond that enables the painter to free the cub and then to relate the story to a young mountain guide, the future author Howard O'Hagan.

If anything, the idea of a community of interest between humans and wild animals is even more central in "Grey Owl." In his review of the first edition of *Wilderness Men*, the distinguished librarian Bruce Peel asserts that, of O'Hagan subjects, none is "more interesting" than the enigmatic English-born conservationist and nature writer Archie Belaney who pretended to be Indigenous (79). It is certainly difficult not to notice the author's identification with the man that came to be known as Grey Owl. O'Hagan opens his text by stating that while the wilderness is a place where misanthropes like MacNamara can escape society, it can also serve as "a stage" where people can reinvent themselves (*Wilderness* 95). One such individual, he argues, is Belaney, the begetter of Grey Owl. This is the reason that the professed death of Grey Owl on April 13, 1938, marks the demise of someone "who had never, in fact, been born" (95). Grey Owl could not die physically because he was Belaney's "imaginary man" (113), the creation that would so categorically overshadow its maker.

To this day, the most polemical aspect of the story of the trapper-turned-conservationist is his self-fashioning as someone of mixed Indigenous and Scottish ancestry, a transformation that has led some critics to label him nothing less than "a wanton cultural appropriator" (Taylor 120). O'Hagan does not deny that Belaney deceived people about his ethnocultural background, including his wives and his publishers, not the least O'Hagan's old Jasper friend Lovat Dickson. Yet he maintains that the imposture should not be allowed to eclipse Belaney's/Grey Owl's achievements as someone who used his books to urge "tolerance towards the Indian" and who was instrumental in saving "the beaver from extinction" (*Wilderness* 96). O'Hagan goes as far as contending that Belaney "not only impersonated an Indian, he became one to such an extent that his true identity was lost in the process . ... Only by being an Indian could he speak forthrightly for them and for their 'little people,' the beaver" (97). In other words, for O'Hagan, Belaney's metamorphosis into Grey Owl is not so much an act of cultural appropriation as an act of self-abnegation, one for which he surrenders his own identity.

O'Hagan's affinities with Grey Owl have much to do with the latter's success as a writer. While admiring Grey Owl for his conservationism on behalf of wild animals like the beaver, O'Hagan is particularly impressed by his extraordinary ability to find an international audience for his tales about Canadian nature. During the Great Depression no less, Grey Owl became "a 'best-seller'" with books such as *Men of the Last Frontier* and *Pilgrims of the Wild*, which were read avidly around the world (95). Even more notable, he not only produced a series of widely popular books but gave the world a new literary territory, "'Grey Owl country,' a nebulous region of forest and stream in the Canadian hinterland" that, by the late 1930s, "was already in common use" (113). The currency of the term internationally is reflected in the fact that, when *Tay John* was published in Great Britain in 1939, a London newspaper carried an advertisement billing it as "A Novel of the Grey Owl country" (qtd. in Fee, "Canonization" 98; see also

Dickson 20).[6] Whatever his ethical shortcomings, Grey Owl is clearly a literary precursor.

In contrast to Grey Owl, the even more elusive individual at the centre of "The Man Who Chose to Die" attempted to form a community of interest with neither humans nor nonhumans. The man who came to be known to history as Albert Johnson was also a product of the Great Depression. He appeared mysteriously in the Northwest Territories hamlet of Fort McPherson in the summer of 1931 and before the end of the year would trigger one of the most famous manhunts in Canadian history. After a Gwich'in trapper alleged that Johnson had tampered with his traps, the Mounted Police first attempted to notify Johnson of the charge. When he ignored them, they decided to serve him with a warrant for his arrest, but he responded by shooting at them. This precipitated a forty-eight-day pursuit across parts of the Northwest Territories and the Yukon, in the depths of an Arctic winter, which would end with Johnson's death on February 17, 1932 (North 3-47). In addition to Indigenous and white trappers, the Mounties were assisted by the First World War ace pilot Wilfrid "Wop" May. Still, by the time the chase was over, they had lost one constable and two were wounded.

The extensive radio coverage of the pursuit of the so-called Mad Trapper of Rat River turned him into an international hero. People were in awe of his seemingly superhuman endurance and, considering that millions "walked in gloom, not

---

6   Considering O'Hagan's friendship with Lovat Dickson, who became Grey Owl's publisher in the United Kingdom and who was instrumental in his gaining an international readership, Margery Fee states that she finds it "difficult not to speculate what would have been different for O'Hagan had he sent [*Tay John*] to Dickson, rather than to Laidlaw and Laidlaw" (note to Dickson 20).

understanding the [economic] disaster that had come upon them," the one-sided "struggle of Albert Johnson against the forces which hunted him across the Arctic wastes became symbolic of their own" (O'Hagan, *Wilderness* 65). O'Hagan asserts that, regardless of "his other qualities, Johnson was a man forged in the classic tradition of the North. Hardship was his daily bread and middle name" (75). Like a doomed figure out of classical Greek literature, he was "a man against the world, and against himself, one who chose to die and yet, until his last breath, fought to live" (80). Nevertheless, there remain many mysteries about the Mad Trapper. For instance, after he died, it was discovered that he carried "almost three thousand dollars" (65), which makes it even more puzzling why "he robbed the traplines of others" (68).[7] For an individual at least temporarily living in the Far North, a predominantly Indigenous region, he conveyed the impression of being someone "who lived beyond, and independent of, the community of his fellows" (66). In short, he neither respected the rights of the local people nor made an effort to be part of the community.

The greatest riddle about the Mad Trapper is his identity, both individual and collective. While he has come to be known as Albert Johnson, one of the few certainties about him is that it is almost surely not his real name. Nationally, he has been "identified as a Swede, a Russian, an American, a Dane, a Finn, a Norwegian, and a Canadian" (North 45), although the most recent forensic evidence suggests that he hailed either from the US Midwest or from a Scandinavian country (Smith 115-16; see also Stolze). Yet, despite his being given a name, his personal identity remains a total enigma, a fact

---

7   In light of his predatory practices, and echoing the title of a 1938 magazine article, Barbara Smith claims that a more appropriate moniker name for Johnson would be "the 'Fiend of Rat River'" (153).

that incidentally complicates some of the most celebrated postulates in O'Hagan's best-known book. Whatever else it may be, *Tay John* is a meditation on names and naming, a rather sophisticated one at that. "It is physically exhausting to look on unnamed country," famously writes O'Hagan. "A name is the magic to keep it within the horizons. Put a name to it, put it on a map, and you've got it. The unnamed—it is the darkness unveiled" (*Tay John* 80). Or as he encapsulates his stance, "Without a name no man is an individual, no individual wholly a man" (87). But in "The Man Who Chose to Die," he seriously undercuts this ostensible link between naming and identity. Following the logic articulated in *Tay John*, O'Hagan states that the reason the Mad Trapper styles himself as Albert Johnson is that "for a man to exist in the world of men must have a name" of his own. At the same time, he counters that "[n]amed, he is nameless" (*Wilderness* 64). That is, a name does not necessarily shed light on what it labels; it merely creates the illusion of such a connection.[8]

Not surprisingly perhaps, not all the sketches *Wilderness Men* are successful, either dramatically or stylistically. This is very much the case of the remaining texts about people of European descent. "The Man Who Walked Naked across Montana" depicts the story of John Colter who early in the nineteenth century escapes a large Blackfoot contingent by, as the title implies, fleeing stark-naked across what is now the state of Montana. But since O'Hagan never conveys why Colter eventually has "enough of Indians and mountains" (93), it is

---

8   As the noted forensic anthropologist Owen Beattie remarked during the 2007 exhumation of Johnson's body, to test his DNA, "If you can't put an actual name to an individual, that's a break in that [identity] chain. 'Albert Johnson' is a first and last name, but is it the *right* first and last name?" (qtd. in Smith 107).

difficult to discern what motivates him or why readers should care. "The Grass Man and Walker among Trees" is arguably even feebler. The story of the pioneering botanist and plant collector David Douglas, after whom the Douglas fir is named, it details his journey from his native Scotland, through North America, to its fatal end in Hawai'i, where he falls into a pit and is horrifically "mangled" by a trapped bullock (155). Yet O'Hagan seems so disengaged from Douglas that he reproduces whole pages of the scientist's own writings, making considerable parts of the text read like an uninspired undergraduate term paper.

O'Hagan, though, is far more successful in the three sketches he devotes to Indigenous historical figures, possibly because those individuals challenge his very concept of the legendary loner, something of which he is fully aware. At the beginning of the book, in the opening paragraphs of the "Old" MacNamara piece, O'Hagan identifies critical differences between his Indigenous and non-Indigenous subjects, differences that arise from their contrasting visions of the individual's relationship to the community. According to O'Hagan, North American Indigenous people at the turn of the twentieth century had "a collective, or tribal conscience ... Life outside the group had little meaning for the tribesman deprived of its social nourishment" (9).[9] This is reflected in the fact that historical "records reveal few 'loners,' as distinct from 'outcasts,' among the tribes of the West—solitary men, voluntarily shunning the company of their fellows. 'Loners,' or 'wilderness men'—are the product of the civilization whose

9   This is one of the reasons that Albert Johnson's isolation appears almost unnatural. Rudy Wiebe, who has written extensively on both Almighty Voice ("Where") and Johnson ("Death," *Mad Trapper*, "Naming," and "Refusing"), maintains that "a Kutchin or Inuvaluit 'loner' seems incredible. It is a contradiction by very concept ... It seems in the Arctic that everyone lives in a community" ("Refusing" 318).

society they have, in large part, rejected" (9). In other words, not only is the social conflict between O'Hagan's Indigenous and non-Indigenous subjects dissimilar, it is not even clear that the former constitute "wilderness men."

One of the most striking aspects of the Albert Johnson story is that the Mounted Police sided so unequivocally with Indigenous people against a white foe. Needless to say, this is not the typical response by Canadian police (or military) forces whenever there is a clash between Indigenous people and settlers in Canada, as O'Hagan's sketches pointedly illustrate. "The Singer in the Willows" chronicles the undaunted resistance against Canadian authority by Almighty Voice who, rather than being "a 'loner,' ... made a lonely stand" (29). For twenty months in 1897 and 1898, just over a decade after the Métis defeat at Batoche, the young Saskatchewan Cree withstood the power of the Mounted Police in "the last pitched battle between the white man and the Indian on the North American plains" (31). Almighty Voice's initial transgression, as O'Hagan underlines, was "the shooting of a white man's steer," but "his more grievous fault was that he had been born an Indian in a tepee of buffalo hides" (31). By the time the struggle ended, with the death of the protagonist and his two even younger Cree companions, three Mounted Police constables and one volunteer had also been killed and several wounded. The settlers in the region and most people across the country, who feared that the skirmish might portend the beginning of an Indigenous uprising, presumably were relieved by the outcome and got set to enjoy Queen Victoria's imminent Diamond Jubilee—like the group of Mounties who learned at their farewell dance in Regina that the "grave news from the North" required that their departure for London be postponed (56). However, O'Hagan notes that for Indigenous people, Almighty Voice's stand "was not a crime, but a deed, and its perpetrator, far from being a murderer was a victim and in time a 'martyr' of the manhunt organized against him" (48). This is the reason that he would emerge as "a legend for his people" (30), starting with his mother, Spotted Calf, who fearlessly follows him to the end and attempts to motivate him to fight with her haunting chants (57).

O'Hagan singles out one Corporal Dickson as the catalyst for Almighty Voice's violent response to his incarceration, by intimating that the prisoner would hang from a scaffold and crows would "peck at his eyes as his body dangled in the autumn winds" (43). But O'Hagan leaves little doubt that the struggle waged by Almighty Voice was not just against one individual, or even a police force, but "a nation, an empire" (30; see also 60-61). That said, he does not exonerate the Mounted Police, who, by turning their modern weaponry on Almighty Voice, "were duly performing the function for which they had been formed" (31). For O'Hagan, the battle in the Minnichinas Hills, north of Saskatoon, was simply the latest in a long series of wars against Indigenous peoples in Canada and the United States. These conflicts may have varied in strategy from one country to the other but they had the same aims, to suppress the First Nations and their cultures. "The Americans," he writes, "killed the Indians in the thousands." The Canadians, in contrast, "took away the Indian's source of living and slowly starved him to death" (38). The Mounted Police, in conjunction with priests and bureaucrats, was of course the main instrument by which the Canadian government was able to enforce its policies.

The settlement of the Canadian West is often associated with civilization and progress, best symbolized by the expansion of the agriculture frontier and the building of the transcontinental railroad. But this is a stage of social organization whose main proponents never seem to have anticipated an active role for Indigenous people. As O'Hagan writes, "By definition, 'to civilize' … means to make a citizen of. 'Civilization' brought no such privilege to the Indian. He was made a social outcast in his own country" (39). The Canadian Confederation evidently did not have a place for Almighty Voice as a citizen, much less as a member of an autonomous ethnonational collectivity within its own borders. The same is true of Simon Gunanoot,[10] the subject of "The Little Bear That Climbs Trees," which is the English transliteration of his Gitxsan name. A well-to-do merchant and rancher from the Hazelton area of northwestern British Columbia, Gunanoot was hunted by the BC Provincial Police for thirteen years between 1906[11] and 1919. Unlike Almighty Voice, Gunanoot ultimately surrendered, but the impact of his conflict with the Canadian authorities was no less devastating.

Gunanoot's ordeal began when two mixed-race ne'er-do-wells, Alex McIntosh and Max Leclaire, got killed separately after leaving a roadhouse near Hazelton. Gunanoot, who was then in his early thirties and physically imposing, was "a distinguished character" in the region who "prided himself on his family" (122). The recipient of a Catholic education, he was married and had two young children. Along with his wife, he owned a small store in Kispiox village, which she ran when he was away prospecting or trapping. Gunanoot had sold his cache of winter furs a few days earlier and stopped at the roadhouse for a drink with his brother-in-law to celebrate. McIntosh and Leclaire had been on "an all-night drunk" and, before long, McIntosh started to cast aspersions on the sexual

---

10 Although O'Hagan spells the surname of his protagonist "Gun-an-noot" (117 ff.), I have adopted the now common spelling of Gunanoot.

11 Early in the text, O'Hagan writes that Gunanoot's hunt lasted for "thirteen years," between "June 19, 1908" and "June 24, 1919" (118), which is only eleven years. However, he later correctly states that the episode began on "June 19, 1906" (119). See Ball.

mores of Gunanoot's wife, claiming that "all [women] have their price ... Yes, even your Christian squaw" (122, 124). He further boasted that "any one of [the women] on the reserve can be bought. I know because I've done it—and Mrs. Gun-an-noot, too" (125). Gunanoot became so incensed by the taunting that he "picked McIntosh up and hurled him, like a sack of flour, into a corner of the bar" (125). A free-for-all ensued and the other patrons forced the combatants out of the premises, but not before Gunanoot was heard shouting: "McIntosh, someday I'll fix you good!" (125). Thus when a few hours later both Leclair and McIntosh were found shot to death, Gunanoot became the primary suspect—indeed, "the only" suspect—and was summarily convicted of "wilful murder" (126).

Gunanoot refused to surrender, however, and disappeared into the familiar neighbouring wilderness, becoming "a phantom, a frequenter of a strange, shadowed land" (128; see also 138). As O'Hagan captures the fugitive's semi-mythical status with one of his signature phrases: "Shadowed, he became the shadower" (130). Tellingly, throughout the manhunt, Gunanoot continued to provide for his family, sometimes by appropriating the supplies left by the parties sent to arrest him. This perhaps explains why he achieved such broad support within the larger community, both Indigenous and non-Indigenous. O'Hagan writes that even after "a price of a thousand dollars" was placed on his head, "none of the several people from outside who met him, nor any of the many trappers and prospectors who knew his whereabouts, attempted to turn him in" (132). Despite his justifiable apprehensions about Canadian justice, Gunanoot was eventually persuaded by his friends and a prominent Vancouver defence lawyer that he would receive a fair trial, and he turned himself to the police. While he was acquitted of the charges against him, by then he was "a broken, beaten man" (138) and would die a few years later.

Almighty Voice and Simon Gunanoot are obviously not loners who try to flee civilization but rather casualties of a political and legal system that appears to be structurally designed not to deal with Indigenous people in an equitable manner. Consequently, they are embraced as heroes by their peoples. This, however, is not quite the case of the protagonist of O'Hagan's last text on Indigenous historical figures. "Shwat—The End of Tzouhalem" relates the death of a despotic Indigenous war chief, by one of his intended victims. Tzouhalem, whose story unfolds in what is now the Duncan area of Vancouver Island in the first half of the nineteenth century, is unquestionably the oddest personage in *Wilderness Men*. The Cowichan leader is notorious for his violence, being a sadistic hunchback "whose twenty-year record of pillage, rape, murder, and torture is probably unequalled on the West Coast north of the Tropics" (158). He is particularly infamous for his mercenary relations to women, acquiring "some fourteen wives, most of whom had been widowed by him" (Akrigg 174). Fittingly, he was slayed while procuring yet another consort, the Shwat[12] of the title.

O'Hagan opens "Shwat" with a macabre scene in which a young Cowichan man, standing alone in one of Vancouver Island's rocky inlets early one fall evening, discovers his bride of three months floating dead in icy but calm waters. The body of the sixteen-year-old lay lightly on a bed of kelp and, when the man waded into the water, he "saw that the soles of the feet were black and charred, as if they had been slowly roasted. Feeling them, he noticed that in places the flesh was gone and under

12 The spelling of the name of Tzouhalem's avenger varies widely from source to source. The anthropologist Chris Arnett, for instance, calls her "Tsae-Mea-Lae" (46). To avoid confusion, I have decided to follow O'Hagan's spelling.

the instep his fingers touched exposed tendons" (*Wilderness* 158). For the contemporary reader, the scene is likely to evoke *Apocalypse Now* and, through it, the work of one of O'Hagan's favourite authors, Joseph Conrad, especially *Heart of Darkness* (Geddes 86). Yet O'Hagan proceeds to imply that Tzouhalem's life of crime and violence may not have been a total aberration, but partly caused by his cultural environment. Growing up in a part of the Pacific coast where a "caste system prevailed ... and slaves were a form of wealth," the low-status Tzouhalem profoundly resents that he and his family have "no place in the hierarchy of the Cowichans" (*Wilderness* 161, 163). This sense of grievance leads him to wander for years, becoming alienated from his people. Then when he returns home around 1835, after having been away for about two decades, he emerges as "an apostle of violence." Supported by a small army of followers, he "set[s] out to avenge himself upon those who, as he thought, had denied him" (169). Since a leader's prestige depended on "the number of women he had," he becomes determined to "have more than any other" (169). For ten years, he and his followers would behead men and kidnap women almost at will. If the women resisted, he would have them tortured and then killed. He did so until he encountered a woman named Shwat, whom he came upon while she was digging for clams with a shovel-like stick. When Tzouhalem attempted to seize her, Shwat "ran yelling up the path to her cabin," but did not let go of her stick. By the time her husband responded to her urgent calls for help, "Shwat had pinned Tzouhalem's arms to the log wall with her clam-digging stick" and in no time her husband "split the intruder's skull wide open" with his axe (173), putting a decisive end to Tzouhalem's campaign of terror.

Although somewhat idiosyncratic in relation to the other texts in the collection, "Shwat" is a compelling piece of writing. First, in his simultaneously ethnographic and poetic exploration of Tzouhalem's descent into barbarism, O'Hagan dramatizes what Freud terms the fundamental struggle between the individual's "urge for freedom" and "the will of the group" (*Civilization* 50). No less significant, by having women at the centre of "Shwat," O'Hagan illustrates how limited is the male-dominated world of most of his other sketches, which is one of the reasons the conflict between the individual and the group becomes so pronounced. In "The Singer in the Willows" there is already a strong female presence. Even though Almighty Voice is the grandson of Chief One Arrow, who was imprisoned for three years following the Northwest Resistance of 1885 (O'Hagan, *Wilderness* 37), his primary source of inspiration is not his grandfather but his mother. Thus when he defiantly howls his "death chant" at the end of his confrontation with the Mounted Police, it is "Spotted Calf, fifty yards distant on a hillock, [who] joined with him in a quivering treble" (30), having surreptitiously ascended the bluff during the night (57). But while pivotal, Spotted Calf's role is that of the supportive mother. In contrast, the women in "Shwat" are engaged in a war of the sexes, a brutal contest for which many of them pay with their lives. Finally, O'Hagan suggests that the memorialization of people and deeds does not necessarily have much to do with either group achievement or ethics. Given his protracted resistance to his persecution by the authorities, it does not come as a surprise that Simon Gunanoot would have a mountain named after him as testimony to his "endurance and cunning" (119). O'Hagan, though, points out that "Tzouhalem [also] has left his name on a mountain" (159; see also 164). So, judging by collective memorialization, there is little discernible difference between a victim of ethnocultural oppression and a sadist.

Admittedly, some of the sketches in *Wilderness Men* reveal that O'Hagan was not always ahead of his time. Thus the reason Almighty Voice and his people feel "the awful shadow of a

collective doom" (29) is not that they have not yet developed
strategies for dealing with the alien forces that have invaded
their world. Rather, it is that by the late 1890s "on the Canadian prairie a race of men was dying—and with it a way of life
which had endured through the centuries" (32). Similarly, one
moment the Métis are a people who are persuaded to follow
their frenzied leader Louis Riel because, "having no voice in
the laws being foisted upon them from afar, [they] had little
to lose and a country of their own to gain" (37). Yet the next
moment they become a venal hybrid collectivity "who, for a
consideration, would betray those to whom they were allied by
blood" (46).[13] Again, O'Hagan at times is not able to rise above
the dominant stereotypes of the day. Or to phrase it differently,
he can both resist and echo the prevailing national narratives.

To be fair, many of the social contradictions that surface
throughout the collection are really reflections of the systemic
contradictions in Canadian society itself. As mentioned earlier, O'Hagan explains that the main difference between his
Indigenous and non-Indigenous subjects is their dissimilar
attitude toward the larger community. But there is another
critical distinction between the two groups: the non-Indigenous
figures, with their roots elsewhere, have themselves invaded that
which they come to see as paradise. No matter how benevo-
lent their intentions, and how deep their love of the landscape,
they are trespassers on other people's territory, and they know
it. Likewise, regardless of how passionate one may be about
Canada, one cannot avoid the fact that it is a settler society.
Besides, it is not just a society in which diasporic ethnocultural

---

13 Along the same lines, in "Montana Pete Goes Courting," O'Hagan asserts
    that "French *voyageurs* and Scottish traders ... mixed their blood with
    that of the native Cree Indians, as if so to atone for the ingenious rascal-
    ity of their trading" (*Wilderness*1958: 238-39).

groups have dominated its Indigenous inhabitants politically and culturally for generations, but one historically dependent on a staples economy, specifically an economy that trades on the death of nonhuman animals. As Margaret Atwood has a character ask in one of her early novels: "Do you realize ... that this country is founded on the bodies of dead animals? Dead fish, dead seals, and historically dead beavers" (39-40). But we do not need to turn to Atwood to discern the centrality of wild animals in the Canadian economy and, one might venture, the Canadian imagination; it is already there in O'Hagan's sketches. After all, most of his wilderness men engage in that most Canadian of professions, trapping, an activity that is much more imbricated in the civilization-nature divide that people care to acknowledge.

O'Hagan is often praised for his "scornful sense of irony toward civilization," exposing "all civilization as ephemeral and tragic" (Ondaatje 265, 268). But critics tend to ignore that in the author's literary universe life is, if anything, even more evanescent than civilization. This is especially true of nonhuman life. Not only is the trapping of wild animals completely naturalized in the world O'Hagan depicts but, as we have seen with MacNamara, even bona-fide wilderness men can smash the "brains out" of a four-legged creature like a porcupine on a whim. Such nonchalance about killing other animals is probably the result of the fact that, for many of O'Hagan's subjects, trapping is not just part of the economy—it is the economy—as it has been for much of Canada's history. As Harold Innis posits in his magnum opus *The Fur Trade in Canada*, it is not by "accident that the present Dominion coincides roughly with the fur-trading areas of northern North America" (392; see also 262). By killing wild animals for a living, people are therefore not transcending Canadian civilization but rather inserting themselves into its core.

Freud contends that "it is the principal task of culture, its real *raison d'être*, to defend us against nature" (*Future* 8, 26).[14] O'Hagan, however, seriously complicates this idea by showing how dependent Canadians have always been on nature. Moreover, this dependency is evident in the relations to fur-bearing animals by both non-Indigenous and Indigenous Canadians. In "The Singer in the Willows," O'Hagan writes not only that "[t]he white man walked west in North America on a carpet of beaver skins" but also that First Nations, notably the Cree, "lay the carpet at his feet as he crossed Canada" by trapping, hunting, and guiding him through an "intricate [chain of] waterways" (*Wilderness Men* 32). The early entanglements between Indigenous peoples and Europeans in what is now Canada involved significant financial as well as technological exchanges, the latter of which could have devastating environmental impacts. The adoption of even a relatively simple technology like steel traps could hasten the "exhaustion of the beaver fields" (Innis 263), irrevocably altering an ecosystem and underscoring how humans always set the terms of engagement that govern their "communities of interest" with wild animals. Indeed, one of O'Hagan's achievement in his sketches is that he shows not just that Canada owes far more to nonhuman animals than it does to the transcontinental railroad but also how both Indigenous and non-Indigenous peoples have been enmeshed in this economy. By dissecting the relationship between human and nonhuman animals in Canada, Howard O'Hagan identifies at least one commonality between the country's two true solitudes. Unsurprisingly perhaps, it is largely not a positive one.

---

14 Freud, who perceives human culture as comprising "all those respects in which human life has raised itself above animal conditions and in which it differs from the life of the beasts," stresses that he "disdain[s] to separate culture and civilization" (*Future* 8-9).

Works Cited

Akrigg, G.P.V., and Helen B. Akrigg, *1001 British Columbia Place Names*. Discovery Press, 1973.

Arnett, Chris. *The Terror of the Coast: Land Alienation and Colonial War on Vancouver Island and the Gulf Islands, 1849-1863*. Talonbooks, 1999.

Atwood, Margaret. *Surfacing*. McClelland and Stewart, 1972.

Ball, Georgiana. "Simon Peter Gunanoot." *The Canadian Encyclopedia*, 2 June 2008. Accessed 2 March 2019. https://www.the canadianencyclopedia.ca/en/article/simon-peter-gunanoot

Dickson, Lovat. "A Letter from Lovat Dickson." 1985. Fee, *Silence*, pp. 19-20.

Fee, Margery. "The Canonization of Two Underground Classics: Howard O'Hagan's *Tay John* and Malcolm Lowry's *Under the Volcano*." Fee, *Silence*, pp. 97-108.

----. Introduction. Fee, *Silence*, pp. 7-14.

----, ed. *Silence Made Visible: Howard O'Hagan and Tay John*. ECW Press, 1992.

Freud, Sigmund. *Civilization and Its Discontents*. 1930. Edited and translated by James Strachey. W.W. Norton, 1989.

----. *The Future of an Illusion*. 1928. Edited by James Strachey and translated by W.D. Robson-Scott. Martino Publishing, 2010.

Geddes, Gary. "The Writer that CanLit Forgot." *Saturday Night*, vol. 92, no. 9, 1977, pp. 84-92.

Innis, Harold. *The Fur Trade in Canada: An Introduction to Canadian Economic History*. 1930. The University of Toronto Press, 1999.

North, Dick. *The Mad Trapper of Rat River*. Macmillan, 1987.

O'Hagan, Howard. "Accepted by the Penguins." Fee, *Silence*, pp. 50-54.

----. *The School-Marm Tree*. Talonbooks, 1977.

----. *Tay John*. 1939. McClelland and Stewart, 1989.

----. *Wilderness Men*. Doubleday and Company, 1958.

----. *Wilderness Men*. 1958. Talonbooks, 1978.

O'Hagan, Howard, and Keith Maillard. "An Interview with Howard O'Hagan." Fee, *Silence*, pp. 21-38.

Ondaatje, Michael. Afterword. O'Hagan, *Tay John*, pp. 265-72.

Peel, Bruce. Rev. of *Wilderness Men*, by Howard O'Hagan. *Saskatchewan History*, vol. 13, 1960, p. 79.

Smith, Barbara. *The Mad Trapper: Unearthing a Mystery*. Heritage House Publishing Company, 2009.

Stolze, Dolly. "Who Was the Mad Trapper of Rat River?" *Forensic Magazine*, 6 June 2018. Accessed 22 Feb. 2019. https://www.forensicmag.com/article/2018/06/who-was-mad-trapper-rat-river

Taylor, Drew Hayden. "James Owl or Grey Bond." *Further Adventures of a Blue-Eyed Ojibway: Funny, You Don't Look Like One Two*. Theytus Books, 1999, pp. 119-21.

Trilling, Lionel. *Beyond Culture: Essays on Literature and Learning*. Viking Press, 1968.

Wiebe, Rudy. "The Death and Life of Albert Johnson: Collected Notes on a Possible Legend." 1978. *Figures in a Ground: Canadian Essays on Modern Literature Collected in Honor of Sheila Watson*, edited by Diane Bessai and David Jackel. Western Producer Prairie Books, pp. 219-46.

----. "Louis Riel: The Man They Couldn't Hang." Wiebe, *River of Stone*, pp. 188-215.

----. *The Mad Trapper*. McClelland and Stewart, 1992.

----. "The Naming of Albert Johnson." Wiebe, *River of Stone*, pp. 74-91.

----. "On Refusing the Story." Wiebe, *River of Stone*, pp. 303-20.

----. *River of Stone: Fictions and Memories*. Vintage, 1995.

Howard O'Hagan in His Own Words

On *Tay John*'s publication and reception

From Howard O'Hagan's interview to Keith Maillard:[1]

Keith Maillard: I wanted to ask you how you managed to get published in London. Did you have an agent in England?

Howard O'Hagan: Yes. It was a chancy proposition. I met someone in Berkeley, California. I was introduced to Margaret Peterson, who is now my wife [to someone who] had the name of this Margaret Watson, and she sold the manuscript of *Tay John* to Laidlaw and Butchart, a very small publishing firm in London. This was in 1939. It got top of the column in the literary supplement of the *Times* of London. They said it was a novel that would be long remembered, among other things. And Frank Swinnerton wrote it up in the *Observer* paper, but it received no notice whatever in the United States and very little in Canada. it's still on the shelves, as McClelland and Stewart published it ...

  [...]

Maillard: Can I ask you something about the reception that *Tay John* had? You said it was reviewed in the *Observer* and the *Times*.

O'Hagan: Yes, it was the literary supplement of the *Times* in London. The top of a column. The book didn't sell worth a damn.

---

1 For the full text of the interview, please see: Maillard, Keith. "An Interview with Howard O'Hagan." *Silence Made Visible: Howard O'Hagan and* Tay John, by Margery Fee, ECW, 1992, pp. 21-38.

Maillard: But was there any notice taken of it in Canada?

O'Hagan: Very little. The *Edmonton Journal* and the Vancouver *Province* were the ones I remember. But I didn't subscribe to a clipping bureau, so I don't know.

Maillard: Did you meet anyone because of *Tay John*? Did anyone come around and talk to you after that?

O'Hagan: No. No one showed any interest in *Tay John* at all until about four years ago. We had just come back from Sicily, and we went out to lunches and dinners and whatnot, and people were talking about *Tay John*. Of course, they hadn't read *Tay John*, but they were looking forward to reading it. Anyway, I wondered what sparked this interest. … when I learned about George Woodcock having put two or three paragraphs [about *Tay John*], I wrote him to tell him why I was surprised, and so on. He wrote me back that he was not the only one who admired *Tay John*, there was Michael Ondaatje, and he sent me Michael's article in *Canadian Literature*. …

On writing *Tay John*

From Howard O'Hagan's interview to Keith Maillard:

Maillard: How did you come to write it?

O'Hagan: Well, that I really don't know.

Maillard: Let me try the question a different way. Is there a specific kind of book you were planning to write, or was it something you just felt you had to do?

O'Hagan: No, I don't know. Milton and Cheadle wrote *The Northwest Passage by Land*. They went across Canada on the route now taken by the Canadian National through Yellowhead Pass and down. They had to eat their horses. And they found a skeleton by a fire—by the remains of a fire. The skeleton had no head. And they searched everywhere for the head, but they couldn't find it. So I started this book as a diary by the man who had lost his head, you know. And they wrote the first four chapters on that. And I saw it didn't work, so I rewrote the first chapter, and the second, third, and fourth stayed as they were. But I had no prevision of what the book was going to be at all.

[...]

Maillard: Had you always wanted to write a novel, or did this one sneak up on you?

O'Hagan: I really can't say whether I wanted to write a novel or not. I was doing it.

[...]

When I finished the first part, its utterance was faintly biblical ... mainly. When I got to the end of the fourth chapter, I saw I couldn't go on with this omniscient ...

Maillard: Narrator?

O'Hagan: Yeah. And I was out walking in the Hills behind Berkeley, California, where you overlook San Francisco Bay and can see the fog coming in on a summer day—beautiful sight—pouring through the Golden Gate. And Jack Denham, which was the name of the marine Reporter of the *San Francisco Chronicle*—a man whom I had never met—began to talk to me while I was up there alone. You know, as crazy as this sounds, apocryphal I know, it's so. And I got back to my flat in Berkeley about five o'clock, and I was just full of this but I always worked in the morning and I was determined that I wouldn't start on it until the next morning. I spent a sleepless night, and it was as though this thing had been (this is the fifth chapter, "The Bare Foot") ... as though I were just copying something down. Samuel Taylor Coleridge started to write "Kubla Khan" after he had had an anodyne, and he woke up with his thing right before his eyes and started to copy it down. And he was interrupted by a man on business who held him in conversation for an hour or so, and when he came back there was nothing left to write ...

[There was] a group of us in Berkeley—they were professors. Most of them had PhDs. I just have a BA, LLB. Each man, once a month (we met once a month), had to write the minutes. I was chosen this particular time, and it was just about Mr. Blizzard and Mr. Weatherweary—the dialogue between these two. One of the professors asked me how I did it. He said he couldn't imagine. I said if I knew how I did it I could never do it. And it's the same with writing in general, as distinct from articles.

[...]

There are a lot of things in *Tay John* I wish I'd never written at all. For instance, he has just one hand. No, it's impossible ...

From Howard O'Hagan's interview to Rebecca Wigod:[2]
O'Hagan: It's full of flaws [about *Tay John*] ... I accept my short stories, but *Tay John* is full of flaws ... I don't know how they can teach writing with it.

On possible literary influences

From Howard O'Hagan's interview to Keith Maillard:
Maillard: What sorts of things did you like to read? What other novelists were you reading, or had you read?
O'Hagan: Oh, well, W. H. Hudson, *Far Away and Long Ago*, and Cunningham Graham White, who wrote about the Argentine. It was very odd. I should have read them because I went down to the Argentine to become [chief of publicity for the] *Ferrocaril Central Argentino*. It's an English-owned railroad ... Oh, and I read Joseph Conrad. I'm not a great reader. There are lots of things I haven't read that I should have read. Ecclesiastes has

2   Wigod, Rebecca. "How a Man of Wilderness Became a Man of Words." *Times-Colonist* [Victoria, BC], 9 July 1982, p. 21.

always interested me. It has no real place in the Bible, as far as I can make out, but it's a beautiful job.

[...]

Faulkner was an outstanding writer, no doubt about that. Hemingway, I don't think he's so much of a writer. People can write in the style of Hemingway. No one except Faulkner can write like Faulkner. ... The year Faulkner got the Nobel Prize, Hemingway said, "I would prefer to have worked on *The Old Man and the Sea* then to have got the Nobel Prize." What a petty thing to say. And of course he wouldn't. [...] and his breast beating to make himself a man. I've known other writers who are the same way. They make a profession of being a man. I don't know. That seems to me what you more or less take for granted.

Maillard: Yeah. Ernest really work that way. He overdid it.

O'Hagan: I think some of his short stories are stupendous ...

On the Indigenous motifs in *Tay John*

From Howard O'Hagan's interview to Keith Maillard:

Maillard: ...Was any of the material in *Tay John* based on your personal knowledge of Indians or Indian myth?

O'Hagan: No. Well, of course Tête Jaune was an Iroquois half-breed who had the cache west of what is now Jasper at the juncture of the Swiftwater and the Fraser. He was a trapper and a hunter. But the myth of Tay John's birth is from the Carrier Indians near where what is now Prince George. It was written up by Diamond Jenness, and I think the title is *The Indians of Canada*, but I'm not sure. Anyway, I wrote [Jenness] and told him that I was writing a book and I would like to use this in it. Of course, I didn't need to ask permission because, after all, happenings aren't copyrighted. It's only the writing that's patented. And it's my writing—it's not his writing. But anyway, he wired me that I was welcome to it. So that's about as far as the actual Indian myths concerned me, but I went into Vancouver because instead of calling these people, you know, Broken Knee, or Sitting Bull, or whatnot, I wanted their actual names. And I went to the University of British Columbia to see a professor of anthropology. Damn, but I forget his name now [it was Charles Hill-Tout]. He gave me the names that I've used, which was very decent of him. I think the anthropologists, people who have really studied the Indians, look with some disdain on a man who is an outsider and has only a casual knowledge of it. But I worked with half-breeds on the trail (that's a horrible term—half-breed), and I've heard them maligned and I have found them impeccably honest all the way through. I remember one evening—and of course in those days (60 years ago) they couldn't go into the liquor store—this man ... Plante, who was half Cree and half French Canadian, was [drunk], and he fancied the neckerchief that I was wearing, which was worth probably $0.50. He said he would give me his bridle for it. And his bridle was rolled, with the curbed bit, and worth probably $25 or $30. The next morning I said, "Isaac ... you were pretty drunk last night, weren't you?" He said, "Yes, Howard, I was pretty drunk." I said, "Look, this bridle is worth money." He said, "that neckerchief you're wearing isn't worth anything, so let's just exchange things and put them back where they were." And he spoke perfect English. At another time when I was managing this dude ranch, I took a very well known Edmonton lawyer and politician and his wife to visit Isaac at his teepee. And there were drums sounding in the foothills. Very impressive sound. It seems to come through the ground. I've heard it in Fiji too. And this man spoke pidgin English to Isaac.

Maillard: The people around there would be what—Shuswap?

O'Hagan: No, there were half-breed Crees that lived between Fish Lake, near Brulé and 200 miles north on the Smoky River at a place called Grande Cashe where they went in the wintertime. In the spring and summer they were near Fish Lake, near Brulé. But they weren't true Indians. No, the Shuswaps are a branch of the Salish tribe who settled just under Mount Robson. Most feudal campground I've seen anywhere. Milton and Cheadle encountered them there. And there were a couple of them working for Fred Brewster's outfit, for which I was working. I was at Jasper. They were very different than the Crees. They were short, squat people. The Crees were generally tall and slender ...

On *The School-Marm Tree*

From Howard O'Hagan's interview to Keith Maillard:
O'Hagan: ... [B]ut my interest right now is not so much in *Tay John*. *The School-Marm Tree* is a simple sort of story. George Woodcock wrote it up in a review in the *Times* of Victoria. He complained that the characters were types. Dickens's too. And he said the plot, well you would see it stretching ahead of you. Of course. I mean what's a plot? A plot—you remember the clothes hangers they used to have in the old days standing in the hall or whatnot? That you hang your things on? A pole with hooks? Well, that's what a plot is. A pole with hooks. It's not interesting itself at all. It depends what's hung upon it. But George Woodcock made no such concession. He spoke highly of the work generally, and he liked the short stories especially. He compared them to Camus and Sartre. But you know when you write a book you just set yourself up as a target. You have to accept what's coming. [...] And it doesn't really matter to me so much. But this *School-Marm* is a story whose theme ... is the same theme as *Maria Chapdelaine* by Louis Hémon, a Frenchman, who died in a speeder accident on what was then the Canadian Northern in northern Ontario.

240 The Mountain Man of Letters

And it's the same theme as *Wild Geese* by Martha Ostenso, except that both these heroines … had their attention fixed on the United States as the place to go, whereas my character, Selva, has—she's in the mountains—her attention riveted on Montreal or an eastern Canadian city. But it's essentially the same. They're trying to get away from where they are and to go somewhere where life is.

On the wilderness tourists and the environment

From Howard O'Hagan's interview to Keith Maillard:
O'Hagan: … Well, I have been a guide in the Rocky Mountains for many, many years off and on, and I took charge one summer of a dude ranch in the foothills near Brulé, just east of Jasper. and I had a good cook, that was the main thing. When you're out on the trail in the mountains with tourists, your horses come first, but here on this dude ranch I had to keep these people occupied from half past seven or eight in the morning until ten or eleven at night, and this just drove me half cuckoo. They weren't interested in me or in the country—that is, most of them. They were interested in talking to one another about hotels where they both stayed or almost stayed, you know—exchanging credentials. We were just servants, and I remember taking one couple in—this was the time of Roosevelt's presidency in the United States—and they spoke to me of the cripple in the White House and I said "your president is very highly regarded up here." They cancelled the reservation. They had to stay one night, anyway. And I took them back to the railroad station the next morning. They didn't think that a mere guide should have an opinion.

[…]

Maillard: In the little introduction that P. K. Page wrote to *The School-Marm Tree* …

O'Hagan: It was pretty good, wasn't it?

Maillard: Yeah, it was. She said you were talking about a presence in the mountains. Could you talk a little about that?

O'Hagan: Well, it's very hard to talk about that. I fully notice it when I've been alone in the wintertime. And it would seem that there was something keeping time with my snowshoes, just off a distance. I couldn't see him. But this has been better portrayed than I could ever do it by a French-Canadian writer whose name I've forgotten [in a poem] called, as I remember, "The Walker on the Snow." It's set in a canyon north of Montreal or Québec, I forget. When men went through that canyon, they felt this presence, or they heard this man snowshoeing in unison with them. The faster they went, the faster he kept up with them. ... It was a very moving poem. But now, you know, the yippies and peace and God knows whatnot have taken over places like the Thompson Valley. ... There are hundreds of them now. We used to go in there with horses, and we'd be the only people there except possibly a park warden, and we have this silence and the flies and mosquitoes, too, to ourselves. But now these people are so poorly bred that they have made a devastation of this beautiful, beautiful valley on its ...

Maillard: Its northern face, isn't it?

O'Hagan: Southern. They are so precipitous that in the wintertime they are still black. They don't hold the snow ... These people have no respect for silence or the rivers running or anything. Why the hell do they go in there at all? I don't know. One has not the authority to keep them out, but there must be some way to discourage them. They destroy the valleys for other people.

Maillard: Edmund Wilson once said that most Americans look on Canada as a playground that, luckily, is situated directly to the north. Well, in some sense, aren't the people you're talking about just modern versions of the tourists who came up to

Jasper? There are more of them now. There is a similar kind of disregard for the environment.

O'Hagan: No. The people I took out (this is before the highway was through—I think the highway people are much the same as these hippies, or whatever they're called), with one or two exceptions, they had high respect for the mountains and everything that went on, and they were full of questions. too many for me to answer. But these other creatures, they don't ask any questions. They think they know it all. ...

On the female characters in *Tay John* and *The School-Marm Tree*

From Howard O'Hagan's interview to Keith Maillard:
Maillard: The one tourist [in *The School-Marm Tree*] who seems to come off fairly sympathetically is the mountaineer. His name's Branchflower?

O'Hagan: Oh, yes.

Maillard: Most of them don't come off too well. But he comes out fairly well. He comes up and he climbs the mountain and makes a pass at Selva and then he goes home.

O'Hagan: Yes, he tried to make a pass at Selva. I don't think he did, did he?

Maillard: Well, she didn't go to his cabin. She says to him ...

O'Hagan: Oh yeah, that's right. And you know why I pulled that out? This girl was typing it for me in a college just on the edge of Duncan near Cowichan Bay. She said, "I think, Mr. O'Hagan, that would destroy my conception of Selva." So I cut it out.

Maillard: Oh—on the original draft Selva went?

O'Hagan: Yeah. [The typist] didn't want to copy it out.

[...]

Maillard: The interesting thing to me about *The School-Marm Tree* was that you had written from a woman's point of view, which seemed very different from *Tay John*. Did you find that hard to do?

O'Hagan: No, I didn't find it hard to do. No, we had George Woodcock again. He says he found it impossible that the girl like Selva who had been just a maid in someone's house should take charge of a dude ranch in the mountains. Well, we had a girl like Selva in the house for four years. She used to do all the shopping. At first my mother kept track of the accounts, but after that she didn't. We had eight or twelve people in to dinner, and this girl Mitzi attended to everything. She looked after the shopping, she did the washing. It was slave work. Twenty-five dollars a month.

[...]

Maillard: I was thinking about two books together in my mind. In *Tay John*, there are only two women—there's the wife ...

O'Hagan: The wife of Swamas, The Indian woman ... I thought she was pretty good. But the other women in *Tay John* are terrible. Just terrible.

Maillard: You mean terribly drawn or terrible people?

O'Hagan: Terribly drawn.

Maillard: You think so?

O'Hagan: Yeah.

Maillard: I thought the wife, Julia Alderson, was well drawn, because you paint her very quickly and you can see her very quickly. She has her high heeled riding boots on, and there is a very quick description of her, but the picture comes quite alive—her chubby hands, that is the one detail. As a character she seems quite real to me. I had a little trouble with Ardith Aeriola.

O'Hagan: I had trouble with both of them. They don't seem to me to be agreeable at all. I mean this Alderson woman comes into the clearing where Tay John is, and her perfume—well it pervades her, it pervades the place. First of all, that's no way to perfume. And secondly, it wouldn't prevail over the smell of horse.

Maillard: But the effect that both those women have on the plot is ... The feeling I had was that it was a very male world with all these men around; McLeod has a picture of a woman on his wall in his cabin just sort of like a vision or a dream. When the real women appear, the whole focus of attention is turned on them, and of course they both cause the plot to happen. It seemed very interesting to me that, having looked at women from that point of view, you should later write another book from inside a woman's mind—*The School-Marm Tree.*

O'Hagan: That's because I didn't get inside the women's minds at all in *Tay John*, except for the Indian woman, Hanni, who was dying. And she said, "Speak to me loudly, for my head lies on a river." I think that's a beautiful line. I don't know where in the hell it came from.

On O'Hagan's short stories and sketches

From O'Hagan's foreword to Wilderness Men, *dated "February 14, 1958, Victoria, B.C.":*[3]

The nine men whose lives are traced in the following pages are of the West. The three Indians—Almighty Voice, Gun-an-noot, and Tzouhalem—being born there, knew no other world than their limited tribal range, except for Gun-an-noot, who had a brief and deadly glimpse of the "outside."

The six others, white men, were westward-seekers, who sought out the West and came to know it. The three Indians, by circumstance, lived up on the fringes of the society which bore them, Almighty Voice and Tzouhalem leaving bloody

---

3   O'Hagan, Howard. *Trees Are Lonely Company*. Talonbooks, 1993, pp. 9-10.

trails in their wake. Similarly, the six white men, though more as a matter of choice, scouted the western rim of civilization in whose cities they found no peace. One of them was to hang his name upon a tree. Another to have his partner's lungs slept across his face. Still another heard death come to him from overhead as he trudged up a river in the far northern tundra.

These nine men, Indian and white alike, have a further bond of union: they met life alone in the somber forests of the Pacific slope, in the uptilted land of the Rockies, on the northern prairies, or in the waste of the Arctic. Even Tzouhalem, with his gang of cutthroats, was a man apart, and Grey Owl, though often married, kept to himself the imposture which enabled him to confront mankind.

The writer knew two of these men as persons. I was the "doctor's son" who went with "Old" MacNamara up the ghostly Grantbrook in Chapter 1. Jan Van Empel, the Dutch-born artist of Chapter 9, I knew in Jasper, Alberta, and later met him while I was taking a pack outfit by Berg Lake behind Mount Robson, British Columbia. The device of the third person was used to preserve the same point of view throughout the book.

From Rebecca Wigod's sketch and interview with O'Hagan:
Back in the 1920s, when he was a young man, O'Hagan worked out of Jasper as a mountain guide and packer. Sitting in his James Bay kitchen, with a glass of watered whiskey close, he remembered how he was called to art in the Rockies.

"The first short story I'd written ("The Tepee"), was based on an evening I spent with Montana Pete. If he has another name, I don't know it. His cabin was on the Little Hay, in the foothills East of Jasper. As you always do, approaching a cabin, you don't knock on the door. You shout to let them know you're coming."

O'Hagan and his lifelong friend Fred Brewster found the mountain man perched on his bed, surrounded by Imperial

Mixture tobacco tins. "He sat on this upper bunk like a Buddha." In the buttery lantern-light, Montana Pete must have unreeled the powerful skein of verbiage. When he told it," said O'Hagan, "I had no idea writing would become a way of life for me."

From Howard O'Hagan's interview to Keith Maillard:
O'Hagan: [...] the pieces I've had published—short stories and so on—I've rewritten four or five times.

   [...]

We were living in Lucerne—my mother and my father and me and my sister. There was an old trapper across Yellowhead Lake ... This old man—he was about 60, the youngster to me now (I'm 77)—and these mountain goats were over on the north side of the Seven Sisters, which is a range above a lake. And just before the first snow came, two or three days before, the goats would come over into the south side of the mountain because they have sort of a built-in barometer. They knew what was coming. And they would trickle down through the gulleys of Seven Sisters. There were about 40 or 50 of them and they were as white as snow. They'd shed their winter coats, and they were growing new, and they were as white as the snow, whose harbingers they were. And Daniel MacNamara [the old trapper] would go up to the trap line, and he took me on one of these occasions. Before taking me up, he described to me what it was like above his cabin, which was really like a doghouse when I got to it. He described the pools up in the alp lands of water where the caribou came down to drink. And they were as blue as the sky. I saw them. they were like pieces of sky falling down into the alp lands. The old guy was illiterate, but he had this feeling—although it was a tough life as a trapper—for his environment.

On the writing process

From Howard O'Hagan's interview to Keith Maillard:

Maillard: [...] You've just got me thinking now about some of the images of violence in both your books, and they're very sudden, and they're quite extreme, and they seem to me quite realistic. I think you intended them to be. Did you?

O'Hagan: I don't think one has any intention, you know. Again, aside from my articles, then you have an intention. No, one only sees what he's going to write when he's written it. At least that's been my experience—in what I regard as my good writing. That isn't true of all of *Tay John*. I think *The School-Marm Tree* is better written as a whole.

[...]

O'Hagan: I used to write 1000 words in the morning between nine and twelve or one. Now it's down to about 300. I'm trying to write about my early days in the Rockies. It's coming pretty damn hard. But you know a writer has a wonderful privilege. He can leave his life twice.

Maillard: Yeah, I've found that true myself. People ask me how I can remember certain things; I have a great memory for details because I'm sitting writing about them.

O'Hagan: When I was five or six years old in the Crownsnest Pass in Southern Alberta [our maid] used to take me for walks, and brought me in this night and showed me a little barn owl ... and showed me the first crocus of the spring. It was like a chalice of snow, and I saw water running down ... put my hand out to grab it ... first of the season.

Maillard: You studied under Leacock.

O'Hagan: What a wonderful guy he was. I guess he didn't like the Irish. "Mr. O'Hagan, your handwriting is painstaking enough in its way, but it has a peculiar cussedness."

My handwriting was bad. In law school, the professor gave up trying to read it and asked me to read my paper to him ... If I had read all my papers [aloud] I think I would have got better then second-class honours.

Selected Bibliography

Books:

O'Hagan, Howard. *Tay John*. Laidlaw, 1939.

----. *Tay John*. 2nd ed., introduction by Harvey Fergusson, Clarkson N. Porter, 1960.

----. *Tay John*. 1960. Introduction by Patricia Morley, McClelland and Stewart, 1974.

----. *Tay John*. 1960. Afterward by Michael Ondaatje, McClelland and Stewart, 1989 (reissued in 2008).

----. *The School-Marm Tree*. Introduction by P.K. Page, Talonbooks, 1977.

----. *The Woman Who Got on at Jasper Station, and Other Stories*. Swallow, 1963.

----. *The Woman Who Got on at Jasper Station, and Other Stories*. Talonbooks, 1977.

----. *Trees Are Lonely Company*. Talonbooks, 1993.

----. *Wilderness Men*. Doubleday, 1958.

----. *Wilderness Men*. 2nd ed. Talonbooks, 1978.

Short stories and sketches:

----. "A Mountain Journey." *Queen's Quarterly*, no. 46, 1939, pp. 324-33.

----. "Accepted by the Penguins." *Silence Made Visible*, edited by Margery Fee, ECW Press, pp. 50-53.

----. "Conquest of a Rock." *Toronto Star Weekly*, 22 Aug. 1942, p. 3.

----. "Cuidado Con Los Golpes." *John O'London's Weekly*, 20 May 1938, pp. 245-46.

----. "Her Father's Daughter." *Weekend Magazine*, 29 Jan. 1955, pp. 8, 18, 22, 30.

----. "Her Name... Was Mary." *Event*, no. 5, 1976, pp. 84-96.

----. "How It Came About." *Sydney Mail*, 27 July 1927, p. 16.

----. "Ito Fujika, the Trapper." *Prairie Schooner*, no. 19, 1945, pp. 310-17.

----. "Savoir-Faire." *Maclean's*, 1 Dec. 1939, pp. 7-9, 46-47.

----. "Slim from the Chilcotin." *Silence Made Visible*, edited by Margery Fee, ECW Press, pp. 47-49.

----. "The Colony." *Circle*, no. 7, 1946, pp. 65-67.

----. "The Fabulous Journey." *Weekend Magazine*, 13 Mar. 1954, p. 34.

----. "The Love Story of Mr. Wimple." *Berkley*, no. 2, 1948, pp. 3-5.

----. "The Mad Trapper of Rat River." *Argosy*, Sept. 1954, pp. 32-33, 81-84.

----. "The Man Who Stayed Invisible for Thirteen Years." *Maclean's*, 5 July 1958, pp. 20-21, 34-39.

----. "The Pool." *Story*, Nov.-Dec. 1939, pp. 42-46.

----. "The School-Marm Tree." *Event*, no. 5, 1976, pp. 49-83.

----. "The Stranger." *Queen's Quarterly*, no. 47, 1940, pp. 296-310.

----. "The Tepee." *New Mexico Quarterly Review*, no. 15, 1945, pp. 304-12.

----. "The Warning." *Weekend Magazine*, 21 Nov. 1953, pp. 18-19.

----. "The Warpath of Almighty Voice." *True*, Mar. 1954, pp. 29-31, 79-83.

----. "The White Horse." *Maclean's*, 1 Nov. 1945, pp. 13, 34, 37-39.

----. "Trees Are Lonely Company." *Tamarack Review*, no. 9, 1958, pp. 29-45.

----. "Ursus." *Malahat Review*, no. 50, 1979, pp. 49-64.

Articles:

----. "The Cowboy: A Disappearing Factor." *Sydney Morning Herald*, 9 Apr. 1927, p. 11.

----. "Conquerors of Nature's Giants." *Canadian National Railways Magazine*, Oct. 1930, p. 9.

----. "The Weird and Savage Cult of Brother 12." *Maclean's*, 23 Apr. 1960, pp. 22-23, 34, 36, 39.

----. "The Packhorse on the Moose?" *Islander* [Victoria *Colonist*], 7 May 1961, pp. 12-13.

----. "The Cubs of the Swiftwater." *Islander* [Victoria *Colonist*], 21 May 1961, pp. 2-3.

----. "Dwellers in the Dusk around Us." *Islander* [Victoria *Colonist*], 4 June 1961, pp. 3, 10.

----. "Not All the Pioneers Were Valorous Souls." *Islander* [Victoria *Colonist*], 11 June 1961, pp. 7, 15.

----. "Where the Tide Whispered." *Islander* [Victoria *Colonist*], 25 June 1961, p. 2.

----. "Stephie." *Queen's Quarterly*, no. 68, 1961, pp. 135-46. Reprinted in *McGill News*, vol. 42, no. 3, 1961, pp. 20-22; no. 4, pp. 22-24.

----. "... To Follow Knowledge Like a Sinking Star..." *Islander* [Victoria *Colonist*], 28 Oct. 1962, p. 4.

----. "Parks Need Protection." *Islander* [Victoria *Colonist*], 11 Nov. 1962, p. 4.

----. "Hero of the Long Chase." *Islander* [Victoria *Colonist*], 18 Nov. 1962, p. 16.

----. "Steam Revival for the P.G.E." *Islander* [Victoria *Colonist*], 25 Nov. 1962, p. 3.

----. "Woman with Her Turkies." *Islander* [Victoria *Colonist*], 2 Dec. 1962, p. 13.

----. "When She-Bear Asked for Help." *Islander* [Victoria *Colonist*], 9 Dec. 1962, p. 10.

----. "Death Lurks in Silence." *Islander* [Victoria *Colonist*], 23 Dec. 1962, p. 12.

----. "Coyote's Song to Perish?" *Islander* [Victoria *Colonist*], 30 Dec. 1962, p. 13.

----. "Strange Portents on a Mountain Trail." *Islander* [Victoria *Colonist*], 6 Jan. 1963, p. 16.

----. "The Man Who Took Chilcotin to Australia." *Islander* [Victoria *Colonist*], 13 Jan. 1963, p. 5.

----. "Pushing Back the Frontier." *Islander* [Victoria *Colonist*], 27 Jan. 1963, p. 3.

----. "Reach Up... towards the Stars!" *Islander* [Victoria *Colonist*], 3 Feb. 1963, p. 16.

----. "Breakfasts Must Be Eaten Alone." *Islander* [Victoria *Colonist*], 10 Feb. 1963, p. 3.

----. "Little Duck Abandoned." *Islander* [Victoria *Colonist*], 10 Mar. 1963, p. 11.

----. "For Every Mile a Life Was Taken." *Islander* [Victoria *Colonist*], 17 Mar. 1963, p. 12.

----. "What's Wrong with Walking?" *Islander* [Victoria *Colonist*], 14 Apr. 1963, p. 2.

----. "Diesel Locos Came to Stay." *Islander* [Victoria *Colonist*], 5 May. 1963, p. 13.

----. "The Artist Has a Language All Her Own." *Islander* [Victoria *Colonist*], 12 May. 1963, p. 5.

----. "Writers Need Experience!" *Islander* [Victoria *Colonist*], 2 June 1963, p. 11.

----. "Train-Running: My Most Strenuous Crossing of Canada." *Times* [Victoria, BC], 12 Sept. 1963, p. 4.

----. "New Voice in the Wilderness." Review of *Royal Murdoch*, by Robert Harlow. *Colonist* [Victoria, BC], 30 Dec. 1962, p. 15.

----. "Nobody Has More Fun than an Otter." *Maclean's*, 14 Apr. 1956, pp. 38, 72, 74, 76.

----. "The Wily Wraith that Trappers Hate." *Maclean's*, 1 Dec. 1954, pp. 36, 63-66.

----. "The Long Night." *Islander* [Victoria *Colonist*], 18 Dec. 1960, p. 2.

----. "Roads from Athabasca Tar Sands." *American City*, Sept. 1928, pp. 121-22.

----. "Grizzled Gentlman." *Maclean's*, 1 Jan. 1949, pp. 11, 40-41.

----. "The Strangest Hunt of His Life." *Argosy*, May 1953, pp. 25, 65-67.

----. "The Ghostly Sentinel of Peaks." *Maclean's*, 26 Nov. 1955, pp. 30-31, 46, 48, 52-53.

----. "The Bear Cub Is Everybody's Baby." *Maclean's*, 21 July 1956, pp. 22-23, 34-36.

----. "Cold Disaster." *Islander* [Victoria *Colonist*], 3 Jan. 1960, p. 5.

----. "His Worship the Mayor." *McGill New*, vol. 44, no. 1, 1962, pp. 31-32.

----. "The Hard Way." *Islander* [Victoria *Colonist*], 4 Nov. 1962, p. 16.

----. "Bannock Baker." *Islander* [Victoria *Colonist*], 24 Feb. 1963, p. 16.

----. "Why Have We Lost the Joy of Walking?" *Maclean's*, 11 May 1957, pp. 32, 58, 60, 62.

----. "Man in a Bear Trap." *Islander* [Victoria *Colonist*], 20 Jan. 1963, p. 13.

----. "Color Bar in Canada." *Islander* [Victoria *Colonist*], 17 Feb. 1963, p. 11.

----. "A Secret in the Barn." *Islander* [Victoria *Colonist*], 3 Mar. 1963, p. 5.

----. "Death at His Heels." *Islander* [Victoria *Colonist*], 21 Apr. 1963, p. 11.

----. "The Trail Blazers." *Islander* [Victoria *Colonist*], 21 Oct. 1962, p. 4.

----. "The Chinese Laughed." *Islander* [Victoria *Colonist*], 16 Dec. 1962, p. 11.

----. "We Are Not Alone." *Islander* [Victoria *Colonist*], 25 Oct. 1959, p. 12.

----. "Slow Men Working." *Islander* [Victoria *Colonist*], 28 Apr. 1963, p. 16.

Books, articles, and book chapters on Howard O'Hagan:

Arnold, Richard. "Howard O'Hagan: An Annotated Bibliography." Fee, *Silence Made Visible*, pp. 127-59.

Asai, Akira. *Asian Shadows in Canadian Literature: A Comparative Study of Howard O'Hagan's* Tay John. NCI, 1986.

Atwood, Margaret. "Canadian Monsters." *The Canadian Imagination: Dimensions of a Literary Culture*, edited by David Staines, Harvard UP, 1977, pp. 97-122.

Beddoes, Julie. "The Train We Mythed: Crossed Lines in Howard O'Hagan's *Tay John*." *Open Letter*, no. 7, 1990, pp. 74-83.

Bentley, D. M. R. "The Wide Circle and Return: *Tay John* and Vico." *Dalhousie Review*, vol. 73, no.1, 1993, pp. 34-53.

Braz, Albert. "Fictions of Mixed Origins: *Iracema*, *Tay John*, and Racial Hybridity in Brazil and Canada." *AmeriQuests,* vol. 10, no. 1, 2013, pp. 1-9.

Davidson E. Arnold. "Being and Definition in Howard O'Hagan's *Tay John*." *Études Canadiennes*, vol. 15, 1983, pp. 137-47.

----. "Silencing the Word in Howard O'Hagan's *Tay John*." *Canadian Literature*, vol. 110, Fall 1986, pp. 30-44.

Fee, Margery. "Howard O'Hagan's *Tay John*: Making New World Myth." *Canadian Literature*, vol. 110, Fall 1986, pp. 8-27.

----. Introduction. *Silence Made Visible*, edited by Margery Fee, pp. 7-14.

----. "A Note on the Publishing History of O'Hagan's *Tay John*." Fee, *Silence*, pp. 85-91.

----, ed. *Silence Made Visible: Howard O'Hagan and* Tay John. ECW, 1992.

----. "The Canonization of Two Underground Classics: Howard O'Hagan's *Tay John* and Malcolm Lowry's *Under the Volcano*." Fee, *Silence*, pp. 97-108.

Fenton, William. "Parody in O'Hagan's *Tay John*." *Canada: Ieri e oggi 2*, edited by Giovanni Bonnanno, Schena, 1986, pp. 55-73.

----. "The Past and Mythopoesis." *Re-Writing the Past: History and Origin in Howard O'Hagan, Jack Hodgins, George Bowering and Chris Scott*, Bulzoni 1988, pp. 15-64.

Fergusson, Harvey. Introduction. *Tay John*, by Howard O'Hagan, Potter, 1960.

Granofsky, Ronald. "The Country of Illusion: Vision, Change, and Misogyny in Howard O'Hagan's *Tay John*." Fee, *Silence*, pp. 109-126.

Geddes, Gary. "British Columbia, Writing in." *The Oxford Companion to Canadian Literature*, edited by William Toye, Oxford UP, 1983; 2nd ed., edited by William Toye, Oxford UP, 1997, pp. 144-45.

----. "The Writer That CanLit Forgot." *Saturday Night*, Nov. 1977, pp. 84-92.

Hancock, Geoff. "O'Hagan, Howard." *The Oxford Companion to Canadian Literature*, edited by William Toye, Oxford UP, 1983; 2nd ed., edited by William Toye, Oxford UP, 1997, pp. 880-81.

Harrison, Dick. *Unnamed Country: The Struggle for a Canadian Prairie Fiction*. U of Alberta P, 1977, pp. ix, ff.

----. "The Deep Pool of the Unconscious: *The Man Who Killed the Deer* and *Tay John*." *Studies in Frank Waters VII: An Appreciation*, edited by Charles L. Adams, Frank Waters Society, 1985, pp. 45-55.

Hingston, Kylee-Anne. "The Declension of a Story: Narrative Structure in Howard O'Hagan's *Tay John*." *Studies in Canadian Literature/Etudes en Litterature Canadienne*, vol. 30, no. 2, 2005, pp. 181-92.

Jones, D. J. *Butterfly on Rock: A Study of Themes and Images in Canadian Literature*. U of Toronto P, 1970, p. 7, ff.

Kaltembeck, Michèle. "L'Expansion vers l'ouest dans *Tay John* de Howard O'Hagan." *Essays on Canadian Writing*, vol. 21, 1995, pp. 193-204.

256   The Mountain Man of Letters

Keith, W. J. *A Sense of Style: Studies in the Art of Fiction in English-Speaking Canada.* ECW, 1989, pp. 23-39.

----. *Canadian Literature in English.* Longman, 1985, pp. 138-39.

----. "Howard O'Hagan, *Tay John,* and the Growth of Story." Fee, *Silence,* pp. 73-84.

Kroetsch, Robert. "The Veil of Knowing." *The Lovely Treachery of Words: Essays Selected and New,* Oxford UP, 1989, pp. 179-94.

Maillard, Keith, and Howard O'Hagan. "An Interview with Howard O'Hagan." Fee, *Silence,* pp. 21-38.

Maud, Ralph. "Ethnographic Notes on Howard O'Hagan's *Tay John.*" Fee, *Silence,* pp. 92-96.

Mitchell, Ken. "Howard O'Hagan." *The Canadian Encyclopedia,* 3 April 2014, https://www.thecanadianencyclopedia.ca/en/article/howard-ohagan/.

Monkman, Leslie. *A Native Heritage: Images of the Indian in English-Canadian Literature.* U of Toronto P, 1981, pp. 44-48.

Morley, Patricia. "Introduction to the New Canadian Library Edition." *Tay John,* by Howard O'Hagan, McClelland and Stewart, 1974, pp. vii-xiv.

Moss, John. *A Reader's Guide to Canadian Literature.* McClelland and Stewart, 1981, 221-22.

Ondaatje, Michael. Afterword. *Tay John.* Toronto: McClelland, 1989, pp. 265-72.

----. "Howard O'Hagan and the 'Rough-Edged Chronicle.'" *Canadian Literature,* vol. 61, Summer, 1974, pp. 24-31.

Page P. K. Introduction. *The School-Marm Tree,* by Howard O'Hagan, Talonbooks, 1977, pp. 7-10.

Pivato, Joseph. "Forest of Symbols: *Tay John* and *The Double Hook.*" *Sheila Watson: Essays on Her Works,* edited by Joseph Pivato, Guernica, 2015, pp. 181-196.

Roberts, Kevin. "VOIR DIRE as Fictional Structural Procedure in "Tay John." *Canadian Literature,* vol. 214, Autumn 2012, pp. 194-98.

Robinson, Jack. "Myths of Dominance Versus Myths of Re-Creation in O'Hagan's *Tay John*. *Studies in Canadian Literature/Etudes en Litterature Canadienne*, vol. 13, no. 2, 1988, https://journals.lib.unb.ca/index.php/scl/article/view/8084/9141

----. "Dismantling Sexual Dualities in O'Hagan's *Tay John*." *Alberta*, vol. 2, no.2, 1990, pp. 93-108.

Scobie, Stephen. *Signature, Event, Context*. NeWest, 1989, p. 141.

Stouck, David. "The Art of the Mountain Man Novel." *Western American Literature*, vol. 20, 1985, pp. 211-22.

Tanner, Ella. *Tay John and the Cyclical Quest: The Shape of Art and Vision in Howard O'Hagan*. ECW, 1990.

Yakovenko, Sergiy. "A Deceptive Initiation: An Ecological Paradigm in Howard O'Hagan's *Tay John*." *Le Simplegadi*, vol. 15, 2017, pp. 284-94.

Zichy, Francis. "Crypto-, Pseudo-, and Pre-Postmodernism: *Tay John, Lord Jim*, and the Critics." *Essays on Canadian Writing*, vol. 81, Winter 2004, pp. 192-221.

---. "The 'Complex Fate' of the Canadian in Howard O'Hagan's *Tay John*." *Essays on Canadian Writing*, vol. 79, Spring 2003, pp. 199-225.

Selected book reviews:

Bilan, R. P. Review of *The School-Marm Tree*. *University of Toronto Quarterly*, vol. 47, 1978, pp. 331-32.

Fischman, Sheila. "A Mountain Celebration." Review of *The School-Marm Tree* and *The Woman Who Got on at Jasper Station*, by Howard O'Hagan. *Montreal Star*, 11 Mar. 1978, p. 39.

Hancock, Geoff. "Short Stories Back with a Bang." Review of *Wilderness Men*. *Toronto Star*, no. 31, D7.

Harrison, Dick. "The O'Hagan Range." Review of *The School-Marm Tree. Canadian Literature*, vol. 81, 1979, pp. 116-18.

Hill, Jane W. "The Man Who Digs Mountains." Review of *The School-Marm Tree* and *The Woman Who Got on at Jasper Station*, by Howard O'Hagan. *Books in Canada*, vol. 7, no. 4, Apr. 1978, pp. 18-19.

Keate, Stuart. "Intruder in the Wilderness." Review of *Tay John. New York Times Book Review*, 13 Mar. 1960, p. 34.

----. "With Trap-Line and Gold Pan." Review of *Wilderness Men. New York Times Book Review*, 19 Oct. 1958, p. 48.

Keith, W.J. "Where Men and Mountains Meet." Review of *The School-Marm Tree* and *The Woman Who Got on at Jasper Station*, by Howard O'Hagan. *Canadian Forum*, vol. 58, no. 681, June-July 1978, pp. 27-28.

Markin, Allan. Review of *Wilderness Men. Canadian Book Review Annual*, Peter Martin, 1978, pp. 30-31.

Morash, Gordon. "Life, Death and Struggle." Review of *The School-Marm Tree* and *The Woman Who Got on at Jasper Station*, by Howard O'Hagan. *NeWest Review*, Apr. 1978, p. 9.

Novak, Barbara. Review of *The School-Marm Tree* and *The Woman Who Got on at Jasper Station*, by Howard O'Hagan. *London Free Press*, 25 Mar. 1978, p. B4.

Peel, Bruce. Revie. of *Wilderness Men*, by Howard O'Hagan. *Saskatchewan History*, vol. 13, 1960, p. 79.

Powers, Gordon. "Of Men vs. Mountains, Minus Machismo." Review of *The School-Marm Tree* and *The Woman Who Got on at Jasper Station*, by Howard O'Hagan. *Ottawa Citizen*, 11 Mar. 1978, p. 42.

Robertson, George. "Mountain Man Mythology." Review of *Tay John. Canadian Literature*, vol. 9, 1961, pp. 65-66.

Schmuck, John. Review of *Tay John. Library Journal*, 1 Apr. 1960, p. 1474.

Stow, Glenys. "A Discordant Heritage." Review of *Tay John*. *Journal of Canadian Fiction*, vol. 16, 1976, pp. 178-81.

Swinnerton, Frank. "New Novels." Review of *Tay John*. *Observer*, 19 Mar. 1939, p. 6.

Thompson, John. Review of *The School-Marm Tree* and *The Woman Who Got on at Jasper Station*, by Howard O'Hagan. *The Globe and Mail*, 4 Mar. 1978, p. 41.

Watt, F. W. "Letters in Canada: Fiction." Review of *Tay John*. *University of Toronto Quarterly*, vol. 30, 1961, pp. 414-15.

Woodcock, George. "Howard O'Hagan and Living Wilderness." Review of *The School-Marm Tree* and *The Woman Who Got on at Jasper Station*. *Times* [Victoria, BC], 18 Mar. 1978, p. 14.

----. "You Can't Judge a Book by Its Past." Review of New Titles in the New Canadian Library Series. *Maclean's*, May 1974, p. 100.

Contributors

D. M. R. BENTLEY is a Distinguished University Professor and the Carl F. Klinck Professor in Canadian Literature at Western University. He has published widely in the fields of Canadian literature and culture and Victorian literature and art, and on the importance of the Arts and Humanities in society. His recent and forthcoming publications include essays on Thomas Moore, Archibald Lampman, Gabrielle Roy, Alice Munro, Dante Gabriel Rossetti, Algernon Charles Swinburne, Aubrey Beardsley, and T.S. Eliot. In 2015 he was awarded the Killam Prize in Humanities.

ALBERT BRAZ is Professor Emeritus of Comparative Literature and English at the University of Alberta. A comparatist whose research focuses on Canadian and inter-American literature, he is especially interested in the relations between national/regional and world literature. In addition, he has worked extensively on translation and the status of real-world figures in literature. Among other texts, he is the author of *Apostate Englishman: Grey Owl the Writer and the Myths* (2015) and *The False Traitor: Louis Riel in Canadian Culture* (2003).

KYLEE-ANNE HINGSTON is an Assistant Professor of English at St. Thomas More College, University of Saskatchewan, where she teaches on Victorian literature, children's literature, and disability in literature. Her book *Articulating Bodies* (2019) examines how Victorian fiction articulates concepts of disability through patterns of focalization and narrative structure. Her current research centres on the intersection of disability and theology in Victorian popular religious magazines.

RENÉE HULAN is a Professor of English Language and Literature at Saint Mary's University in Halifax, Nova Scotia. She is author of *Climate Change and Writing the Canadian Arctic* (Palgrave 2018), *Canadian Historical Fiction: Reading the Remains* (Palgrave 2014), *Northern Experience and the Myths of Canadian Culture* (MQUP 2002), and editor of *Native North America: Critical and Cultural Perspectives* (ECW 1999), and *Aboriginal Oral Traditions: Theory, Practice, Ethics* co-edited with Renate Eigenbrod (Fernwood 2008). From 2005-2008, she co-edited the *Journal of Canadian Studies* with Donald Wright.

JOSEPH PIVATO is Professor Emeritus of Literary Studies at Athabasca University where he taught courses in Canadian Literature and Comparative Literature that included Indigenous writers at both the undergraduate and graduate levels. In 1985 he edited *Contrasts: Comparative Essays on Italian-Canadian Writing,* the first critical analysis of this emerging literature and that stimulated further work on ethnic minority authors. He published *Echo: Essays on Other Literatures* (1994 & 2003) and edited books on George Elliott Clarke, Sheila Watson, Mary di Michele, Caterina Edwards, F. G. Paci, and Pier Giorgio Di Cicco, all with Guernica. In 2018 he published *Comparative Literature for the New Century* co-edited with Giulia De Gasperi. Many of the chapters in this collection focus on Anglophone and Francophone Canadian authors as well as ethnic minority writers.

DR. JACK ROBINSON is an Associate Professor who has served as English Department Chair from 2007-2013. He has taught Modern Canadian Literature and more recently Indigenous Literature, particularly Indigenous Literature of Residential Schools in Canada, and has published in those areas.

CARL WATTS holds a PhD from Queen's University and currently teaches at Huazhong University of Science and Technology. His research interests include whiteness, modernity and development, and constructions of experimental and mainstream poetry. His scholarly articles have appeared in journals such as *British Journal of Canadian Studies*, *Canadian Poetry*, and *Studies in Canadian Literature*; he has published poetry in *The Cincinnati Review*, *The Cortland Review*, *Grain*, and *The Best Canadian Poetry 2014*, as well as in a chapbook, *REISSUE* (Frog Hollow, 2016).

SERGIY YAKOVENKO completed his PhD in Comparative Literature at the University of Alberta. He also holds a Candidate of Philology degree from the Institute of Literature at the National Academy of Sciences of Ukraine. He currently teaches in the Department of English at MacEwan University. His research interests include Canadian literature, English literature, Slavic literatures, and literary theory. He has published on Sheila Watson, Howard O'Hagan, Charles G. D. Roberts, Roy Kiyooka, and Michael Crummey. He also is an author of two comparative monographs (in Ukrainian) on Polish and Ukrainian prose fiction of the twentieth century and modernist literary criticism.

Acknowledgements

I am grateful to all the authors who have contributed to this collection of essays. I would like to thank Michael Mirolla, of Guernica, and Joseph Pivato, who entrusted this exciting project to me, for their guidance and generosity. Thank you, Professor Pivato, for reviewing my work and for your invaluable suggestions. I am equally thankful to Professor Jack Robinson, my mentor and colleague, with whom I share a long-standing passion for Howard O'Hagan and *Tay John*, for his feedback on my essay and our inspiring discussions on various topics in Canadian literature.

The following texts were previously published:

D. M. R. Bentley's "The Wide Circle and Return: *Tay John* and Vico" was previously published in *Dalhousie Review*, vol. 73, no.1, 1993, pp. 34-53, and is republished here with the author's permission.

A revised version of Kylee-Anne Hingston's "The Declension of a Story: Narrative Structure in Howard O'Hagan's *Tay John*" was previously published in *Studies in Canadian Literature/Etudes en Litterature Canadienne*, vol. 30, no. 2, 2005, pp. 181-92, and is republished here with the author's permission.

Printed by Imprimerie Gauvin
Gatineau, Québec